The *Holiday Which?* Guide to

THE LAKE DISTRICT

£4.50

The *Holiday Which?* Guide to
THE LAKE DISTRICT

Edited by Tim Locke

Published by Consumers' Association
and Hodder & Stoughton

Which? Books are commissioned and researched by
The Association for Consumer Research
and published by Consumers' Association,
2 Marylebone Road, London NW1 4DX, and
Hodder & Stoughton, 47 Bedford Square, London WC1B 3DP

Typographic design by Tim Higgins
Cover painting of Grasmere by Linda Schwab
Cover design by Mon Mohan
Touring maps by David Perrott Cartographics
Walks maps by Tim Locke
Acknowledgements to Val Campbell

First edition 1989
Revised edition 1990

Copyright © 1989 Consumers' Association Ltd

British Library Cataloguing in Publication Data
The Holiday Which? Guide to the Lake
    District – Visitors' guides.
    1. Cumbria. Lake District – Visitors' guides
    I. Locke, Tim   II. Consumers' Association
    914.27'804858

ISBN 0 340 54411 2

Typeset by Rowland Phototypesetting Ltd
Bury St Edmunds, Suffolk
Printed and bound in Great Britain by
BPCC Hazell Books
Aylesbury, Bucks, England
Member of BPCC Ltd.

Contents

Introduction

One of the Lake District's most curious and endearing traits is that the better one gets to know it the more one realises how much there is to explore. The Lake District National Park is a mere 30 miles across, yet its deceptive scale and complex topography make it feel much larger. Physically, the district is self-contained and inward-looking. Skirting the east of the lakes, the traffic on the M6 and trains travelling the London–Glasgow line see virtually nothing of the area. To the west and north, the land slopes abruptly down to coastal plains, while to the south Morecambe Bay forms a great natural boundary.

The very compactness of the Lake District is at the same time astonishing and delightful. Much of the charm of the lakes themselves comes from their surrounding blends of upland and lowland, of crag and heather, of sheep-pasture and dry-stone walls, of green valleys dotted with broad-leaved trees, and of sturdy grey-stone farmhouses. This subtle landscape texture is perhaps shown off to best effect around Derwent Water, Borrowdale, Grasmere and the southern end of Ullswater. To the majority of visitors, the fells (upland hills and mountains in most of the rest of England, but in the Lake District they are always called fells) are as memorable a feature of the area as the lakes. Scafell Pike, at 3206 feet the highest mountain in England, has one of the most spectacular outlines; Great Gable's shapely pyramidal form is used as the National Park logo. Helvellyn is one of the most popular with fell-walkers: in sunny weather there can be hundreds of people on its slopes.

In fact, dodging the crowds of tourists can often be a problem, and it's as well to be aware of some of the more frustrating aspects of this much visited area. Roads such as the Hardknott Pass and the routes to Watendlath can get choked with traffic, defeating the purpose of a pleasurable drive. Villages like Hawkshead and beauty-spots like Tarn Hows can get flooded with people, the car-parks full and pedestrians getting in each other's way. But it is possible to avoid such problems – by keeping clear of the more touristy villages, like Grasmere, at peak times, by using less well-known back roads, by using local buses, or even by

7

taking footpaths instead of driving. The lovely western dales – Buttermere, Wasdale, Eskdale and the Duddon Valley among them – get fewer visitors because of their relative inaccessibility: for fine scenery this side of the district probably has the edge over the eastern lakes.

Some times of the year are quieter than others, too. In winter the whole area virtually empties out – not always because of the weather, either. Winter can produce glorious crisp, sunny days with a dusting of snow; summer can be grey, cold and wet. School holiday times are always busy, as is September. Perhaps the quietest times to visit are May and June, October and mid-winter.

The supply of accommodation – in hotels, guest-houses, pubs and self-catering establishments – is plentiful throughout the year. Some of England's finest hotels are in the Lake District, prestigious places like Miller Howe and Sharrow Bay. But smaller and less expensive hotels, which can provide the basis for a delightful holiday, are common. Bed-and-breakfast accommodation proliferates almost everywhere (to a quite spectacular degree in Keswick, particularly) and is mostly good value, though a lot of it tends to be much of a muchness: families would do better to be self-catering.

The Lake District offers plenty of opportunities for sightseeing, particularly in the south-east. Kendal's Museum of Lakeland Life and Industry is an attraction likely to appeal to most visitors – an extremely well-displayed overview of the social history of Lakeland. Stott Park Bobbin Mill, a working museum, is especially absorbing. Of the houses open to the public, Townend is the most quintessentially Cumbrian, while the finest of the stately homes is a three-sided toss-up between Dalemain, Levens Hall and Sizergh Castle. Not surprisingly, the Lakes have drawn a number of distinguished writers and artists over the ages. Some houses of famous local residents make particularly interesting visits, notably two houses lived in by Wordsworth – Dove Cottage and Rydal Mount – and Ruskin's Brantwood.

But scenery will always be the main attraction for people visiting the Lake District, and the area is famous as walking country. The beauty of the lakes and fells and the large areas of unspoilt farmland make the region supremely rewarding for exploring on foot, and there are walks suitable for everyone, from short easy strolls to much more ambitious walks on the fells.

This landscape is a precious asset: the area's natural resources started to be exploited long before the conservation movement came into being. The enlargement of Thirlmere into a reservoir in the last century triggered off a storm of protest: it was this more than anything else that led to the formation of the National Trust, whose first acquisition was a woodland on the shores of Derwent Water. Today the Trust is the major landowner in the Lake District, responsible for large tracts of the best-loved uplands, woodlands and waters; these have been safeguarded against development in perpetuity. Meanwhile, the Lake District National Park Authority exercises careful control over development and tackles the increasingly tricky problem of how to make the area available to visitors without the sheer number of them spoiling the very things they have come to enjoy. It's to the Lake District's everlasting credit that it absorbs its visitors (on the whole) so well.

For people become hooked on the area, soon establishing their own favourite among the lakes, dales, fells and villages. Perhaps the Lake District's greatest attraction is that it is a place to which to return again and again to make fresh discoveries.

About the guide

To break up the main body of this book into manageable sections, the Lake District National Park and its adjacent areas have been divided into four regions – the north-west, the north-east, the south-west and the south-east. Each region is in turn subdivided into touring routes, and each route is accompanied by a road map showing major points of interest. The text fully describes everything on or near the touring route. For quick reference, at the start of each region are highlights of what that region has to offer.

Restaurants, pubs and tea-rooms are mentioned throughout the text as appropriate.

At the end of each of the four regions are hotels and guest-houses worth staying at, together with an indication of the sort of prices you can expect to pay; the key to prices appears below. There is also a short summary of bed-and-breakfast accommodation and which towns, villages and country areas are best for it.

The chapter on walks describes the best walks in each of the four regions. These range from easy strolls on the flat – perhaps around a lake – to more demanding walks on the fells. Outlines only are given of some walks, perhaps because the routes are so self-evident that no detailed directions are needed or because the routes are so popular that it's a case of following the crowds. It's wise to take an Ordnance Survey map (see p. 264) on walks that are not accompanied by their own maps in this guide, and to carry a compass on all fell walks: the weather in the Lake District can be unpredictable, and mist and rain can reduce visibility alarmingly.

Some of the walks outlined refer to *The Holiday Which? Good Walks Guide*, also edited by Tim Locke and published by Consumers' Association and Hodder & Stoughton; the walks are described in full in that guide.

Key to accommodation prices

£ Less than £25   £££ £35 to £45   £££££ Over £55
££ £25 to £35   ££££ £45 to £55

These prices, current in summer 1990, are for bed and breakfast, per person per night, in a double room with private bathroom (if available).

The natural setting

The rocks

What sort of chisels and in what workman's hands were used to produce this large piece of precious chasing, or embossed work, which we call Cumberland and Westmorland?

To Ruskin's sentimental question there are very long geological answers. Broadly speaking, three bands of basic rock slant across the Lake District: in the north, Skiddaw Slates; in the middle, Borrowdale Volcanics; in the south, Silurian Grits. Each type has given the landscape some of its fundamental character – steep domed hills, craggy peaks, gentle farmland – often with a visibly abrupt change of scene where the bands meet. Superimposed on the basic rocks (and increasing their contrasts) is the overall effect of ice.

At the height of the glaciation era it is possible that all Lakeland was covered by a single vast dome of ice. In the course of a million years there were at least three major Ice Ages; during warmer interludes, glaciers ground their way downhill. The weight and pressure of advancing ice scoured V-shaped valleys into deep U-shapes, and as the mountain-side was carved away great fragments travelled on the ice surface, to be deposited miles away as friction-rounded boulders, often quite foreign to the rock of their resting-place. Of these 'glacial erratics', the Bowder Stone in Borrowdale is the most famous and astonishing example.

Lakes formed as ice melted, some in valleys deepened to below sea-level (Wast Water is the deepest), some dammed by mounds of deposited debris, some in pairs, like Buttermere and Crummock Water, with debris or a resistant rocky shelf between them. On the fell slopes, broken 'hummocky' ground is the scattered debris left by the icefield; on open level ground its intermittent drift built up the whale-backed hillocks called drumlins, common in the Windermere and Esthwaite areas.

The last 'mini-glaciation' began a mere 10,000 years ago, and its effects are everywhere apparent. Lingering pockets of ice expanded and spilled downhill, gouging out the corries now filled with tarns, grinding smooth the sides of sharp ridges like Striding Edge, undercutting the high hanging valleys from which waterfalls drop. The Lodore Falls in Borrowdale is a good example – the beck from the hanging valley of Watendlath, in Borrowdale Volcanic rock, here plunges down to the scooped and eroded Skiddaw Slate of the main valley floor. Piledrivers, shears and nutmeg-graters as well as Ruskin's chisels, the glaciers shaped all Lakeland scenery; their most dramatic effects are in the centre, where they met the hardest rock.

The plants

After its aeons of mineral history, the vegetable history of the Lake District was soon influenced by man. When the last Ice Age ended, treeless tundra was succeeded by rich woodland cover: birch grew first, then hazel, then a great spread of oak on lower ground and pine above. Neolithic and Bronze-Age man cleared ever-increasing patches for animals to graze on; bare ground suffered soil erosion, and bogs spread as the climate grew wetter. Almost all that woodland was destroyed, and fertility leached out of the unprotected soil, leaving high bare mountain tops of heath and grassland. Grazing sheep were (and are) the enemy to the natural regeneration of woodland; and medieval man's contribution of coppicing – the systematic planting and cutting of trees and undergrowth – was small compared with his inroads on mature timber for building, fuel and charcoal-burning.

On a larger scale, man has planted and cut timber here from the sixteenth century, when industrial demand began, to the Forestry Commission's activity in the twentieth. As well as useful (if alien) conifers, plenty of broad-leaf woodland was kept up by landowners: pure beech woods, and mixtures including oak, birch and hazel, turn to glorious autumn shades along the lakesides. Holly and yew are native and widely scattered, juniper thickets survive on steep valley sides. Bracken, the farmer's curse and colourist's delight, spreads from hill slopes to pastureland; more delicate ferns flourish among rocks; the heather districts are on the soils of Silurian Grit and Skiddaw Slate. On the highest ground among the mosses and lichens, tiny alpines have a short season among sheep-free crags and corries; the wetter slopes have interesting bog plants and the drier a variety of grasses. Dale meadows are often too carefully controlled for wild flowers to proliferate, but open woodland and lake fringes have scores of species, favouring different degrees of damp and shade – including of course the famous Lakeland daffodils.

Animal life

*Yan, tyan, tethera, methera, **pimp**; sethera, lethera, hovera, dovera, **dick*** (Traditional sheep-counting numbers, one to ten)

Much the most visible animals in the Lakes are sheep. The local native breed is the Herdwick, whose coarse strong wool was the basis of the region's trade in tough durable cloth. Herdwicks are the hardiest of sheep, able to thrive on thin pasture and in the harshest weather – they can survive many days' complete burial in snowdrifts, living off their own fat and, *in extremis*, it is reported, sucking nourishment out of their own oily wool. They're also known for their attachment to their own 'heaf', the pasture where they were born – if sold and moved miles away they occasionally reappear like homing pigeons. Herdwicks are the brindled black ones with white faces. These days they are outnumbered by other breeds and crossbreeds including the black-faced Swaledales, for Herdwicks are not particularly profitable to the modern farmer. Their wool is not copious, and they produce relatively small numbers of lambs.

One Herdwick specialist was Beatrix Potter, who became a full-time prizewinning sheep farmer on the proceeds of her much-loved children's books about Peter Rabbit, Squirrel Nutkin, Mrs Tiggy-Winkle and other small natives of her favourite countryside. She bequeathed her flock (and 4000 acres) to the National Trust, who run their considerable Lakeland holdings on conservationist lines and have done much to prevent the Herdwick from becoming a rare species.

The sheep graze on fellsides high and low – it is for their control and protection that those dry-stone walls snake up and over such slopes – except for regular engagements down on the farms: mating in November, dipping in February, lambing in April and May, clipping and marking in July, dipping again in August. There are also fairs, 'meets' and shows. Whatever the occasion for manoeuvring a flock off the fells, the performance of shepherd and swift wily dogs is absorbing to watch.

There are red deer still in the Lake District, whose
ancestors pre-date its human habitation. They mostly roam
the forests, but some have adapted to the high fells: the
Martindale herd lives on a reserve east of Ullswater. Roe deer
are smaller and shyer. Numbers of both are controlled, for
they have no natural predators since British wolves died out
and might become too many for their food supplies. Foxes
are all too plentiful, and enthusiastically hunted. A most
attractive native is the red squirrel, whose survival can be
attributed to the island qualities of this corner of Britain:
competitive grey squirrels which dominate everywhere else
have been slow to cross the treeless miles of moor to north
and east – though they now threaten the National Park's
boundary.

Conservationists think that badgers and otters are slowly
increasing in number; rabbits and hares have plenty of
predators including stoats and weasels, which often share
the shelter of dry-stone walls with the lizards and
slow-worms. The adder is common, and much more
frightened of man than man need be of it.

Lakeland's largest bird, the golden eagle, made a
comeback in the 1970s and its nesting sites are protected.
Buzzards' effortless circling flight is almost equally
impressive; ravens too are high fliers, practising noisy
aerobatics in the air-currents among the summits. Carrion
lamb forms a large part of the ravens' diet, and naturalists
observing the birds feared the effects of post-Chernobyl
contamination on their breeding cycle, but any threat seems
to be receding. In the woodlands, woodpeckers prefer the
hardwoods and goldcrests the conifers, and the most
unusual summer visitor is the pied flycatcher. The lakes
attract a great range of waterbirds, including Canada geese,
whooper swans in winter, and the great crested grebe. Fish
of interest to anglers are chiefly of the salmon family – sea
and brown trout, and the deep-water char; perch and pike
can also be found.

Nature reserves and conservation

Considerable areas of the Lake District – over 14 per cent of
the National Park – have been designated by the Nature
Conservancy Council as sssis – Sites of Special Scientific
Interest. There are nearly 70 sssis, some huge and some tiny.

Access to them is not necessarily restricted, and plant and animal life by no means all rare or unusual; these areas are cared for partly because they represent the character of the countryside that visitors come to see. The NCC also designates National Nature Reserves to which access is, inevitably, restricted. So far there are four of these in the Lakes.

Blelham Tarn near Windermere (a field research station) has various habitats of fen, bog and wet woodland, and the great crested grebe nests here. Esthwaite North Fen is an area in slow transition: from water to woodland, from reed-swamp to regenerated alder and willow and oak. At Rusland Moss further south, this process was completed long ago and a native species of pine covers its drying peat. In Roudsea Wood near Haverthwaite – accessible on rights of way only – roe deer and red squirrels inhabit the wonderfully varied woodland: one side of the valley is basically slate, the other limestone.

Limestone flora and fauna can also be appreciated from rights of way at Whitbarrow Scar, where there are crags and screes and a wide expanse of limestone pavement. This is in part designated a Local Nature Reserve: bylaws limit the climbing areas of the crags to avoid destruction of plants, and enforce a close season so that breeding birds are left in peace. There is another LNR at Drigg Dunes on the coast near Ravenglass.

Thirteen nature reserves (some including land designated sssi) have been established by the Cumbria Trust for Nature Conservation, a vigorous voluntary body; and on land owned or leased by the National Park Authority, about 15 other deserving areas with no specific designation are sure of 'sympathetic management'.

Man's Lakeland history

Prehistoric activity

It was long thought that prehistoric settlers in the Lake District farmed only the coastal plain where Neolithic and Bronze-Age burial mounds are found in concentration, ignoring the inhospitable mountains. The most dramatic and mysterious remnants, their great stone circles, were raised on sites high and lonely but relatively easy of approach – even Castlerigg, so spectacularly surrounded by central peaks. But in the 1940s and 1950s Neolithic enterprise was discovered in the high heart of the fells: Pike of Stickle among the Langdale crags is littered with evidence of axe-making on a large scale. Here and at similar sites the hardest volcanic rock, capable of a sharp durable edge, lay about in great boulders at the foot of a precipice with no need for quarrying: axeheads were chipped and shaped on the spot and sent to the coastal settlements for polishing. Then they found their way all over Britain. Examples in the distinctive Langdale rock have turned up on the Channel coasts. Their Lakeland distribution reveals that much of the central mountain fastness was well trodden in prehistoric times. Certainly Neolithic settlers used their stone axes to clear living space among the forests; finds of burial urns and fragments of woollen cloth nearly 3000 years old suggest a culture more advanced than that of later Celtic settlers, who seem to have missed out altogether on the Iron Age. A single earthwork, at Carrock Fell, was probably built by the Brigantes who controlled most of northern England by the arrival of the Romans in the first century AD.

Roman interlude

Roman occupation of the Lake District was limited to the strategic. To the north, Hadrian's Wall was the limit of their empire, where the Scots were kept at bay; in Cumbria the Brigantes alternated between co-operation and rebellion.

Roman ports and a coastal chain of signal stations were
defences against incursions of Scots and Irish; Roman forts
inland marked political control of this impenetrable Celtic
backwater, linked by patrol and supply roads. High Street
took a nonchalant ridge route north from Ambleside fort
(Galava) towards Brougham, but the main artery was west to
Ravenglass, across the Wrynose Pass and the Hardknott
Pass. Mediobogdum, the half-way fort at Hardknott, must
have been one of the loneliest in the Roman Empire. Its
position looks impregnable, but it was sacked at the end of
the second century and never re-occupied. Ambleside and
Ravenglass were strengthened, and the Romans kept control
for another hundred years, but they had no interest in
settling the region – even to exploit its minerals, of which
they were aware. When the final withdrawal came, in
around AD 400, they left little behind.

Celts and Christianity

During the Dark Ages that followed the Roman occupation, a
Celtic twilight glimmered faintly. The epic poetry of Wales
records a Celtic kingdom called Rheged in the north-west. A
Welsh tribe, the Cymru, gave Cumberland its name; a few
other Celtic placenames survive, mainly for natural features
– the mountain Blencathra, the rivers Eden and Derwent,
Leven and Usk. Christianity was brought by Celtic saints –
the linking of Patterdale with St Patrick has little support, but
the missionary visit of St Ninian in the fifth century is
undisputed, and St Kentigern (seventh century) has eight
ancient dedications including the church of Crosthwaite,
Keswick's former parish.

From across the Pennines, English-speaking Anglians
migrated. Bede recorded two centuries later how King
Aethelfrith of Northumbria set about systematically
conquering and colonising. By the end of the seventh
century Northumbria controlled the whole of the north-west
and ruled it until the tenth. The Anglian farmers preferred
the lowlands, where they built villages in an English cluster
around a central green. They seem to have accepted
co-existence with a very different people, who found
high central Lakeland so much to their liking that initial
raiding parties from the sea became a long influx of
pioneer settlers.

Placenames

There was a great prince called Llewellyn
Whose ancestors came from Helvellyn.
But the Welsh thought, forget it,
He'd only regret it –
And they all kept a vow not to tell 'im.

If ever a placename looked Welsh, it's Helvellyn; but that is not official, because not enough evidence exists – no early spellings or variants – to trace its Welshness. The analysis of placenames is a scholarly business, of use to geographers and biologists as well as historians and linguists. Satisfying the mild curiosity of the non-specialist is rather difficult to do with any accuracy: the slimmest booklet about placenames has in common with the fattest academic volume a great many conflicting interpretations, speculative theories and general ifs and buts.

*In the Lake District there is a concentration (unique in Britain) of Old Norse placename elements, well mixed up with bits of British/Celtic, Welsh, Old English, Old French and Middle English. Local dialect can be a linguistic law unto itself; and quite a few spellings date from the eighteenth century and are condemned as 'errors' – ghyll, for instance, which is more properly gill, from Norse **gil** (a narrow ravine or the stream in it).*

*Every beck and bridge, wood and crag has a name, and there are many duplicates: 28 Raven Crags have been recorded. Each dale had its self-sufficient community and no inhabitant was likely to confuse his local Blea Tarn or Sour Milk Gill with the one across a couple of intervening fells. For a single feature of the landscape, a different name distinguished how men used it: a track up a hill might be a steep footpath, a **stig** (as in Styhead); or originally the route to a pasture for animals, a **reik** (Lady's Rake, Scots Rake); or in later local dialect a 'trod': Moses' Trod commemorates a quarryman called Moses who smuggled precious plumbago from Borrowdale to Ravenglass.*

*It is one thing to acquaint oneself with the commonest placename elements, another to make the right deductions. Satterthwaite is easy: **saetre**, a shieling or summer pasture, plus **thwaite**, a clearing. But take Seathwaite: in Borrowdale, it's 'the clearing among the sedges', but in the Duddon Valley it's 'the clearing near the lake', and to trace why you have to know what they called each*

Seathwaite in the Middle Ages. Then there is the Inversion Compound, an Irish habit some Norsemen had picked up: feature first, name or adjective second. We do it with rivers (the River Thames); they did it in Seat Allen and Seat Sandal, the shielings of Alein and Sandulfr, and in plenty of other places. There's some confusion at that celebrated beauty-spot Tarn Hows as to whether the tarn describes the haugr, hill, or vice versa.

Distinguishing vegetation is often part of a name: alder trees (alor) at Seatoller, oaks (derw or derwentio) at Derwent Water, birch trees at Birker or Birkrigg – but not Birkett Fell, which was named after the conservationist Lord Birkett in 1942. Animals often feature: griss and svin, pigs and swine, appear in Grizedale, Mungrisdale (the 'mun' part is for St Mungo's church) and Swinside. Cat Bells was probably where the wildcats had their dens (bield, a shelter); Ickenthwaite abounded in squirrels (ikorni) and Yewbarrow has nothing to do with yew trees but is the hill where ewes were pastured.

If Ullock Pike, Ullscarf and Ulpha all have exciting connections with real wolves (ulfr), it is disappointing to learn that Ullswater hasn't – it just belonged to a Norseman called Ulfr. Hawkshead was Haukr's shieling, Finsthwaite Finn's clearing, and so forth all over Lakeland. It seems it was almost exclusively the men who were remembered, except for one lady called Dufa, who pioneered in her own right at Dowthwaitehead. There was also Portinscale, where the portcwene (harlot) kept house; and Nan Bield is allowed to have been the shelter of an unfortunate called Ann.

Some names sound deceptively modern. Lodore Falls ought to be romantic nineteenth-century coinage, but no – it's a literal low door (lagr and duru) or gap in the ridge through which the water flows. And some deserve an anecdote – but Great Cockup means nothing more entertaining than the valley (hop) where woodcock were plentiful, and Dollywaggon Pike has no explanation at all.

Worst of all, the experts let us down on some of the best-known names. Helvellyn isn't the worst of it: look up Scafell or Skiddaw and you find 'much speculation', 'alternative suggestion', 'most likely explanation', 'a little obscure' – and other such unsatisfactory hedgings. Nor have they yet entirely accounted for Watendlath or Wrynose. But in spite of the gaps, a short glossary of placenames to accompany a map gives you a glimpse of 'history on the ground'.

The Viking settlement

The land-hungry Norsemen arrived from Ireland and the Isle of Man, where they had already mixed and intermarried with the Celts and often became Christian converts: a tall Viking cross survives at Gosforth, sculpted with both the Crucifixion and a dragon-slaying legend from Nordic myth in a style much livelier than the formal scrolls and foliage of English carving. In the long narrow valleys between the highest mountains they set up the individual communities loosely linked, which had always been their lifestyle. Over many generations they cleared away trees and scrub and glacial boulders to make farms and pasture, completing the creation of the present landscape and naming it too – fell, force and tarn; nab, knott and gill; scar, scree and beck. Hundreds of Lakeland placenames are the record of their local history, telling where stones were particularly troublesome to clear, where alders grew, where pigs were bred, and which patriarch first established his family in the dale. The Herdwick strain of Lakeland sheep was probably Norse, and the sheepfarmer's 'lug' marks come from the Norwegian word for law.

Conquerors and monasteries

A quarter of a century after the Battle of Hastings, the Norman conquerors of England turned their attention to the north-west. William II defeated its Northumbrian overlord and 'sent thither very many English peasants with wives and stock to dwell there and till the ground'. He sent a good many Border barons here too – considerable force was needed for a couple of centuries against the war-raids and cattle-reiving of the Scots – and parcelled off much of Cumbria into their estates. But the major Norman influence on the Lake District was the establishment during the twelfth century of powerful, land-owning religious houses all around it. Among a dozen abbeys and monasteries, the greatest and most centrally powerful was at Furness, whose eventual domain was not only the peninsula where it stood but all the land between Windermere and Coniston Water, the whole of Borrowdale, and upper Eskdale.

An outlying monastic sheep farm was called a 'grange'.

20

These were often high on the slopes, above the Norse 'thwaites', and the constant grazing of monastery flocks contributed to the retreat of vegetation from the fells. Forests, however, were important to the Norman nobility as hunting grounds, and under the medieval Forest Laws great tracts were preserved and extended, within whose bounds new building and farming were forbidden, and woodcutting for fuel or fences strictly controlled – at least in theory. In practice, over a long period, much 'forest' intended for the preservation of deer became common grazing land for the expanding population of peasants and tenant farmers which – particularly in the dales – was at its highest concentration.

Medieval and Tudor upheavals

The Lake District was losing its island-like immunity from the nation's affairs, and the fourteenth century brought much social misery. Plague, the Black Death, arrived in 1348 and twice in the 1360s: the expanded dale communities for whom new chapels had been built perished in sufficient numbers to require new graveyards, and the Bishop of Carlisle reported a critical lack of priests. In war with the Scots, Carlisle was repeatedly besieged, and one rich abbey after another was plundered, burnt or held to ransom as Scottish armies ravaged their way south. After the English defeat at Bannockburn the 'frontier' castles (Kendal, Appleby, Brough) were much strengthened and extended, and a military style of domestic architecture also appeared – the peel tower. This was a three-storey stone-built refuge: cattle could be herded into the windowless ground floor, access to living-quarters was up a narrow spiral staircase, and the battlemented roof served as a defensive platform. Versions of these towers were built chiefly along the threatened north-east fringe of the Lake District, but examples have been found in the lower valleys and even along the coast, surviving as the core of a farm or its unusually massive outlying barn.

Peace and some prosperity returned under the Tudors. Scottish raids diminished after the Battles of Flodden and Solway Moss to the stuff of border ballads, and ceased to concern Cumbria. Henry VIII's dissolution of the monasteries was a major upheaval of its social and economic patterns, causing unemployment, poverty, real distress and

Underground industry

Though the most visible and permanent, the pastoral way of life is not the only tradition of the Lakes: industry has roots here too. Kendal was the cloth manufacturing centre for cottage spinners and weavers; from the Middle Ages the various kerseys, friezes, linsey wolseys, 'spotted cottons' and 'Kendal green' were famous for their durability and excellent dyes. But more central than the fulling mills and contributing much more to the region's character were its mines and quarries.

Iron was the mineral worked here first – possibly by the Romans, certainly since the medieval monks who smelted it on open charcoal hearths called bloomeries. The rich copper deposits in Newlands Valley, explored in the thirteenth century, became of major national interest in the reign of Elizabeth I. Lead too was found in the Newlands mine, and more copper at other sites near Coniston and on the Caldbeck fells north of Skiddaw. The ore was hauled by packhorse-train to smelting works at Brigham near Keswick, which by the 1560s amounted to an industrial suburb (destroyed later during the Civil War). Elizabeth had imported German expertise from the mines of Augsburg – many of the German miners married into local families – and in 1561 The Society for the Mines Royal was set up, providing impetus and finance.

It may have been the Germans who first exploited the 'wadd holes' of Seatoller Fell. Wadd was the local name for the carboniferous

less tangible loss of local pride – Henry 'found the north poor, and he robbed it of the only treasure it possessed in the wealth of the abbeys'.

The Statesmen era

Out of the redistribution by the Crown of monastic lands there presently emerged a middle class of yeomen farmers locally called 'statesmen'. The fixed-rent tenant of a lord, with independent rights over his estate and its management, could grow wealthy by the sale of wool, cattle and timber in the rapid inflation of the sixteenth century; he could pass on his swelling possessions to his next of kin; and he could, and many did, rise through the ranks of freeholders, squirearchy, gentry and aristocracy.

*deposit called plumbago, graphite, black-lead or 'black cawke'. It was
first used to make moulds for coinage – since when is debated, as it
was much employed by Elizabethan counterfeiters – and even by the
late sixteenth century was also described as 'a kind of earth or
hardened glittering stone which painters use to draw their lines and
make pictures of one colour'. The Keswick pencil industry cannot be
traced back so far; its first manufacturer is recorded in the eighteenth
century, by which time wadd was also in demand for 'the casting of
bomb-shells, round shot and cannon-balls'. The wadd holes provided
phases of work for local mining families from the 'Old Men' of the
seventeenth century, whence there are tales of wadd stealing and
smuggling, until final closure in the middle of the nineteenth.
Stockpiles of 'the purest Borrowdale lead' for Keswick pencils lasted
until 1906.*

*There are other rare deposits in the Lake District, their value
discovered much later: wolfram (tungsten), used for the filaments of
lightbulbs and extensively in armament production during both
World Wars, and most recently barytes, whose uses include the
coatings for specialised papers.*

*Slate quarrying in the region – as an export rather than for purely
local use – got under way in the 1770s and proved more consistently
profitable than the mines. Dark blue slate from near the coast on
Kirkby Moor roofed much of the industrial north of England. Some
inland ventures closed, but the quarries above Honister Pass have
been worked continuously since 1643, and the grey-green slate of
central Lakeland is a prized building material.*

Statesmen family groups held their Lakeland territories
with clan-like stability, and theirs was the final major
influence on the landscape we see today. From the
mid-sixteenth century to almost the end of the nineteenth
they continued to create the irregular patchwork of fields
that covers each flat valley floor, replacing the old open
agriculture; and as the farmers prospered they improved
their homes. England's 'Great Rebuilding' era reached the
Lakes by 1650, and was so total in these dales that barely a
barn survives from an earlier date. Stone-built, long and low
with a heavy slate roof, the 'statesman plan' farmhouse and
its variations, so satisfactory a part of the scenery, symbolises
the sturdy independence of Lakeland tradition.

In their snug and practical basic plan, the farm's front door
opened on a wide passage called the hallan, dividing the

building into 'firehouse' and 'downhouse', the latter being a large open area where fuel was kept and washing, baking and brewing accomplished – a utility area. In the living-quarters, the social hub of the farm was the fireplace, built against the stone wall of the hallan with a huge sheltering hood to sit under and its own small window. Buttery and best bedchamber opened off the main room; children and servants slept in the loft, up a slate staircase. The house would be massively furnished with settles, chests, a long oak table built *in situ* because it was far too big to pass through the doors, and the important bread cupboard, often built into the chamber wall – a status symbol, this, whose elaborate carving would incorporate the date of the building and the initials of its owner. The 'statesman plan' was extended according to family fortune and demands: more partitions, more rooms, more outbuildings. Sometimes an outside 'spinning gallery' was tucked under the eaves; these picturesque features were useful for storage and access to the upper floor as well as for the housewife's daylight spinning and the hanging of finished cloth.

'Towards the head of these Dales was found a perfect Republic of Shepherds and Agriculturalists, among whom the plough of each man was confined to the maintenance of his own family, or to the occasional accommodation of his neighbour . . . an organised community, whose constitution had been imposed and regulated by the mountains which protected it.' But the society thus eulogised by Wordsworth was not immune to market forces. By the time of his writing, the secure prosperity of the statesmen had eroded away. From the mid-eighteenth century the building of turnpike roads brought outside competition to their market towns, and opened their region to the beginning of industrial progress.

Picturesque tours

The new roads brought carriages as well as market wagons: travel for pleasure had begun, and when the French Revolution made a tour abroad impracticable, many explored Britain instead. Early writers had little good to report of the region – Daniel Defoe rejected Westmorland as 'a county eminent only for being the wildest, most barren and frightful of any that I have passed'. But a vividly descriptive *Journal in the Lakes* by the poet Thomas Gray, published in 1775, appealed to romantic sentiment. It was presently incorporated into a bestselling *Guide to the Lakes* by a local priest and antiquarian, Thomas West, who recommended a tour of his region as not inferior to grand excursions in the Alps. West's route from viewpoint to viewpoint (he called them 'stations', rather as in a pilgrimage) set the pattern for decades of visitors. Fashionable tourists were presently assisted in their appreciation of the scenery by William Gilpin's influential *Observations relative to picturesque beauty* (1786), which instructed them to regard a landscape as if it were a picture, in terms of foregrounds and perspectives, tone and line. A 'Claude glass' assisted judgement: this was a framed mirror, slightly concave and sometimes tinted, in which – turning his back on the scenery – the viewer would search for a composition that looked like a painting by the famous Claude Lorraine. There were exclusive standards: 'Mountains . . . rising in regular lines, or in whimsical, grotesque shapes, are displeasing.' The Lake District had in abundance the right kind of mountains and the wrong; its 'prospects' were admirably irregular, precipitous, immense, stupendous, horrid and sublime. Travel-writing had acquired a convention and a vocabulary; guidebooks multiplied and so did tourists.

Economic backwater

Between the mid-eighteenth century and the mid-nineteenth the picturesque backwardness so agreeable to visiting 'Lakers' ceased to be an obstinate local quirk – it reflected decline and distress. In the dales there was a spurt of wall-building; the enclosure of common farming land was efficient agricultural practice, but in many areas there were also attempts to reclaim some of the fellsides to grow more food. In the villages population steadily dropped as the demand for rural crafts and industries was undermined by town manufacturers. Work was to be had along the coast in the eighteenth-century industrial ports; nearer at hand, Cockermouth and Kendal expanded into small industrial quarters, water-powered well into the nineteenth century by their respective rivers, the Derwent and the Kent.

Inner market centres became obsolete as the local textile industry collapsed. Hawkshead, where wool was brought from the fell-farm spinning-wheels to be sold, was left completely stranded when its market died. Keswick had served the northern fells, a centre for the spinning and weaving trade; it survived the collapse partly through its pencil factory and partly by being well situated to cater for picturesque tours. Ambleside, which had shared with Hawkshead the wool trade from the southern fells, was both sheltered and attractively set: it pleased not only tourists but new residents, and became a thriving little Victorian town. While wealthy industrialists built homes along the shores of Windermere, the whole neighbourhood of Ambleside was popular with genteel independents, from retired clergymen to successful writers.

The presence of the poet Wordsworth in successive homes at Grasmere and Rydal made the neighbourhood a place of literary pilgrimage within his own long lifetime. He wrote with a passionate faith of nature as teacher and healer, of beauty as a moral force offering joys far beyond a trivial pleasure in the picturesque. Their attitude to landscape thus

The Lake Poets

One impulse from a vernal wood
Can teach us more of Man,
Of moral evil and of good
Than all the sages can.

Three nineteenth-century poets – William Wordsworth (1770–1850), Samuel Taylor Coleridge (1772–1834) and Robert Southey (1774–1843) – were later grouped for critical or biographical convenience as The Lake Poets; only Wordsworth wrote 'Lake poetry'. Coleridge was an ardent explorer of the high fells for the few years he lived among them; Southey preferred his library apart from a gentle local walk each day. Both loved the region and were much inspired there to write. But Coleridge's imagination, assisted by opium, flew to more exotic scenes; and Southey's prodigious output included history, biography and reviews. His long dramatic poems were esteemed by the Romantics, and though a comparatively undistinguished Poet Laureate (from 1813 to his adjusted, admirers of his poems flocked to see the places that inspired them. For the further illumination of 'persons of taste, and feeling for landscape, who might be inclined to explore the District of the Lakes with that degree of attention to which its beauty may fairly lay claim', Wordsworth also wrote his own *Guide to the Lakes*. By the 1830s it had become an indispensable introduction; the final version, published in 1835, is a classic of its kind. More than an eloquently descriptive topographical guide, it is a valuable (if idealised) record of the region's traditional life, and an early plea for the preservation of its landscape. He deplored the planting of trees for profit, in solid tracts with no regard for the lie of the land; he found larch trees particularly unsightly. Foreseeing that 'in a few years the country on the margin of the lakes will fall almost entirely into the possession of gentry, either strangers or natives', he made the interesting suggestion that the Lake District might be deemed 'a sort of national property, in which every man has a right and interest who has an eye to perceive and a heart to enjoy'.

death in 1843; Wordsworth succeeded him) he was as much as Wordsworth a focus of literary interest in his Lakeland home.

In Wordsworth's poetry, inspiration and subject-matter were one. Before their poetic paths diverged, he and Coleridge jointly produced the Lyrical Ballads, *a deliberately innovative collection of poems written in 'language really used by men', about 'incidents of humble and rustic life', where 'the passions of men are incorporated with the beautiful and permanent forms of Nature'. Not all Wordsworth's later products of this poetic theory were admired – parody and mockery greeted some of his rustic simplicities. But his convictions were unshaken, and his true innovation in English poetry was his explicitly autobiographical verse, 'The Prelude'. Written over five years but revised for nearly forty and published after his death, this is a vivid and triumphant account of his boyhood in the Lakes and the profound effect of natural beauty on 'the growth of the poet's mind'. In the sonnets and narrative poems of his most fertile years, the moral profundities of nature-worship which so appealed to Victorian taste can seem irritatingly obscure today, but the evocation of Lakeland scenery is a lasting delight. For Wordsworth-lovers there is a Lake District of the mind, enhancing with remembered images the reality they see.*

The Lake Poets CONTINUED

'Plain living and high thinking'

Wordsworth's life and biographical connections with the other Lake Poets absorb academics as they fascinated contemporary gossips. Born and brought up in the Lakes, he went to Cambridge, sowed some wild oats in France, joined Coleridge in Somerset during their youthful poetic collaboration, and was enabled by a legacy to return with his sister Dorothy to live at Dove Cottage, Grasmere, in 1799. Coleridge followed his friend, bringing his family to Greta Hall, Keswick; he and Robert Southey had married sisters, and by 1803 the Southeys had joined the Coleridges. Southey amused the assorted children with the story of 'The Three Bears' and a breathless poem beginning 'How Does the Water Come Down at Lodore?' (from 'Eddying and whisking, Turning and twisting' to 'Pouring and roaring, Waving and raving' in 200 crescendo lines).

At Grasmere the overcrowded intricacies of Dove Cottage in the Wordsworths' early years included the Hutchinson sisters, Mary and Sarah: Wordsworth married Mary in 1802, while Coleridge fell inconveniently in love with Sarah. (This and his opium habit broke up his already unhappy marriage, and in 1804 he took to travel abroad, leaving Southey to support the whole Keswick ménage.) Dorothy Wordsworth, who loved her brother William in a more than sisterly way, kept a repressed but revealing journal of their frugal, contented life at Dove Cottage from 1800 to 1802. She was his factotum and his inspiration: her vivid records of their walks and scenic discoveries were of material help to his poetry. Her writing, never intended for publication, ended after Wordsworth's marriage, which brought her close to breakdown. Thereafter, visitors found her odd but stimulating – all gipsy tan, wild eyes and impetuous stammer, in contrast to Mary's domestic serenity.

Thus cosseted by devoted women, Wordsworth wrote his finest poems at Dove Cottage, and it is today the principal shrine for his literary pilgrims. But it was undeniably too small for his expanding family and frequent visitors; Sir Walter Scott was once driven to the

The railway age

A railway loop around the Lake District was completed by 1857: the last link was the Furness line with its viaducts and views of Morecambe Bay. Lines branching inland were usually planned to serve industrial interests, with *local pub by its cramped and spartan regime. Wordsworth moved twice to larger Grasmere premises – necessity overcoming his aesthetic objections to the prominent white house called Allan Bank – before settling in much grander Rydal Mount. This was the tourist attraction during his lifetime, for 37 decreasingly productive but much venerated years. Latterly, as many as a hundred visitors a day would arrive for a glimpse of him. By 1843, when he was made Poet Laureate, he had ceased altogether to write poetry, and he never composed an official line.*

When the Wordsworths moved out, the tenancy of Dove Cottage was taken for a while by Thomas De Quincey, a brilliant essayist of feckless character addicted, like Coleridge, to opium (he claimed Coleridge's daily dose was 10 times his own) and best known for his Confessions of an English Opium Eater. *His admiration for Wordsworth's work amounted to worship, but he never managed to become the poet's friend – few did. After De Quincey married a local girl of lowly stock, William and Dorothy would barely speak to him. Before this offence he took full part in the excursions and tabletalk of Grasmere and Keswick: his* Recollections of the Lakes and the Lake Poets *is a compilation of critical studies, rambling biographies, local anecdote, flagrant gossip and devastating personal descriptions of the whole Lakes coterie. Briefly allowing that Wordsworth had a noble face, he spends two enjoyable pages deploring his figure and particularly his legs, which were serviceable but shapeless, and his walk, which 'had a wry and twisted appearance; and not appearance only – for I have known it, by slow degrees, gradually to edge off his companion from the middle to the side of the highroad'. De Quincey calculated that the Wordsworthian legs 'must have traversed a distance of 175 to 180,000 English miles – a mode of exertion which, to him, stood in stead of wine, spirits and all other stimulants whatsoever to the animal spirits; to which he has been indebted for a life of unclouded happiness, and we for much of what is most excellent in his writings'.*

passengers a profitable sideline, but the 1847 line to Windermere – and possibly to Ambleside – was proposed expressly to give access to people unable to afford other means of travel. Wordsworth's was the most powerful voice raised in protest at this violation, in a sonnet (see p. 167) and in two resounding epistles to the *Morning Post*. Chief among his lengthy arguments was that insoluble crux of mass tourism: that 'transferring at once uneducated persons in large bodies to particular spots' was of doubtful benefit to the persons and immediately destroyed the desirability of the spot. Ambleside was spared, Windermere village much stimulated, and there were those who welcomed the effect of the railway on the local economy. Wordsworth's worst fears of 'trains pouring out their hundreds at a time along the margin of Windermere' came true after his death: from 1869 the branch line to Lakeside at the southern tip of Windermere brought excursions all summer from Barrow and the Lancashire cotton towns, to steam up the lake for tea at Ambleside.

Further west, a line from Broughton to Coniston opened in 1859 following renewed interest in local copper. Its station was set inconveniently high for lakeside traffic, but gave access to the fells. Walkers carried a popular new guidebook, Murray's *Handbook to the English Lakes*, which in successive editions as the railway lines opened gave new routes to be explored from them. By 1864 the Cockermouth–Keswick–Penrith line was encouraging active tourists to visit the less frequented northern lakes; but protest deflected the proposed branch to Buttermere. In Eskdale a line built in 1875 to transport iron ore from Boot failed when reduced to passenger traffic, but was relaid as a narrow-gauge railway in 1915, and in miniature form still carries tourists today.

By the late nineteenth century schemes for further railway expansion were abortive. Opposition was strong, including John Ruskin from his new home at Brantwood and Canon Rawnsley, vicar of Crosthwaite and co-founder of the National Trust, who in 1883 helped form the Lake District Defence Association. This society, which defeated a proposed railway along Ennerdale, failed in its primary object – to prevent the expansion of Thirlmere into a reservoir supplying water to Manchester. It did, however, attract support on a nation-wide scale – but 'poets, artists, bishops and sentimentalists,' claimed Manchester.

Conservation and conifers

Eminent, literary and leisured Victorians continued to retreat to the Lakes from the rigours of the Industrial Revolution, as residents or frequent visitors. John Ruskin bought his property at Brantwood 'sight unseen', declaring any house set with a view of The Old Man of Coniston to be desirable; Matthew Arnold walked the fells from Fox How near Ambleside. Guidebooks appeared for every requirement, from rock-climbing to honeymooning. The classic work for fell-walkers was Baddeley's Guide, unsurpassed in its detailed coverage until the series by the incomparable A. Wainwright began to appear in the 1950s. But in the early years of the twentieth century, with the last mills closed and agriculture (especially hill farming) in steady decline, Wordsworth's gentrified 'offcomers' and Ruskin's tourists 'drunk on Helvellyn' seemed to offer the region its only chance of economic survival.

The National Trust, established in 1895 to 'hold places of historic interest and natural beauty for the benefit of the nation', was from its beginnings closely associated with the Lake District. Having successfully resisted a proposed tramway along Windermere, it made its first appeal for funds and bought a small area by Derwent Water called Brandelhow Park. By 1925 the Trust owned Scafell; steady acquisitions made it not only a guardian of scenery but an important contributor to the recovery of Lake District farming. The Forestry Commission, formed in 1919, also took a strong economic interest in the region. Opposition to the commercial growth of conifers was primed by the results around Thirlmere, heavily planted with spruce by Manchester Corporation. As similar gloomy uniformity grew up in Ennerdale, debate turned into such powerful protest that in 1935 an agreement was reached between the Commission and the conservation bodies that there would be no further plantations in the central mountainous area. Grizedale Forest, the biggest holding, where planting began in 1937, was developed on more enlightened lines, combining forestry with amenities and preserving or re-establishing the original varied use of the area. There are still large tracts of regimented conifers in the Lake District, but while a reservoir is permanent, a plantation is not. Trees are a crop, and apart from their economic value they benefit their site by slowing down erosion and impoverishment of the soil. This long-term view was seldom that of the farmers, who wanted the lower slopes as well as the high mountains as grazing for their sheep.

'National Parks – solitude for the masses'

The masses today mean millions of people within two or three hours' drive of the Lake District, and at peak summer weekends 186,000 arriving for the day to supplement the 50,000 already there on holiday.

In the 1920s and 1930s several more organisations concerned themselves with landscape preservation and freedom of access, including the Council for the Preservation of Rural England, the Youth Hostels Association, the Friends of the Lake District and the Ramblers Association, and largely through their efforts a parliamentary committee first considered the formation of national parks. By 1945 these had a crucial definition: 'an extensive area of beautiful and relatively wild country in which, for the nation's benefit and by appropriate national decision and action, (a) the characteristic landscape beauty is strictly preserved, (b) access and facilities for public open-air enjoyment are amply provided, (c) wildlife and buildings and places of architectural and historic interest are suitably protected, while (d) established farming use is effectively maintained.' The Lake District was the largest of 10 National Parks in Britain established between 1951 and 1957. Thirty years later, under changed and greatly increased pressures, their administration was reorganised at the same time as local government; 10 National Park Authorities (NPAs) had considerably more powers – and staff – to resolve conflicts between their statutory purposes. Emphasis for a while was very much on preservation. In the 1980s, however, a reassessment of problems concluded that 'complete preservation of an area such as the Lake District is neither possible nor necessarily desirable. The task of the NPA is to continue to try to curtail or prevent those changes which are detrimental to the character and qualities of the Lake District and encourage those which are desirable; in short, to try to maintain a harmonious interaction between man and his environment.'

Management today

Some of the activities of National Park staff are obvious: the waymarking and maintenance of footpaths, the repair of dry-stone walls, the provision of car-parks, the coping with ravages of careless visitors – from obstructed farm gates to scattered litter. They provide enormous amounts of information at visitor centres, on courses and guided walks, in programmes for schools. Less visible is the complex interaction of NPA and farmers. To survive, the fell farmer wants to increase his stock, modernise his buildings, perhaps let out fields for tents or caravans, offer bed and breakfast or holiday flats; in all these matters the NPA will advise and help, so that the farm remains viable rather than being fragmented and sold off. But stone walls in good repair are preferable to wire fences, local building materials to concrete, and temporary holiday accommodation to outright second homes. On the fells, control of erosion is not confined to popular tourist paths but is needed on the climbing approaches to the peaks; and with climbers' co-operation, crags with nesting birds are avoided. In woodland areas tree-planting schemes and tree preservation orders are employed, but overall conservation again depends on co-operation.

The lakes themselves, above all, need the NPA's protection to 'maintain a harmonious interaction between man and his environment': walking and picnicking along the lakeshores are the chief attractions in the region for millions of car-touring visitors each year. The concern of the NPA is threefold: to protect lakes and shores from inappropriate development, to control the impact of the more all-out watersports, and to provide access for gentler activities. Windermere, Coniston, Ullswater and Derwent Water, all with public rights of navigation, are in that order the recreational lakes; non-powered boat launching is also permitted on Thirlmere. Windermere is the only one where (in parts) water speeds of over 10mph are permitted – which means waterskiing and fast power-boating. Dinghies, canoes and sailboards create far less disturbance, but noise and wake are not the only considerations: boating in any concentration, with the car-parks and slipways which would become necessary, would soon transform the tranquillity of the smaller lakes.

Physical damage at the water's edge is much less obvious to the eye than an eroded fell track, but can destroy the habitat of wildlife: steep rocky shores are less vulnerable than the soft reedy areas where rich wetland habitats develop. The presence of apparently contented native ducks accepting visitors' crumbs does not mean that more sensitive migrant wildfowl are not disturbed, crucially in the breeding season; the balance of public access and natural conservation needs careful management. Even busy Windermere has such habitats, especially – as at Derwent Water – around its islands; and Windermere attracts a great many wintering wildfowl. Bassenthwaite Lake, owned outright by the NPA since 1979, has a single sailing club at one end and a particularly rich wetland habitat at the other where conservation has overriding priority.

The water itself of the Lake District supports an exceptional variety of plant and animal life: there are over 20 open-water Sites of Special Scientific Interest. Lakes and tarns differ widely in size, depth, altitude and geological basis, and their chemical composition changes with their catchment area. Influx of sewage, leaching of agricultural fertilisers and the effects of acid rain are all researched and monitored. The Lake District's water supply comes from many small lakes and tarns, and without noticeable effect on the landscape Ennerdale Water, Wast Water and Crummock Water supply West Cumbria. The National Park's inviolability was confirmed in 1978 when major new proposals for extracting water from Wastwater and Ennerdale were rejected. The traumatic drowning of a village and the bleak shoreline scar at Haweswater, reservoir for Greater Manchester since the 1930s, will never be repeated. Thoughtful replanning of the shores of Thirlmere, where two lakes were merged and some land lost, have given it more appeal and accessibility; water from Ullswater and Windermere feeds the same supply but abstraction is strictly limited, and managed without perceptible works or change of level. Urban authorities continue however to covet the water of other Lakeland valleys.

The element of the Lake District least under the control of the National Park Authority is the welfare of its living communities. The NPA is powerless to prevent the decline of employment, the closure of village schools and shops or the diminishing of public transport – except by its efforts to limit the takeover of the area by car-bound second-home owners, and its policy of 'containing provision of recreation and tourist facilities . . . to a level compatible with the essential character of the Lake District'. It is just as well that the steep up-curve of tourist numbers is flattening out as the motorways, let alone the destination, reach and pass saturation point.

The modern Lake Poet Norman Nicholson, Wordsworth's successor in his lifelong, loving interpretation of his native region, feared in the 1960s that 'the National Park will become no more than a convalescent home for a sick urban civilisation'. Twenty years on, the various national, regional, commercial and conservationist powers that govern or influence the Lake District have yet to combine on Nicholson's 'real defence against the erosion of tourism: the survival of a living community, long-rooted in the locality, making its own way and at least partially independent of the visitor'.

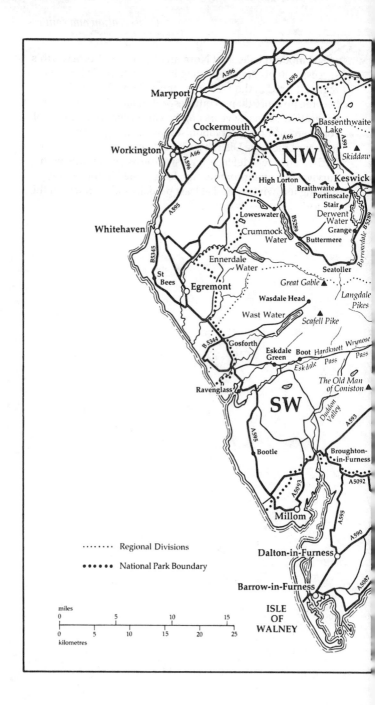

.... Regional Divisions

●●●●●● National Park Boundary

miles
0 .... 5 .... 10 15

0 ... 5 ... 10 ... 15 ... 20 ... 25
kilometres

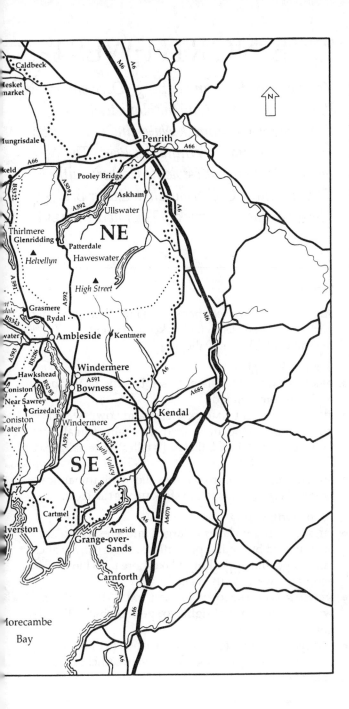

THE NORTH-WEST

Keswick · Skiddaw and Latrigg · Derwent Water · Borrowdale and the Honister Pass · Buttermere, Crummock Water and Loweswater · Lorton Vale and the Whinlatter Pass · The Newlands Valley · Keswick to Cockermouth · Cockermouth · Cockermouth to Calder Bridge · The west coast · Keswick to Thirlmere · WHERE TO STAY

Scenery

Arguably more variety per square mile than any other part of the Lake District: six lakes and some magnificent fells and valleys.

Scenic highlights

- DERWENT WATER for sheer classic beauty. Boat trip highly recommended.
- BUTTERMERE, CRUMMOCK WATER and LOWESWATER: BUTTERMERE is the finest sited of a chain of small but very beautiful lakes. Lakeland's tallest waterfall, SCALE FORCE, is nearby.
- BORROWDALE – a narrow river valley with romantically wooded crags; leads to the stark HONISTER PASS.

Also worth seeing

- THIRLMERE – two lakes enlarged into a reservoir, surrounded by conifer plantations. A partially artificial landscape, but appealing; a lakeshore path looks across the water to HELVELLYN.
- NEWLANDS and ST JOHN'S IN THE VALE – two valleys with no great natural sights to speak of, but with quiet charm.
- The fell road from ENNERDALE BRIDGE to CALDER BRIDGE, which gets good distant views (including SELLAFIELD).

Best walks

Easy walks

- Any walk around the shores of DERWENT WATER.
- A circuit of BUTTERMERE.
- Woodland and hill walks taking in the floor of BORROWDALE.
- SCALE FORCE and TAYLOR GILL FORCE: both waterfalls involve walks through fine mountain scenery; for immediate setting, TAYLOR GILL FORCE just has the edge.
- Forest walks in THORNTHWAITE FOREST (from Whinlatter visitor centre) and DODD WOOD.
- Low fells with good views include CAT BELLS, LANTHWAITE HILL, LOW BANK, LATRIGG, WALLA CRAG, CASTLE HEAD, CASTLE CRAG and DODD WOOD.
- The clifftop path between WHITEHAVEN and ST BEES provides the best coastal walks in the area.

Fell walks

- Magnificent ridge walks in the triangular area of fells enclosed by BORROWDALE and DERWENT WATER to the east, the BUTTERMERE valley and HONISTER PASS to the south, and the WHINLATTER PASS to the north.
- Rugged mountain scenery along the RED PIKE to HAYSTACKS ridge.
- SKIDDAW – a marvellous view from the summit. A long plod up along an easy but dullish route if you follow the crowds, but there are more interesting – and more challenging – ways to the top.

Sights

Houses

- WORDSWORTH HOUSE in Cockermouth: Wordsworth's birthplace and a fine house in itself.
- MIREHOUSE: Tennyson connections; pleasantly sited in extensive grounds, close to BASSENTHWAITE LAKE.

Gardens

- LINGHOLM: famous for rhododendrons and azaleas; lovely woodlands; occasional glimpses of CAT BELLS and the BORROWDALE fells.

Best churches

- Nothing unmissable in the National Park; what few medieval churches survive were thoroughly restored in Victorian times. CROSTHWAITE CHURCH is worth a visit for its Southey memorial.
- ST BEES – priory church with Norman doorway and unusual nineteenth-century screen.
- CALDER ABBEY – fine ruins, but privately owned and possible to view only from a distance.

Museums

- FITZPARK and PENCIL MUSEUMS in Keswick – unusual subject-matter, and quite good places to which to take children. The RAILWAY MUSEUM in Keswick is mainly for enthusiasts.
- The ETHNIC DOLL AND TOY MUSEUM in Cockermouth – as its name suggests, lots of dolls; nearly all the toys are model railways.
- WHITEHAVEN MUSEUM – good local museum with displays on maritime history, and coal and china industries.
- Maryport's STEAM TUGS, in the harbour; popular with children. Small NAUTICAL MUSEUM nearby.
- SELLAFIELD – hi-tech razzmatazz, promoting the nuclear gospel. A visually stunning free show.

Archaeology

- CASTLERIGG STONE CIRCLE – sited above KESWICK, with a fine view.

Best villages

- Picturesque vernacular in BORROWDALE, at its best in ROSTHWAITE and STONETHWAITE, and a pretty bridge at GRANGE. WATENDLATH merits a look if only for its location.

Towns

- COCKERMOUTH is off the beaten track but more likeable than KESWICK: a maze of small streets and vestiges of its industrial past make it a rewarding place for a walkabout.
- KESWICK is much more touristy, and frantically busy in

season. Excellent central location for the northern
lakes, and masses of B&B, but disappoints as a place.
A few museums plus the tourist information centre for
rainy days, and a good range of shops.

- WHITEHAVEN – an early planned industrial town, lots
  of eighteenth-century streets, an atmospheric harbour,
  a fine church, a good museum and Cumbria's largest
  second-hand bookshop.
- MARYPORT – not quite another Whitehaven, but a
  planned town of the same period.
- WORKINGTON – a large industrial town, with one
  incongruously pleasant square and a briefly absorbing
  old centre; but there's not quite enough to go out of
  your way for.
- EGREMONT has a ruined castle; otherwise an
  industrial-cum-market town with little to see.

Keswick

With such a range of first-class scenery on the town's
doorstep, Keswick seems the obvious major base for
exploring the northern Lake District. It is handy for public
transport (several local bus services operate from here) and
you will probably want to use the town's amenities; but if
you have a car, there are better places to stay at in the
vicinity. Despite the magnificence of the scenery that
surrounds the town, the neighbouring fells, with the
exception of Skiddaw and Grisedale Pike peering over the
tops of some of the town's many terraces of guest-houses,
don't make their presence felt very much, and Derwent
Water is even more aloof.

Keswick looks unmistakably Victorian – the result of
expansion after the Cockermouth, Keswick and Penrith
Railway made a concerted effort to boost tourism when the
volume of goods traffic on the line eased off, as the west
Cumbrian iron ore industry fell into decline. To the despair
of Ruskin (see p. 144) ('The stupid herds of modern tourists
let themselves be emptied, like coals from a sack, at
Windermere and Keswick stations'), the line doubled its

passenger traffic between 1865 and 1890. What had been principally a small market town, made prosperous with the advent of the mining industries in Borrowdale and the Newlands Valley, found a new role as what Victorian guidebook writers termed (somewhat flatteringly) a 'little Alpine town' in 'British Switzerland': rows of grey-stone lodging-houses appeared on the east side of town and shops received new façades; the Keswick Hotel opened in 1869 and others followed.

If the town's overall appearance is somewhat sombre, its animated centre compensates to some extent, though it is overrun in season. Keswick has some good outdoor shops (notably George Fisher in Lake Road, a long-established three-floor emporium with a vast stock), a couple of tempting old-fashioned bakers (try the cafe upstairs at Bryson's) and two bookshops (both with a large section on local guidebooks). Hand-made chocolates are sold at Ye Old Friars in Main Street.

Lunch places include the converted Old Station Restaurant, good value with a buffet section; and the Dog and Gun, a lively town-centre pub offering mostly meaty bar meals, some local dishes and some more exotic. Most stylish is Mayson's, attached to a small department store: light self-service lunches (good salads) and a cosmopolitan dinner menu in light and airy surroundings with lots of greenery.

The **Century Theatre** is housed in a bizarre makeshift arrangement of huts, nicknamed for obvious reasons 'the blue box', in Lakeside car-park. More a contraption than a building, the 225-seater theatre travelled the roads of England from 1952 to 1975. It is no longer mobile, despite the wheels sticking out of the sides. It runs a season of drama in the summer – usually three plays in rotation (you can book at the Moot Hall). Keswick's diminutive **Alhambra cinema** is in St John's Street just behind the market place. Look out for the grocer's shop opposite, with its display of early enamel advertising signs.

In the centre of Main Street is the rather Tyrolean **Moot Hall** (built in 1819, before Keswick had a parish church of its own, in a very obviously churchy style), which replaced a sixteenth-century courthouse. It is adorned with a one-handed clock; the building's ground-floor arches were originally open and were used as market stalls. The stones used in its construction and its fourteenth-century bell are thought to have been taken from Lord's Island in Derwent Water. The Moot Hall now houses a major National Park **information centre**. Talks on the National Park, walking, climbing, the National Trust and other themes are held here regularly, usually in the evening; these can be an entertaining way of broadening your knowledge of the area. Regular guided walks start from the Moot Hall.

Keswick has three small museums. The **Pencil Museum** (open all year, Mon to Fri, 9.30 to 4; Sat and Sun, 2 to 4.30) off Main Street adjoins the still-functioning Cumberland Pencil factory (now owned by Rexel); the factory has been here for 150 years, though it no longer uses local graphite. This is a good rainy-day place to visit, and children particularly may find it appealing. The display contains some entertaining curiosities, such as the world's largest pencil and the 'secret map' pencil, which showed Second World War fighter pilots how to escape from occupied territory.

Fitzpark Museum (also called the Keswick Museum and Art Gallery; open Apr to Oct, Mon to Sat, 10 to 12.30, 2 to 5.30) in Station Road is an old-fashioned, small-town museum of the parquet floors and glass cases variety – almost a museumpiece in itself. The collection is endearingly miscellaneous, and includes a penny-farthing bicycle, ancient tooth-extracting equipment, a macabre display of snares (including a man-trap), a 500-year-old mummified cat found in a church roof, fossils, stuffed birds, local paintings and quite a lot more. Highlights are the 'Rock, Bell and Steel Band' – a xylophone partly made of Skiddaw slates collected by the Richardson family between 1827 and 1840, and performed before Queen Victoria in 1848 – you can try it out with your fingers (its tuning is remarkably good); Joseph Flintoft's scale model of the Lake District (which took him from 1817 to 1834 to make); and a valuable collection of letters and manuscripts of Wordsworth, Coleridge, De Quincey, Southey and Hugh Walpole, though for the most part only facsimiles are displayed to prevent deterioration of the originals. Among the printed material is the first edition of *The Story of the Three Bears* (which Southey translated from the German; Goldilocks, incidentally, was a later, English addition to the tale).

The **Railway Museum** (open Easter to Oct, daily, 2 to 5) in Main Street, run by the local railway society, houses a small display of railway signs, old tickets, photographs and signal-box equipment; there are also two model railway layouts and a video.

Keswick Spa leisure complex in Station Road has a wave-effect swimming-pool with waterslide, a solarium and a restaurant. You can buy a ticket for the day; evening rates are a little cheaper.

Keswick's most famous residents lived at **Greta Hall** (now part of Keswick School). The house is not open to the public, but can be glimpsed by taking the riverside path through Fitzpark (off Station Road, close to the Fitzpark Museum), crossing the next footbridge and turning right along a residential road, which soon enters trees; the house is just beyond. Coleridge, his wife and four-year-old son moved here in July 1800 in order to be within visiting distance of Wordsworth, who was then at Dove Cottage, Grasmere. The Hall was at that time inhabited by a William Jackson, a well-to-do carrier, and his housekeeper; Jackson retired in his forties to devote more time to his books, and let off the southerly (better) half of the house. When he found out that his future tenant was none other than Coleridge, he was so pleased that he charged no rent for the first six months.

Wordsworth had tried, unsuccessfully, to encourage Charles Lamb and his sister Mary to travel from London to stay here, but Lamb would have none of it. Coleridge himself finally enticed Lamb to come, but Lamb could share none of the lyric poets' enthusiasm for the scenery:

We have clambered up to the top of Skiddaw, and I have waded up the bed of Lodore. In fine, I have satisfied myself that there is such a thing that the tourists call romantic, which I very much suspected before; they make such a spluttering about it.

As Coleridge's health was failing, he abandoned the Lakeland climate for the warmth of Malta, and Southey and his wife joined Sara Coleridge and the younger Coleridge. The arrival of the Southeys was precipitated by their grief following the death of their daughter. Plaques to Wordsworth, Coleridge and Southey are by the door to Greta Hall.

The Southeys used to attend church services at **Crosthwaite** parish church; as a child Ruskin came to the same services in the hope of catching a glimpse of the famous poet. (Crosthwaite constitutes the western end of Keswick, but the whole town was in its parish until the more central St John's was built in 1838.) The fourteenth- and

sixteenth-century church, half a mile north-west of the Moot
Hall, contains a white marble monument to Southey; the
poet's son Cuthbert said it was the best likeness of the man
that had ever been made. Wordsworth wrote the inscription,
but changed the ending after the carving had been
completed – the erasure in the penultimate line is still visible.
Southey's grave in the churchyard is well signposted, and
there is a lovely view from here over the Derwent fells. One
aisle is dedicated to Canon Rawnsley, one of the founders of
the National Trust and for many years vicar of Crosthwaite.

In the churchyard of Keswick's nineteenth-century parish
church in St John's Street is the grave of Sir Hugh Walpole –
another resting-place carefully chosen for its outlook.

Old Windebrowe (open by appointment only), which
stands under the A66 bridge on the east side of town, was
the home of William and Dorothy Wordsworth for a short
time before they moved on to Dove Cottage in Grasmere.

Skiddaw and Latrigg

For nineteenth-century tourists, the track up **Skiddaw** from
Keswick was the most popular climb in the region, and,
before the central fells became more accessible, Skiddaw was
in fact the only summit most visitors would consider
attempting. The route up today is more clearly defined than
ever, although the 'half-way house' which used to provide
refreshments has fallen into ruin; your best bet for tea
hereabouts now is to try the Underscar Hotel, a spectacular
Italianate mansion in fine grounds with views of Derwent
Water; the hotel is just east of Applethwaite.

Though it's a long (two-hour) plod to the top, Skiddaw is
by far the easiest ascent of the four 3000-foot Lake District
peaks, and there are no hidden dangers on the way. It isn't a
very varied walk up, however (much better on the way down
with Derwent Water and Borrowdale to look at), though you
can be rewarded with astonishingly wide views at the top,
covering the Scottish lowlands, the Isle of Man, the western
Pennines and most of the major Lakeland peaks. (Other,
more exciting routes to the top are a little harder – see p. 227.)
You can start at either of two points. Purists who want to
start from the bottom should take a track on the north side of
Keswick (to reach it, follow Station Road, which bends right
soon after the museum – ignore the entrance to Keswick Spa

straight ahead – continue on the road, which soon passes under the old railway bridge, until you reach a small housing estate; park on the verge – the track is on the right signposted Skiddaw). If you prefer to cut out the first 700 feet of ascent (the worst part, because of the traffic noise from the A66), use the small car-park east of Applethwaite and follow the signs for Skiddaw. From this car-park it is an easy 10-minute stroll on to **Latrigg**, a foothill of Skiddaw; follow the bridleway signposted from the car-park (leading away from Skiddaw), which descends before being joined by conifers on the right, then fork left after 400 yards, on a gently ascending grassy track to the summit. The panorama from Latrigg is an impressive one, including Derwent Water, Castlerigg stone circle, Borrowdale, Scafell, Helvellyn and Pillar.

Skiddaw, Blencathra and the fells to the north collectively make up a vast unpopulated upland, roughly six miles square and crossed by no roads. Depending on taste, it appears as direly austere or magnificently remote: to the north of Skiddaw there are no dramatic major peaks, just vast expanses of rolling moor and forgotten fells. In the middle, and approached by a 1½-hour walk from the Skiddaw car-park (just east of Applethwaite, a hamlet to the north of Keswick) is a solitary farmstead, Skiddaw House, nestling in a windbreak of trees, and now functioning as a very simple youth hostel. A track leading to the house from the west passes Whitewater Dash (also known simply as The Dash), a waterfall which Coleridge visited and admired ('more completely atomised and white than any other I have seen . . . they are the finest water furies I ever beheld').

Derwent Water

Two and three-quarter miles north to south and one mile west to east at its widest, Derwent Water is roughly oval – the least elongated of the lakes. Its captivating views – reedy shores, islands and a surrounding backdrop of mixed woodland and craggy volcanic and smooth slate fells – never quite look the same twice, and there are lots of vantage-points from which to drink it all in. No one should miss out on a boat trip: from the Lakeside car-park near Keswick a launch makes a 50-minute circular tour of the lake, stopping at six landing-stages on the way (services operate alternately clockwise and anti-clockwise); additionally, you

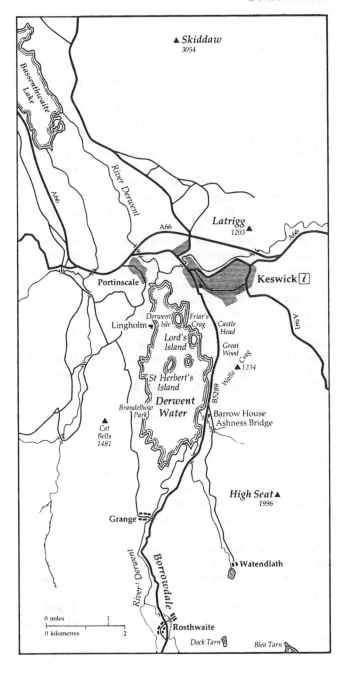

can hire a power- or rowing-boat, which enables you to land on the islands.

Derwent Water also deserves to be at least partially explored on foot, for the sequence of its delights passes by quickly, and some of the finest views of the lake and surrounding fells are just off the road. There are lakeshore paths only around parts of it, though it's possible to devise a day-long circuit using various paths and roads.

Four of the lake's islands are large enough to support the growth of trees; there is also the 'floating island' near the southern end – a tangle of vegetation periodically brought to the surface by marsh gas. **St Herbert's Island** is the largest, so named because that saint lived on it from 685; remains of his hermitage are still just discernible, although the island is overgrown; to the east of it lies **Rampsholme Island**. **Lord's Island** was once the site of the Earl of Derwentwater's house. A colony of German miners specially brought over to work on the Goldscope mine when it opened in 1565 lived on **Derwent Isle**, where they grew vegetables and brewed beer. Joseph Pocklington, scion of a Newark banking family, acquired the island in 1778 and built a house on it together with, in the true romantic spirit, some follies and a stone circle. Pocklington very much made his mark on Derwent Water, building a villa at Portinscale, and Barrow House (1781) and the cottage by the Bowder Stone (1789). He and Peter Crosthwaite, the owner of a museum in Keswick, put on numerous regattas, including a mock sea battle, on Derwent Isle.

The west side of the lake

Immediately west of the point where the B5289 meets the A66 is a minor turn to **Portinscale** (curiously, its name derives from the Norse for 'prostitute's hut'), a large village of villas and small hotels which feels almost like a suburb of Keswick. From here, the Grange road running south ducks into woods and loses sight of the lake. Shortly on the left is the entrance to **Lingholm**, home of Lord Rochdale, whose woodlands and imaginatively planted formal gardens are open to the public (Apr to Oct, daily, 10 to 5); they are known particularly for their rhododendrons and azaleas, as well as fine mixed woodlands; from the terrace are views of Cat Bells and towards Borrowdale. Plants and shrubs are on sale at a nursery here, and there is a tea-room (open to non-visitors).

Beatrix Potter wrote *Squirrel Nutkin* at Lingholm; the hero of the book crossed Derwent Water on a raft.

The abrupt ridge straight ahead as you emerge from the woods is **Cat Bells**, which comprises two large grassy humps, narrow enough to straddle at its northern end; it joins on to Maiden Moor, making a north–south ridge of nearly four miles. In its entirety, the views are best if it is walked from south to north, but the 1000-foot ascent of just the Cat Bells end is superb either way round – and it's just elevated enough to feel like a real fell walk. The tallest hump actually requires a short scramble – not difficult, but be careful (there are more accidents on this hill than on many of the more major peaks). There is a small car-park reached by forking right (signposted to Skelgill and car-park) just after the road crosses a cattle-grid. The path up is popular to the point of alarming erosion, but the sharp contrast of the view west to east, with the Newlands Valley and the smooth green ridges of Causey Pike and Knott Rigg to the west and Derwent Water to the east, explains why so many visitors head here (see walk on p. 225). A path by the cattle-grid and a National Trust sign for Hawes End leads down to the lakeshore and boat landing-stage: turn right at the bottom on the driveway to Hawes End, then immediately left through a kissing-gate to reach the lake.

Between Cat Bells and the lake is an attractive patch of woodlands, with a path following the shore offering waterside views. In 1902, **Brandelhow Park**, which forms part of these woods, became the first National Trust property in the Lake District. Nearby is Brackenburn (not open), where Sir Hugh Walpole made his home for the last 17 years of his life, from 1924 to 1941. The road continues to Grange (see p. 53) at the entrance to Borrowdale, near which the B5289 is joined. Turning left is the route for the east side of Derwent Water.

The east side of the lake

The southernmost car-park on this side of the lake is Kettlewell car-park – a very fine viewpoint. Continuing north, the entrance to **Barrow House** youth hostel is reached. The hostel is a superbly sited Victorian country house looking over the lake. In the nineteenth century dynamite was used to blast out rock in order to enhance the waterfalls at the back of the house. Cheating this may be, but in fact the result is no less pleasing than its infinitely more famous neighbour at Lodore.

Immediately north of Barrow House there is a right turn to **Watendlath**. In season this is a nightmarish drive, as the road is very narrow and there are few passing places; you may be better off starting from Rosthwaite and walking up from there (see p. 53). The Watendlath vale is a classic hanging valley – a subsidiary valley left high above the main one (Borrowdale) after the latter had been deepened by a glacier, with the result that Watendlath Beck tumbles down over the Lodore Falls (see p. 51) to join the River Derwent in Borrowdale. Soon after the initial ascent of the road from the B5289, it crosses the tiny **Ashness Bridge**, which together with the backdrop of Derwent Water and Skiddaw provides a scene which competes with Tarn Hows as being Lakeland's most photographed view. Very shortly after, just off the road to the right, is **Surprise View**, surprising not for its subject (Derwent Water and Skiddaw again) but for the dizzying drop below. **Watendlath** itself is a tiny hamlet of farmsteads encircled by small hills and with its own tarn; a nicely sited cafe provides a leisurely way to take in the scene. The hamlet is so remote that electricity did not arrive here until recent years, and telephones were not installed until 1984. A mile or so further south, and reachable only by path, are two more tarns – **Dock Tarn** and **Blea Tarn**, more remote but less appealing. A footpath along the brook on the other side of a small stone bridge a few steps beyond the end of the road provides a pleasant (and far less frenetic) way to see the valley you have just driven up. Watendlath's setting clearly made a strong impression on Hugh Walpole, and provided the setting for his novel *Judith Paris* (part of the *Rogue Herries* chronicles); a house by the car-park bears a plaque identifying the fictional heroine's home.

The road soon enters woodland, skirting **Great Wood**, whose National Trust car-park is the starting-point for walks up **Walla Crag**, a series of crags just beyond the topmost part of these mixed woodlands.

Two of the finest low-level views of Derwent Water are close to Keswick. From Lakeside car-park at Keswick, a track leads past the landing-stages and soon narrows into a lakeside path. After a few minutes you reach a small wood at **Friar's Crag**, whose outlook of the four islands Ruskin rated as one of the three finest views in Europe; his earliest

memory (as the nearby memorial records) was of being taken
here by his nurse. Adjacent is an idyllic beach. **Castle Head** is
a small wooded hill immediately east of the B5289, and a
15-minute walk from Lakeside car-park. To reach it, take a
woodland path by the Century Theatre in the car-park (by a
National Trust No Camping sign), immediately fork left and
follow a path inside the edge of the woods until taking a path
on the left running between fields; cross the road, and take a
gate opposite into the woods of Castle Head, and ascend to
the summit. The view includes the whole of the lake and its
surrounding fells, plus Scafell, Borrowdale and Criffel in
Dumfries & Galloway; there is a view indicator on top.

Borrowdale and the Honister Pass

Soon after we came under Gowdar-Crag [sic], *a hill more
formidable to the eye, and to the apprehension, than that of
Lowdore* [sic]; *the rocks at top deep-cloven perpendicularly
by the rains, hanging loose and nodding forwards, seen just
starting from their base in shivers. The whole way down, and
the road on both sides, is strewed with piles of the fragments,
strangely thrown across each other, and of a dreadful
bulk.* (THOMAS GRAY, letter written in 1769)

Just beyond the southern end of Derwent Water, the B5289
passes the Swiss Lodore Hotel on the other side of which are
the **Lodore Falls**, accessible by a footpath around the back of
the hotel. After dry weather, these can be a disappointment
as the falls all but dry up, but in the wet season they swell to
a gushing torrent, more impressive still if the trees around
are not in leaf; but even then the description in Parson and
White's Directory (1829) as 'the Niagara of England' is
perhaps a bit over the top. Southey's 200-line onomatopoeic
poem 'How Does the Water Come Down at Lodore?', written
for children, became a popular nineteenth-century parlour
piece.

The road soon enters **Borrowdale**, whose hugely romantic
appeal immediately endeared itself to early-nineteenth-
century tourists and landscape painters in search of the
picturesque, and has been a favourite Lakeland valley ever
since. The essence of its special character is in its irregularly
shaped crags, broad-leaf woods and fine river scenery along
the Derwent. The woods, which comprise chiefly oak, birch

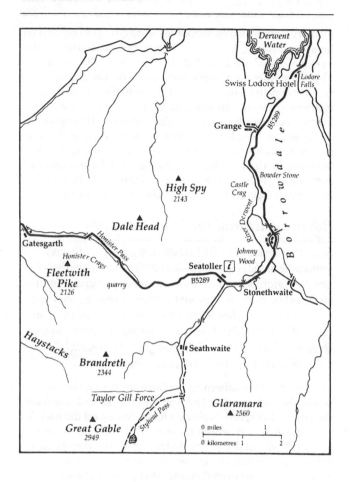

and hazel, plus others including rowan, ash, holly and alder, are not natural but are the result of planting and coppicing, much of it taking place in the nineteenth century. At that time the valley was still a busy centre for mining: the sixteenth-century mining boom depleted the natural woodlands, which supplied charcoal for smelting lead, copper and gold. Plumbago, used as a remedy for colic and as a drawing material, was also mined here for the Keswick Pencil Company.

Inhabitants of Borrowdale were once known as Borrowdale Gowk, 'gowk' being a Cumbrian word for cuckoo. Locals once tried to imprison a cuckoo to ensure that it would always be spring. This they did by building a sturdy stone wall around the bird, which promptly flew out of the top.

Grange village, just to the west of the main road, has a lovely double-arched stone bridge at its near end, and a pretty group of stone cottages around a small green nearby. Grange Bridge Cottage makes a good stopping-off place for snacks or light lunches, while the Borrowdale Gates Hotel, at the north-west end of the village, is ideal for leisurely afternoon tea. There is quite a lot of B&B accommodation in the village. From 1209 the village was a grange – or abbey farm – for Furness Abbey; this was the abbey's most remote of its estates in the Lake District.

Grange is the easiest access-point for exploring this end of Borrowdale on foot. In particular, you can follow paths to the **River Derwent** and on to **Castle Crag**, the finest viewpoint of Borrowdale (see walk on p. 219). There was once a hill fort on top, a defensive base used by the Britons against the Romans (*Borrowdale* or *Borgardalr* means 'valley of the fort').

Continuing south on the B5289, you pass the shop for Lakeland Rural Industries, which specialises in beaten silverwork, although there are many other crafts on display (not all local, but all made in the UK). A little further on, look out for a National Trust sign on the left for the **Bowder Stone**. This 'erratic block' – a 2000-ton boulder moved from its previous site by glacier and deposited here – stands a few yards from the road. It is balanced, somewhat improbably, on its corner and is 36 feet high; a flight of 29 steps ascends it, though the views over Borrowdale are slightly better from an adjacent grassy platform. Victorian tourists made a point of visiting the stone and photographing themselves shaking hands through the overhang.

Borrowdale soon broadens out. At **Rosthwaite** stone cottages are packed in a small tangle of lanes just off the main road – rather pretty in a small-scale way. The signposted bridleway along the drive to Hazel Bank Hotel (just north of the post office) provides a lovely route to Watendlath (see p. 50); a steady but not steep ascent provides good views, and the walk takes an hour there and back. Accessible by path from here or from Seatoller is **Johnny Wood**, generally reckoned to be the finest of Borrowdale's woodlands, given the status of Site of Special Scientific Interest because of its rich variety of ferns, liverworts and mosses in the predominantly oak and sycamore woods.

Stonethwaite lies at the end of a cul-de-sac, and is sufficiently tucked away to get missed by many (the relative obscurity of the fells surrounding it, compared to the giants further west, probably helps keep the crowds away too). Again, it's humble and picturesque – one tea-shop and a couple of B&Bs.

Seathwaite is another very small hamlet off the B5289, but much more frequented owing to its excellent position as a walking centre; there is some parking here, plus a basic cafe (which also sells fresh and smoked trout). The Styhead Pass, an ancient packhorse route, links Seathwaite to Wasdale – 4 miles on foot, while the quickest way by road is about 35 miles. Fortunately temptations to build a coach road over the pass in the last century came to nothing. Great Gable, Scafell Pike and Glaramara are three major attractions which can be reached from here. A much easier walk is to **Taylor Gill Force**; this is one of the most dramatically sited of the Lake District's waterfalls (see walk on p. 222). Seathwaite is notorious for its weather – it is the wettest place in Britain where rainfall is recorded (averaging 125 inches a year); not that it rains more frequently here, it's just that the rain comes down particularly drenchingly when it does. The Wadd Mine which used to operate at Seathwaite was one of the major Borrowdale graphite mines.

Seatoller, on the B5289, has a National Park **visitor centre** housed in an old barn by the car-park; its wildlife and geology displays are worth a look. Yew Tree Country Restaurant, a whitewashed cottage with beams and a flagstone floor, has long been a favourite lunch or tea stop for walkers and motorists; it's also open for early dinners.

The **Honister Pass** is the road route linking Borrowdale to the east end of the Buttermere Valley. Although it has a one-in-four gradient on the west side, it is not either as scary or as demanding a drive as the Hardknott and Wrynose Passes. But the scree-covered slopes which plunge 1500 feet and more are quite formidable.

As you drive over the 1176-foot pass from the Borrowdale end, the dividing line between the smooth, green slopes of the Skiddaw Slate fells on your right and the more rugged Borrowdale series, which includes the striking Honister Crags, on your left is at its most obvious. At the top of the pass are the (working) quarry of the Buttermere and Westmorland Green Slate Co. Ltd (open by appointment only) and a car-park close to the ugly youth hostel and quarry buildings; it's worth getting out here to take in the scale of this somewhat mournful landscape. With so much height gained, this is a relatively easy way to walk up a well-defined track to the top of Fleetwith Pike (2126 feet) ahead and to the left of the road and Haystacks (see below) – both give excellent views down the valley.

More significantly, this is a good starting-point for the easiest route up Great Gable, which lies to the south; the ascent, which is well graded and consistently interesting, heads up Brandreth and Green Gable before the final section to this much-climbed summit.

Slate was first produced here in 1643 and there has been continuous extraction ever since; its fissile nature, splitting cleanly to produce even flakes, makes the stone ideal for commercial use. Before the Honister Pass began to be used in the nineteenth century, slate was taken by a high fell route known as Moses' Trod, which ran directly to Wasdale and then on to the sea at Drigg, near Ravenglass. This route is still used by walkers. The Trod was named after a quarryman called Moses, a part-time whisky smuggler, who may have also had a hand in the illegal removal of graphite from mines nearby and who used this route to his advantage.

Although from the slate quarry the scenery seems just vast and very bare, punctuated only by the crags and the intrusion of the quarry's workings themselves, there is an abrupt transition into a more charming landscape at **Gatesgarth**, where the road flattens and the valley, the southern end of Lorton Vale, opens out. From here you can make the ascent of **Haystacks**, one of the region's most popular fell walks (see walk on p. 228).

Buttermere, Crummock Water and Loweswater

These form a chain of small lakes, usually visited in the same outing. All are reserved for peaceful pursuits – walking, rowing and fishing (boat hire and fishing permits for Buttermere are available from Gatesgarth; for Crummock Water, go to Rannerdale Farm; both are on the road and are easy to find. Enquire at Scale Hill Hotel for hiring rowing-boats and for fishing permits for Loweswater).

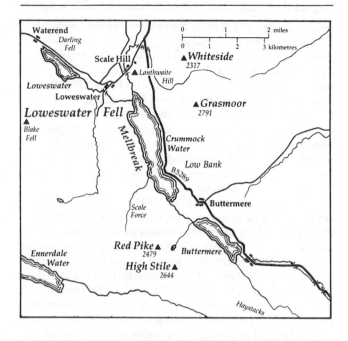

Buttermere is the most popular of the three – hemmed in by fells of sharply contrasting character, and punctuated by patches of woodland. To the east, the deep channel of the Honister Pass leads out of the valley, to the south are the formidable slopes of Red Pike, High Stile and High Crag, while to the north-west is the continuation of the valley to Crummock Water.

Although Buttermere lake is surrounded by imposing fells, there are a few classic easy walks in the vicinity. Most popular of all is the 3½-mile circuit of the lake (see walk on p. 215), which you can start along the track immediately to the left of the Fish Inn in Buttermere village, although it may be easier to park at Gatesgarth and start from there.

Also starting from Buttermere village (and again signposted) is the 2¼-mile walk to **Scale Force**, which at 140 feet is the highest waterfall in the Lake District; the route to it takes the track to the left of the Fish Inn for a short distance before branching right through a gate, then takes the first valley on the left after Crummock Water appears on the right. The falls are in a wooded cleft up to the left, and the path is clear all the way, though it can be boggy in the final stages. Views on the return leg are better than on the way out, but a more interesting (though far more demanding) route to them is from Loweswater village (see p. 58). It is also worth making an effort to see the valley from above. One of the easiest ways of doing this is to walk up on to **Low Bank**, which makes a hugely enjoyable fell walk in miniature: a grassy ridge culminates at the aptly scaled-down crags of Rannerdale Knotts, which involve a token bit of scrambling (see walk on p. 215).

Positioned as it is at the west of the lake, it is perhaps not surprising that tiny Buttermere village gets easily overwhelmed with tourists. The main reason for stopping here is the car-park, which is strategically placed for walks (a fee is payable, however, and there are lots of free, but smaller ones, elsewhere in the valley). In addition to a few guest-houses, the village has two inns.

Tourists have been flocking to Buttermere for a long time. In 1795, J. Budworth published *A Fortnight's Ramble in the Lakes*, in which he made Mary Robinson, the 15-year-old daughter of the innkeeper at the Fish Inn, Buttermere, into a tourist attraction:

Her face was a fine oval, with full eyes, and lips as red as vermilion, her cheeks had more of the lily than the rose . . . She looked an angel, and I doubt not she is the reigning lily of the valley. Ye travellers of the Lakes, if you visit this obscure place such you will find the fair Sally of Buttermere.

On a later visit, Budworth expressed his hope that Mary would not suffer from the stream of sightseers his publication had brought about, adding, 'you are not so handsome as you promised to be and I have long wished, by conversation like this, to do away what mischief the flattering character I gave of you may expose you to'. In 1802 someone purporting to be Colonel the Hon. Alexander Augustus Hope came here and married her, before it transpired that he was a James Hatfield, impostor, bigamist and forger. He was hanged in Carlisle the following year, and Mary gave birth to a still-born child, after which she remained in Buttermere for sightseers to come and gawp at. The case was written up by Coleridge under the heading 'A Romantic Marriage' for the *Morning Post* (and more recently by Melvyn Bragg in his novel *The Maid of Buttermere*). Happily, Mary remarried a local farmer and brought up a large family at Caldbeck, where she is buried. At the time, the saga very much caught the public imagination and there was great sympathy for Mary.

Crummock Water is twice the size of Buttermere and separated from it by just a few flat meadows, low enough to remind us that this was once all one lake. Crummock Water is itself a lake-turned-reservoir. Crummock is surrounded by yet more fells of great beauty. Somehow the lake doesn't quite have the appeal of its neighbour, perhaps because of the wall-like appearance of **Mellbreak** on its west side. Access on foot is possible on both sides, though because of the road the west side makes a more satisfactory walk. The best starting-point is from Lanthwaite Hill car-park, on the Loweswater road (an unclassified road leading west off the B5289) beyond the north end of the lake, just after the road descends by the Scale Hill Hotel; the entrance to the car-park is marked by a bridleway signpost on the left side of the road. From here it takes 10 minutes to walk through the woods via a broad woodland track (ignore left turns) to the head of the lake, where two benches look down the length of the water towards Honister Pass. From here, the lakeside path to the right is the better for open views; the left-hand one is densely screened by trees. Also easy, but more elevated, is the 10-minute walk up **Lanthwaite Hill** – a mere 674 feet (and only 160 feet of ascent), but a surprisingly good viewpoint of the lake and its adjacent fells. To reach its summit from the car-park, follow the road uphill towards the Scale Hill Hotel, just before which take a gate on the right signposted to Lanthwaite Green, picking up a woodland track. After 130 yards, take a narrow path on the left, which rises and soon bends sharp left up rough steps then emerges into open ground; the summit is the larger of two small hillocks in front of you.

The tallest and most shapely fell abutting Crummock Water is **Grasmoor**, at the north-east end of the valley, a graceful pyramid which towers above the lake. To the north is **Whiteside**, whose position as the tallest fell on the north-western edge of the Lake District gives it the most extensive uninterrupted view of the Solway Firth and the Cumbrian coast of any Lakeland summit. See walk on p. 224.

A minor turn on the west side of the B5289, just to the north of Crummock Water, leads to **Loweswater**. Like Buttermere, Loweswater is a smallish lake, abundant in birdlife, which has given its name to a small village.

Loweswater has quiet and pleasant scenery, with none of the fireworks of Buttermere and Crummock Water, so not surprisingly it's also far less frequented. From the road, the lake is screened by a lattice of pine trees; there are a few small parking areas along here. More satisfying views are had from a path on the far side of the lake, particularly looking towards the fells adjoining Crummock Water (Grasmoor, Whiteside and Mellbreak dominate). The three-mile circuit of the lake is easy to follow and interesting most of the way (see walk on p. 216). On the north side of the lake is **Darling Fell**, a little-walked, rather shapeless little hill whose summit is well worth seeking out for its view over the Solway Firth – a reminder of how suddenly the Lake District fells give way to the coastal plain on this side.

Loweswater village is a scattering of cottages and farmsteads around a triangle of lanes. Tucked around the back is the Kirkstile Inn, a cosy low-beamed old pub with an open fire and sundry settles and pews. A cul-de-sac close by gives access to **Loweswater Fell**. This is the name given to a group of four fells, the eastern three of which are ridges splayed out like fingers; the highest is Blake Fell (1878 feet), although only the easternmost of these, Mellbreak, is rewarding to climb.

Lorton Vale and the Whinlatter Pass

North of Crummock Water the B5289 enters a broad, lush vale dotted with farms, and the high drama is over. At **Low Lorton**, immediately to the west of the main road, is Lorton Hall (open by appointment only), a house with a seventeenth-century façade and retaining one of its fifteenth-century peel towers. During the Reformation, this became a house of recusancy, and although the building has been much altered internally its priest-holes and secret escape routes are still there.

Behind the Yew Tree Hall (the village hall) in **High Lorton** (on the B5292) is a yew tree from where George Fox, the founder of the Quaker movement, preached to a crowd of local people, right in front of Cromwellian troops; Wordsworth commemorated the occasion in his poem 'Yew Trees'.

The **Whinlatter Pass** (B5292) goes off east from High Lorton. Apart from a fleeting glimpse of Grisedale Pike to the

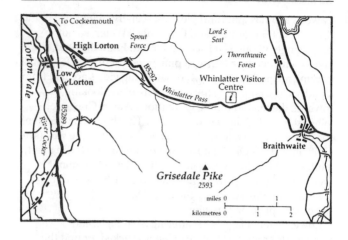

south, and a good view of Bassenthwaite Lake from a lay-by and picnic site near the east end of the pass, this is an uneventful road, enclosed at first by unchanging slopes and then by sizeable Forestry Commission plantations. The **Spout Force** walk and car-park are signposted off the road towards the west end of the pass. This waymarked walk (three miles, according to the signs) follows yellow ringed posts through a pleasantly varied bit of what at first appears to be dull forest; the Force is a 30-foot waterfall gushing into a narrow rocky cleft. A signposted detour to a viewpoint (which turns out to be the cleft from the other side, but the falls are invisible from here) is not really worthwhile.

The Forestry Commission runs the Whinlatter **visitor centre**, where there are displays on trees and forestry management. The adjoining shop is where to pick up the map of adjacent Thornthwaite Forest – if you want to walk here you may get lost with just an Ordnance Survey map; there is a map dispenser outside when the shop is shut. The very first trees planted by the Forestry Commission anywhere in Britain, in 1919, are a few yards away from the visitor centre. Trails and routes ranging from a 1½-mile forest trail to a much longer one taking in the 1811-foot summit of **Lord's Seat** follow very clear marker posts. There are some views out of the forest, notably towards Bassenthwaite Lake, Derwent Water and Skiddaw, and view indicators have been placed along the forest trail.

The Newlands Valley

From Buttermere village a minor road signposted to Keswick
climbs steeply north-eastwards into the uplands of the
Derwent Fells. Though not the most dramatic pass in the
Lake District, this road is the best way of experiencing from a
car the striking emptiness of these hills. At the top, which is
just over 1000 feet, it enters the valley of **Keskadale Beck**,
bounded on the left by Knott Rigg and to the right by the
slopes of Robinson (named after Richard Robinson, who
acquired the estate which included this then nameless fell).
From the car-park at the head of the pass it's a 700-foot climb
to the top of the Knott Rigg ridge; to the east, Cat Bells blots
out any view of Derwent Water from the summit, but
Helvellyn and Blencathra are both in view. Keskadale

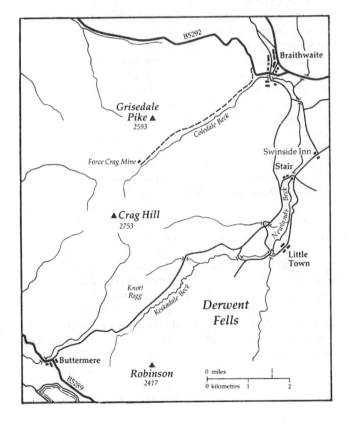

possesses a rare fragment of the primeval forest which once covered most of the Lake District before clearance by early settlers; look out on the left a mile after the head of the pass, just where the road hairpins left – the small patch of oak wood is half way up the side of Knott Rigg.

Keskadale soon broadens and merges with the **Newlands Valley** (so called because of the 'new' lands that were reclaimed after the draining of Husaker Tarn), once one of the most intensely mined areas of the region, but now a scattering of hill farms in a peaceful setting. Its two hamlets are both tiny, but each has a claim to fame. **Little Town**, up the first turn on the right, is illustrated in Beatrix Potter's *The Tale of Mrs Tiggy-Winkle*, while a mile north at **Stair** a farmhouse bears the inscription 'TF 1647', probably that of Thomas Fairfax, commander of the Parliamentary forces, who stayed here.

North-east of Stair is the Swinside Inn, which makes the most of the views of the fells, especially from the picture window of its upstairs dining-room.

The mines in the Newlands Valley were worked intermittently from Elizabeth I's time until well into this century; south and east of Little Town are a number of reminders of the industry. Copper was the first mineral to be fully exploited, when Elizabeth I imported experienced German miners from Augsburg and set up The Society for the Mines Royal to aid mining here and in Borrowdale. Goldscope Mine, in the now-deserted valley south of Little Town, was the most important in early years; lead and a little silver were later worked there.

The minor road from Keskadale joins the B5292 from Whinlatter Pass at **Braithwaite**, a large but not intrinsically interesting village, with a compact centre around a small common and an estate of new houses on its north side. Braithwaite was the original site of the Cumberland Pencil Company, which operated here from 1868 until the factory burned down in 1898, after which it moved to Keswick.

A quarter of a mile west of the village, on the B5292, a path leads off to the left into **Coledale**, a long, corridor-like valley providing easy and quick access to the centre of the fells. The level track close to its floor once served the Force Crag Mine, whose workings mar the far end of Coledale. Originally opened as a lead mine, it was worked for barytes from the 1860s to 1880s, then re-opened by the Coledale Mining

Syndicate in 1912, after which it was operated intermittently until the blizzards of 1947 which flooded the mine. A later attempt to make a new incline was foiled when the bottom fell out of the barytes market. Some attempts at finding new veins were made in the 1960s, but Force Crag is now abandoned.

Keswick to Cockermouth

The A66 between these two towns is convenient but not a road for touring. Sights are minimal, and, to get anything from it, plan to turn off. The A591 is a little slower but has more to offer.

Thornthwaite, a straggly village almost joined on to Braithwaite, lies just west of the A66; Thornthwaite Galleries, a craft shop with coffee shop attached, sells pictures, pottery, ceramics and embroidery, with demonstrations on Wednesdays and Fridays. Opposite the Swan Hotel, high up on the fell, is a whitewashed pinnacle known as the Bishop, painted annually by the hotel's landlord; it gets its name from a story that a bishop entrusted his safety with God and attempted (unsuccessfully) to ride his horse up the steep, scree-covered slopes of Barf Fell.

Bassenthwaite Lake flashes by unspectacularly on your right as you drive along the A66 towards Cockermouth. This most northerly of the major lakes, the fourth longest (at four miles in length, as long as Haweswater and slightly wider), suffers badly from the A66, now upgraded to dual carriageway for much of the lakeside stretch.

In order to protect wildlife, facilities are limited. The southern end is rich in waterfowl; the lake's edges provide breeding ground for over 70 bird species, and in winter there is a sizeable duck population. In the interests of conservation, boating and access to the lake are restricted. Only members of the Bassenthwaite Sailing Club can sail here, and even they have to keep to the northern end of the lake.

The best roadside viewpoints are from the B5291 at the northern end – from Ouse Bridge car-park there is access to the shore and there is a good view towards Skiddaw. Two easily accessible high-level viewpoints are from Dodd Wood (see below) and Binsey (see p. 228).

Bassenthwaite is famous for two things: one is its name – it's the only lake in the Lake District actually called a lake (the

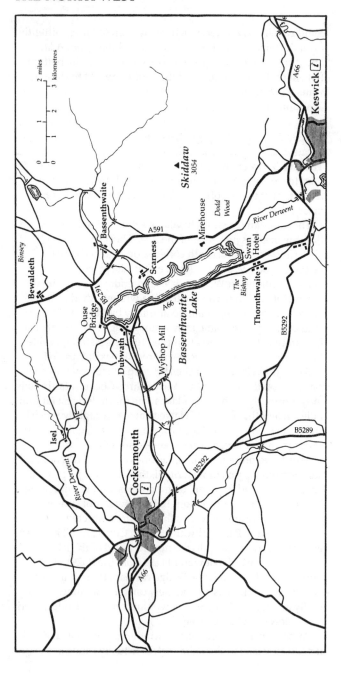

others are waters or meres) – and the other is as Tennyson's inspiration for the death scene of Arthur in 'Idylls of the King' (Tennyson composed the poem in the grounds of Mirehouse, the home of his friend John Spedding: see below).

Mirehouse and **Dodd Wood** are both approached from the same car-park on the A591 north-west of Keswick: look out for Dodd Wood signposts. There is also a tea-room and shop, housed in a converted saw-mill, selling booklets about both places. Dodd Wood is a 1647-foot-high hill afforested by the Forestry Commission, which is mollifying the effect of the unnatural straight lines brought about by the original planting of the 1920s by adopting a more sensitive approach to landscaping. Although there are still some large tracts of unchanging conifer forest here, the waymarked routes (which follow coloured posts) are quite attractively varied. The green route, which is the longest walk, takes in the summit and is gently graded, although the final section is a little steeper; total walking time is about 1½ hours, and there is an excellent view of the north-east fells and Solway Firth (described fully in the Forestry Commission leaflet).

Mirehouse (house open Apr to Oct, Sun, Weds, Bank Hol Mon, 2 to 5; walk open Apr to Oct, daily, 10.30 to 5.30) is a minor country house in pleasant grounds, at their best in rhododendron time (late May to early June). A very gentle waymarked walk leads around the grounds and woods, and to the Tennyson 'theatre', a crude rustic lectern by the lake where 'Idylls of the King' is thought to have been composed; just inside the grounds is an adventure course for children. It's a pretty enough walk, though you may feel that the Lake District offers equally good, less tame ones for which you don't have to pay. By the lake is a beautifully set Norman church (no road leads to it); unfortunately it was given a thorough going over by restorers in 1874. Mirehouse itself has elegantly furnished rooms whose windows make the most of the setting. The mostly eighteenth- and nineteenth-century house contains some manuscripts of Tennyson, Wordsworth, Southey, Carlyle and Hartley Coleridge, plus a collection of ephemera and pictures relating to the Spedding family. There is an engaging identify-the-peculiar-object antiques quiz and often a pianist performs in the music-room.

Continuing along the A591 northwards, there is a turning

off to the left for **Scarness** close to Bassenthwaite 'new'
church. Here is the most satisfactory lakeshore walk on
Bassenthwaite, though admittedly there is not much
competition and even this isn't a Lakeland classic. In its
favour is the extreme quiet – even on a busy Bank Holiday
you are unlikely to meet many people here. Park by the
public footpath sign in front of the entrance to Bassenthwaite
Lakeside Lodges and follow the path to the lake, where you
turn left and follow the shore for ¾ mile until a water course
bars the way ahead; take a stile on the left and head inland
on a clear path close to the water course, then turn left on the
tarmacked lane to get back to Scarness.

Bassenthwaite village has a large modern housing estate
dominating its green, but around the back is the Sun Inn, a
cosy low-ceilinged pub.

Wythop Mill is signposted off the A66 at the north end of
Bassenthwaite Lake. You can follow minor lanes from here to
Cockermouth. The mill (open 10.30 to 6; coffee shop closes
5.30) is fed by a stream and works a belt which can be
harnessed to a saw-mill; wheelwrights' and carpenters' tools
are displayed. There is not a huge amount to see, but it is
worth the effort to come here to visit its coffee shop (cakes
and light lunches available). Nearby, and signposted off the
main road, is the Pheasant Inn, a comfortable inn with
antique furnishings and good bar lunches as well as a
restaurant.

The River Derwent, which joins Derwent Water and
Bassenthwaite Lake, flows out of the north end of the latter
at Ouse Bridge (crossed by the B5291). Quiet, rolling
farmland and conifer woods characterise the Derwent valley
between here and Cockermouth. It's pleasant and unspoilt,
though there are few sights. A minor road crosses the river at
Isel; from the Norman church there is a view across to Isel
Hall, an eye-catching sixteenth-century house with an older
peel tower.

Cockermouth

A market town just outside the north-western corner of the
National Park, Cockermouth tends to be missed by many
visitors, probably because it feels so far removed from the
Lake District. Its gentle pace and untouristy feel can come as
a culture shock after Keswick, which is only 10 miles away.

Many of Cockermouth's compact terraces of colour-washed houses and cottages, most of which front directly on to the street, have been carefully preserved, though some of the town is still in a state of gentle decay.

The town's main claim to fame is **Wordsworth House**, birthplace of William and Dorothy Wordsworth. Set slightly back from the road, this mid-eighteenth-century town house is the most imposing building in Main Street; it seems unthinkable that just before the last war the authorities were proposing to demolish it to make way for a new bus station. Thankfully, the National Trust stepped in and acquired the house, which is now open to the public (Apr to Oct, daily exc Thurs, 11 to 5; 2 to 5 Sun). There's not a great amount of Wordsworthiana inside, but it is beautifully decked out in period furnishings, including some that belonged to Wordsworth and others to Southey. Among the pictures are an early Turner and a number of romantic Lakeland landscapes (some with quaintly inaccurate depictions of Cumbrian mountains). At the back of the house are a walled garden and a terrace, which have a pleasant view over the River Derwent. Wordsworth describes (in 'The Prelude') childhood bathing in an adjacent mill-race. He left the house at the age of eight when his mother died, and was sent to live with an aunt in Penrith, from where he made numerous visits back here.

Cockermouth's other museum is the **Ethnic Doll and Toy Museum** (open Mar to Oct, daily, 10 to 5) in Marketplace, set up by an ex-electrical engineer and his wife; its two rooms house a display of 300 ethnic dolls (mostly modern) from some 60 countries, and a model train layout.

A walk around the town is worthwhile. Broad tree-lined **Main Street** is dominated by the statue of the Earl of Mayo, former MP for Cockermouth and murdered in the Andaman Islands in 1872; this street used to be the venue for cattle and hiring fairs – people came from miles around to hire servants from here. Close by, High Sand Lane leads towards the confluence of the Rivers Derwent and Cocker; just before the footbridge, **Waterloo Street** on the left contains a few relics of the town's industrial past, notably an old linen-mill and a courtyard of restored early Industrial Revolution cottages. The theme continues by the riverside: a brick-built windmill, visible on the other side of the bridge, was probably used in its day for crushing bark for a tannery, and Jennings' brewery just beyond has incorporated a former cotton-mill into its site. The lane which runs through the brewery buildings leads up to **Cockermouth Castle** (open to the public only during the Cockermouth Festival in August), which has been in the hands of the Wyndham family since 1750. The oldest parts are thirteenth century, built by William de Fortibus II to replace an earlier wooden structure. Most of it dates from 1360–70, but there are eighteenth- and nineteenth-century additions. Robert the Bruce made several attacks on the castle, and in the Wars of the Roses the House of York captured it from the Lancastrians. During the Civil War the castle was a Parliamentarian enclave in a strongly Royalist county. The castle retains its oubliette dungeons, so called because they were used for prisoners who were locked away and conveniently forgotten.

From the castle, Castlegate descends to the right to **Marketplace**, the central feature of the town; a street market and cattle auction held on Mondays bring many local people into Cockermouth. Predominantly Georgian and Victorian houses line Marketplace, and the attractive streetscape continues in Kirkgate, a side street by the British Legion building which rises towards the church. John Wordsworth, the poet's father, is buried in the churchyard, and a building near the top side of the churchyard bears a plaque commemorating the site of a primary school attended (at different times) by William Wordsworth and *Bounty* mutineer Fletcher Christian.

Shopping is confined to the area around **Main Street** and Marketplace. Two small complexes are The Old King's Arms Lane (off Main Street), a courtyard containing a second-hand bookshop and a confectioner's, and Cockermouth Antique Market, housed in a building by the river (opposite the Midland Bank), whose three floors make good browsing territory, although the goodies and the junk are comprehensively mixed together. In Castlegate, at the top of the slope, is **Castlegate House**, an eighteenth-century town house containing an up-market art gallery.

For light snacks, it's hard to beat the antique charm of the refreshment room in Wordsworth House, although you have to pay to see the house to use it. Two other pleasant places for coffee or tea are the Court Yard Coffeehouse, an oak-beamed room with a cobbled courtyard outside, just off Main Street, and Over the Top (attached to Fig Tree third-world craft shop: hence all batik and rush matting) in Kirkgate. For evening meals try the gourmet vegetarian restaurant The Quince and Medlar in Castlegate, where the food has Mediterranean influences and the décor is prettily Victorian, or Cheers, an Italian bistro/wine bar in Main Street for excellent pizzas and pasta plus more exotic dishes.

Cockermouth to Calder Bridge

Little can be said for the agricultural scenery along the A5086 for the first few miles south of Cockermouth. The road passes close to **Eaglesfield**, birthplace of both John Dalton, pioneer of atomic theory, and Fletcher Christian, the *Bounty* mutineer. A road from **Mockerkin** is convenient for Loweswater, Crummock Water and Buttermere; the abruptness in which some obscure fells hereabouts rear up from this western flank of the Lake District is quite striking. It is in any case worth turning east off the A5086 to Mockerkin and picking up a minor road running from just east of the village southwards via Lamplugh, Felldyke and Croasdale to Ennerdale Bridge. This road, which runs along the National Park boundary, is more elevated than the main road and gets good coastal views. **Lamplugh** is a tiny village with an odd, reconstructed-looking gateway opposite its church, dated 1595. Half a mile south at **Felldyke** there is a car-park for **Cogra Moss**, a tarn-cum-reservoir hidden away below slopes of densely covered conifer plantations: not everyone's taste, as the forestry borders on the oppressive, though it is certainly an extremely quiet spot. To reach it, take the path at the back of the car-park, turn left on the track a few steps later, then immediately right through a gate; a five-minute walk will get you there, and you can continue along a forestry track along its right-hand side. A higher forestry track above the far end of the water presents an ugly gash across the forest; probably the best feature of a visit to Cogra Moss is the view over the Solway Firth from a field between it and the car-park.

A couple of miles further along this road is **Ennerdale Bridge**, where the Shepherds Arms offers both bar snacks and an interesting set menu. It's the nearest pub to **Ennerdale Water**, which suddenly opens out to the east, with the great crags of Pillar looming just beyond it. Although there are car-parks at Ennerdale Water, the

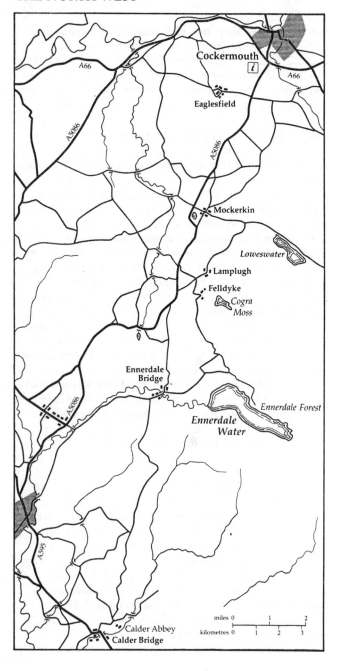

forestry tracks and paths around the lake are for pedestrians only. This, together with Ennerdale's isolated location, mean that the lake is hardly ever overrun; when the central parts of the Lake District become unbearably busy with traffic, this might be a good lake to which to escape. Since it is a reservoir, no private craft are allowed on the lake; the main activities are therefore walking and fishing, and there are tracks and paths around the lake. In Ennerdale Forest the Forestry Commission has set up three self-guided forest trails of varying length – the Smithy Beck Trail, the Nine Becks Walk and the Liza Path.

The fell road from Ennerdale Bridge to Calder Bridge is recommended; although the moors over which it runs are quite bleak, there are excellent views of the adjacent fells and towards the coast (including Sellafield, if that can be called an excellent view), and it is far superior in every sense to the A5086 and A595. It comes down to earth at a T-junction near **Calder Abbey**. Take the cul-de-sac signposted Prior Scales for about 100 yards to get a view of the abbey, which is on private land at the bottom of the valley, but can be seen slightly closer up from a footpath to Calder Bridge from this road. The building is comprehensively ruined, though the tower, west doorway and portions of the transept and chancel are in evidence. It was founded by monks of the Savigny Order (who later amalgamated with the Cistercians) in 1134. The abbey later passed into the hands of Furness Abbey after the monks fled in the Border wars, when much damage was done to the fabric of the building.

At **Calder Bridge** it is necessary to join the A595 for a while if continuing south.

The west coast

This stretch of the Cumbrian coast is heavily industrialised in places, and has only a little in the way of unspoilt cliff and other coastal scenery. But a few features of outstanding interest make it rewarding providing you pick your way carefully. It's best seen by taking a trip on the British Rail coast line, which hugs the coast closely for much of the way and gets views unobtainable from the road. Along most of the coastline it is usually possible to see the Isle of Man.

The coast north of Ravenglass is dominated by the presence of **Sellafield** (visitors' centre open Apr to Oct, daily,

10 to 6; Nov to Mar, daily exc Christmas Day, 10 to 4), which in 1956 was the first nuclear power station in the world. It now occupies 700 acres and employs 20,000 people; the old name of Windscale now applies to just part of the site. Sellafield is still the world's most important reprocessing centre – to where used uranium fuel-rods are brought and processed so that they can be used again. Calder Hall is the name of Sellafield's power station, which provides enough electricity for a city of 150,000 inhabitants.

Sellafield's visitors' centre is dazzlingly futuristic, with a show of technological wizardry that includes simulations of a nuclear chain reaction and what it's like to be inside a nuclear reactor in full operation, and there are computer-operated quizzes and electronically operated displays. This is a didactic and highly professional PR job (the safety aspect is carefully rubbed in), designed to reassure, though nuclear sceptics may be put off further by its sheer slickness. A free coach tour around the site is offered, and operates via a queuing system – get your ticket *before* you start looking at the exhibition, as there may well be a wait; a public address system audible everywhere in the centre will inform you when boarding for the next coach is about to take place. No photography is allowed inside the site.

Extended day-long tours, giving more opportunities to take in the technical details, are also available, but have to be booked a few weeks in advance. Because of the arrays of tempting buttons to press, small children are not admitted to these tours. For details tel Seascale (0946) 773439.

Egremont, inland on the A595, has a somewhat surprisingly pleasant main street, broad and tree-lined – like a lesser version of Cockermouth's. Its one real sight is the ruined castle, which stands on a tump in a public park (take the St Bees road from the war memorial at the southern end of the main street). The most intact features of the castle, which was founded by William de Meschines around 1130–40, are the gatehouse and three arched windows; the walls are partly decorated by herringbone masonry.

Most of the agreeable old part of **St Bees** is ranged along two sloping streets half a mile from the sea, though the village's architectural highlights are on the other side of the railway. One of these is **St Bees Priory**, a large church which once formed part of a Benedictine nunnery founded in the seventh century, and which has a wonderful ornate

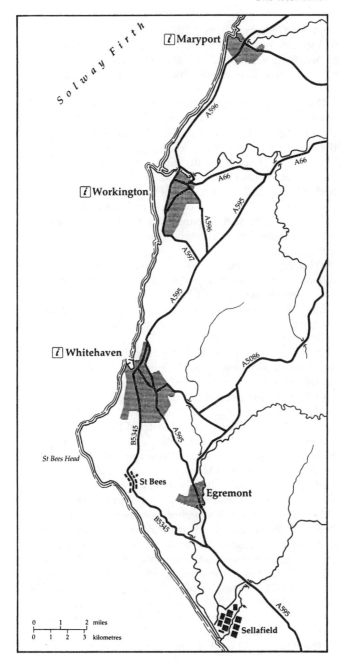

sandstone Norman doorway; the most memorable feature of its Victorian restoration is the handsome screen. The other is **St Bees School**, founded in 1583 and retaining its original schoolhouse in a courtyard reminiscent of an Oxbridge college.

Disappointingly unattractive modern buildings impinge upon St Bees' sea-front, which otherwise is blessed with a pleasant beach of sand and pebbles. The sandstone cliffs to the north from here provide excellent opportunities for birdwatching; there is a nature reserve with lookout points installed at St Bees Head, which among other species harbours England's only colony of black guillemots. A footpath from Whitehaven to St Bees makes an excellent clifftop walk, although it is necessary to use a bus or train to return as there is no worthwhile inland scenery to make it into a circular route.

Whitehaven is a substantial industrial town with a difference. It was the first post-medieval town in Britain to have been planned. The gridiron layout may not appear very original, but the sense of order is nevertheless striking, and the town has managed to conserve quite a lot of its eighteenth-century streetscape.

Whitehaven has several highlights, all in the old centre; a good town trail taking about 45 minutes is available from the tourist **information centre**. The best view of the town is from Candlestick Chimney, which used to be part of the Wellington pit; this operated from 1840 to 1932 and was the scene of the Whitehaven mine disaster of 1910 which claimed 136 lives. It stands above the harbour, on its south side; from here you can get a good idea of the shape of the town, and Scotland and the Isle of Man are also often visible. The harbour, well worth walking around to take in its rough-and-ready character, was attacked in 1778 by John Paul Jones, the Scottish anarchist who became a hero of the American War of Independence. A cannon near the chimney is thought to be from a ship sunk by Jones. The church of St James in Queen Street (not to be confused with St Nicholas, also in Queen Street; the latter, which was largely destroyed by fire in 1971, houses the tourist information centre) stands on a rise overlooking the town. Inside in particular, this is a splendid Georgian church, generous in its proportions and adorned with fine blue and white ceiling medallions.

The civic hall in Lowther Street houses Whitehaven's

excellent **museum** (open all year exc Bank Hol Mon, Mon to Sat, 9 to 5 (4 Sat)), which has displays on the obvious local themes, in particular mining, natural history, ceramics and nautical history. Exhibits to look out for include a view of Whitehaven painted in 1736 by Matthias Read (the town's gridiron plan is already in evidence) and the shroud of a fourteenth-century knight recently discovered in near-perfect condition at St Bees.

No single house or row of houses stands out from the others in the town centre. It is best to just wander around at will. However, the area between the civic hall and the quay has a number of fine streets, including Roper Street, home of what must be Cumbria's largest second-hand bookshop: Moon's Bookshop has a mile of shelves, and makes an ideal place for rainy days. Just off Roper Street is The Good Food Store, a wholefood shop with an alternative-style and cheerfully inelegant cafe attached (patrons are requested not to play chess between 12 and 2). For dinner and good-value lunches try a pizza or some pasta or the daily special at Bruno's wine bar/trattoria in Church Street.

Workington's raw industrial face masks small-scale charm around its old centre, notably tree-fringed Portland Square – all sloping cobbles to the doorsteps of its terraced houses – plus one or two streets of colour-washed terraces leading off. Ruined Workington Hall nearby, set back from a green, stands in ruins, the eighteenth-century additions removed in the 1970s to strip the structure to its fourteenth-century core. St John's church in Washington Street is an enlarged copy, designed by Thomas Hardwick in 1823, of St Paul's, Covent Garden (Inigo Jones' masterpiece, which Hardwick rebuilt to the same design after fire damage). A little further uphill is the Helena Thompson Museum (open Apr to Oct, Mon to Sat, 10.30 to 4; Nov to Mar, Mon to Sat, 11 to 3), an eighteenth-century house, former home of the steward of the Curwen estates, which contains a small collection of costumes, antiques and items of local history.

Further up the coast is **Maryport**, almost a scaled-down version of Whitehaven. It is also built on a gridiron plan, with colour-washed terraces of eighteenth- and nineteenth-century cottages fronting directly on to the street. There is much less of interest than there is in Whitehaven, and Maryport doesn't quite feel as if it is undergoing a Whitehaven-style renaissance. Some character survives around the harbour, though there are plans to turn this into a marina. Here, in the floor above the tourist **information centre**, is Maryport's little nautical museum (open Easter to Oct, daily, 10 (2 Sun) to 5; Oct to Easter, daily exc Weds and Sun, 10 to 12, 2 to 4), which has a facsimile of Captain Bligh's logbook for the *Bounty* open on the fateful day of the mutiny in 1789, plus model ships and displays of nautical equipment. In the harbour are Maryport's latest tourist attractions, three steam-powered tugs, including the *Flying Buzzard*, built in 1951 at Port Glasgow. You are allowed to try out the capstan and sound the telegraph bell and foghorn. Ask the staff on the tugboat to point out any other unusual boats berthed in the harbour, as there are often some antique vessels here.

Keswick to Thirlmere

The most convenient way to make this journey is by the A591, one of only two roads linking the northern and southern Lakes and running through the centre of the region. Scenic though that is, a more interesting route is to take the A591 eastwards from Keswick, to keep left where the A591 bends right towards Windermere, then to turn immediately right on to a minor turn to Castlerigg stone circle, then continue east towards the B5322, and to proceed south down St John's in the Vale, then turn right and immediately left on the minor road which follows the west side of Thirlmere.

Castlerigg stone circle, as Keats put it in 'Hyperion', 'like a dismal cirque of Druid stones, upon a forlorn moor', lies a few steps from the above-mentioned minor road. Late Neolithic or early Bronze Age dates are attributed to the circle, because of the presence of a rectangle of stones within the circle itself. Its purpose is uncertain, though it seems likely that its site – a wonderful one overlooking Skiddaw, Helvellyn, Cat Bells, High Spy, Crag Hill and Grisedale Pike – was deliberately chosen; the two biggest stones apparently mark some kind of entrance. Southey brought his young daughters here; they disproved the legend that no two people can ever count the same number of stones. There were, and still are, 38 in the circle, plus 10 in the rectangle. One or two outliers, including one that used to function as a stile, may or may not be associated with the circle. Sundry

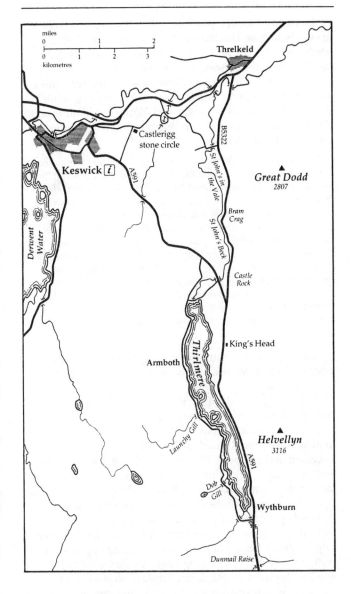

theories of ley-lines passing through Castlerigg exist, including its being on a line between the summits of Skiddaw and Helvellyn.

St John's in the Vale is easily missed, but is worth an

exploration – on foot if possible (see walk on p. 220). This is
the valley linking Threlkeld on the A66 with the A591 at the
northern end of Thirlmere. Blencathra towers above the
northern end; the views are more changing as you travel
north to south, soon leaving the scars left by former mining
activity at Bram Crag. Slopes close in on both sides, while
straight ahead is Castle Rock, a rock-climber's favourite and
shrouded in legends. William Hutchinson's *An Excursion to
the Lakes* sets the scene:

*In the widest part of the dale you are struck with the appearance of an ancient
ruined castle, which seems to stand upon the summit of a little mount, the
mountains around forming an amphitheatre. This massive bulwark shews a
front of various towers, and makes an awful, rude, and gothic appearance,
with its lofty turrets, and ragged battlements; we traced the galleries, the
bending arches, the buttresses; the greatest antiquity stands characterised in
its architecture; the inhabitants near it assert it is an antediluvian structure;
the traveller's curiosity is rouzed [sic], and he prepares to make a nearer
approach, when that curiosity is put upon the rack, by his being assured,
that if he advances, certain genii who govern the place, by virtue of their
supernatural arts and necromancy, will strip it of all its beauties, and by
inchantment [sic] transform the magic walls. The vale seems adapted for the
habitation of such beings; its gloomy recesses and retirements look like
haunts of evil spirits.*

Similarly, Walter Scott's *The Bridal of Triermain* tells the
story of Castle Rock as an enchanted castle inhabited by a
beautiful witch.

On the western side of the valley is St John's in the Vale
church – not an interesting building but in a lovely situation
at the foot of small, hummocky hills. In the churchyard is a
tombstone to John Richardson, a nineteenth-century
Lakeland dialectic poet. The church is thought to have been
built originally by the Knights Hospitallers of the Order of St
John in the thirteenth century; it was entirely rebuilt in 1846.

Thirlmere is a 3¾-mile-long lake-turned-reservoir in a
strikingly pretty woodland setting under the shadow of the
Helvellyn range which rises abruptly from the lake's eastern
side. Its amenities are limited – no swimming or powered
craft are allowed on it (rowing-boats, dinghies, sailing and
windsurfing are permitted, but there are no places by the
lake from which you can hire these). Until recently, access on
foot was virtually non-existent, but the National Park and
water authorities have made efforts to remedy this, and it is
now possible to take a lakeshore path (not shown on current

OS maps) on the west side of the lake from Armboth to Dob Gill – about 1½ miles, and all of it attractive: the path ducks in and out of the woods, and there are a number of small, pebbly beaches. Several small car-parks along this side of the lake give access to the lakeside, and there is also a vantage-point from the nameless car-park at the north end of the lake at a junction of minor roads. As the path is sheltered, it makes for a feasible wet-weather walk. Armboth, which is marked on OS maps, was a hamlet which disappeared under the reservoir when the valley was flooded. Now the name of Armboth survives only for Armboth car-park; a monkey puzzle tree nearby is the sole reminder of Armboth House.

Three-quarters of a mile south of Armboth, from the car-park at Launchy Gill Bridge, there is a very short forest trail up the ravine of Launchy Gill, which tumbles down a series of waterfalls.

The A591 runs close to the eastern side of the lake, and there are some pleasant woodland walks starting from car-parks on this side too. The car-park by Wythburn church is the starting-point for the most popular way up Helvellyn, and further north the King's Head pub (good choice at lunchtimes) displays old photographs of Wythburn village.

Fierce opposition was raised when Manchester Corporation decided to build the reservoir; this, the most central of all the lakes, was a beloved spot from which major poets and artists drew inspiration – two natural lakes, joined at a bridge, and surrounded by deciduous woodlands. Among the campaigners to prevent the scheme were Octavia Hill and Canon Rawnsley, both of whom later became founders of the National Trust; other opponents included William Morris, Thomas Carlyle and John Ruskin. 'What is more truly sanitary to a busy people,' the *Spectator* sounded off in September 1877, 'than the solitude and loveliness of the few natural gardens in which they can forget the thick atmosphere and incessant noise of City life?' Despite the intensity of local and national hostility, the scheme received parliamentary approval in 1879, and the two roads around Thirlmere were built for the use of construction traffic. Two thousand acres of conifers around the reservoir were planted in 1908 by Manchester Corporation (broad-leaf species were then thought harmful to the purity of the water). The corporation may have won this issue, but the debate over

Thirlmere fuelled the conservationist cause, ultimately providing the major catalyst for the formation of the National Trust and the Friends of the Lake District.

Coleridge and Wordsworth had liked to meet at Thirlmere, a half-way house from their respective homes at Keswick and Grasmere. They and members of the Wordsworth family circle carved their initials into a rock. Somewhat symbolically, this 'Rock of Names' was blown up during construction of the reservoir; however, Canon Rawnsley collected the fragments and cemented them into a pyramid. Following landslips in 1984 this was removed to the quarry face behind Dove Cottage in Grasmere.

Just south of Thirlmere, the road reaches the summit of the Dunmail Raise Pass, a traditional north–south dividing point of the Lake District. A cairn in the middle of the dual carriageway marks the site of a battle in 943 when Edmund, King of Northumbria, defeated Dunmail, a Norse king.

Where to stay

For a key to prices, see p. 10

Bassenthwaite Lake
The Pheasant Inn, Bassenthwaite Lake, Cockermouth, Cumbria CA13 9YE. Tel Bassenthwaite Lake (076 87) 76234
Peacefully off the A66 west of the lake, a traditional country inn (and busy pub) dating from about 1600, complete with beams and brass and log fires in its comfortable lounges. Modernised bedrooms, good food and real ale. ££

Borrowdale
Borrowdale Gates Hotel, Grange-in-Borrowdale, Keswick, Cumbria CA12 5UQ. Tel Borrowdale (076 87) 77204
At the northern end of Borrowdale, a modern building in a mixture of rendering and local stone. Inevitably, the views of this lovely valley are the key attraction, and there are plenty of opportunities to enjoy them from the relaxed lounge area and dining-room, with floor-to-ceiling windows, and from a terrace outside. The interior is a successful marriage of modern and traditional, with country crafts, hunting trophies and masses of greenery. The bedrooms are not especially characterful, but are adequate. ££

Loweswater
Scale Hill Hotel, Loweswater, Cumbria CA13 9UX. Tel Lorton (090 085) 232
Overlooking small fells and quiet farmland, a hotel full of reassuringly old-fashioned charm, with a roaring open fire in the evening, lots of cosy corners (some inhabited by cats) in the building's three lounges and conspicuous

absence of TV; daily newspapers are left around for guests' use. Bedrooms are rather plain (the ones at the back of the building have much the best views), but there is a strong temptation in any case to sit downstairs or in the garden. Wholesome country cooking, and enough of it to satisfy the hungriest fell-walker. ££££

Seatoller

Seatoller House, Seatoller, Borrowdale, Cumbria CA12 5XN. Tel Borrowdale (059 684) 218

An informal, old guest-house in a cottage at the foot of Honister Pass, with comfortable bedrooms and a self-service, farmhouse-kitchen dining-room (no smoking in either). It works rather like a chalet party and the atmosphere depends on the company. No children under five. ££

Bed and breakfast

The best areas to head for are the villages of Borrowdale, Buttermere and Lorton Vale, where even the tiniest hamlet has at least one B&B and the surroundings are delightful.

There is a lot of B&B in Keswick, and it should always be possible to find somewhere, but accommodation is nearly all in very suburban-feeling back streets and nothing really stood out among those we saw; convenient for public transport, but if you have a car you could probably do better elsewhere.

Some larger villages near Keswick have a fair amount of cheap accommodation and are quiet, though not especially characterful; these include Braithwaite, Thornthwaite and Portinscale.

There's accommodation in Cockermouth, though not a huge amount, and traffic noise can be a problem in the centre. It's a substantially more likeable town than Keswick, though you might feel you're a bit too far out of the Lakes if you stay here. The A66 makes the northern lakes easily accessible, though it's quite a drive to the southern lakes from here.

THE NORTH-EAST

*South of the A66, north of Ullswater · Ullswater ·
Helvellyn and Fairfield · Back o' Skiddaw ·
North of the A66, east of the National Park
boundary · Penrith · South of Penrith ·
Haweswater and Shap ·* WHERE TO STAY

Scenery

One of Lakeland's finest lakes, and its third highest
mountain. But further to the north and east the
scenery is much less interesting (with a few
exceptions).

Scenic highlights

- ULLSWATER – the second longest lake after
  Windermere, and more captivating because of its
  serpentine shape and the classical grandeur of the fells
  that enclose it. Best seen from a steamer or footpath; by
  car the views are best if you travel from north-east to
  south-west.

Also worth seeing

- The LOWTHER VALLEY – gentle limestone country, quiet
  and very unspoilt.
- BACK O' SKIDDAW – lonely and unfrequented hills
  around the east, north and west sides of Skiddaw and
  Blencathra. Big views north, but no rugged mountain
  scenery to speak of.
- HAWESWATER – a long drive from the central lakes, and
  not much to do when you get there if you don't feel
  like tackling a fell walk. But remote-feeling and
  peaceful lake scenery, best at the southern end of the
  valley.
- SWINDALE – a cul-de-sac, up an idyllic, secretive valley,
  even more inaccessible than Haweswater; fine
  waterfalls at the far end. Parking can be very tricky.

Best walks

Easy walks

- The southern shore of ULLSWATER, from Howtown pier to Glenridding (returning by steamer).
- GOWBARROW PARK (a hill, not a park) and AIRA FORCE. Outstanding short walk; the most satisfying way of seeing the waterfall.
- Other waterfalls worth seeing: THE HOWK, LAUNCHY GILL and WHITEWATER DASH (in that order).
- The LOWTHER VALLEY. Lush limestone country, woods and parkland.
- The best easy fell walks are associated with Ullswater: pick of these are HALLIN FELL and PLACE FELL, both of which can be incorporated into circular walks taking in the lakeshore path.

Fell walks

- HELVELLYN – probably the most climbed mountain in the Lakes. Short and steep from the Thirlmere side, rugged and exposed from the east side. Whichever route you take, plan to walk a section of the six-mile grassy ridge which connects the summits of the Helvellyn range.
- FAIRFIELD, just south of Helvellyn, is not quite as popular, but also has superb views.
- HIGH STREET – huge views southwards from the Roman road on top of this high ridge. Wild, craggy mountain scenery on the ascent from Haweswater via the Nan Bield Pass – the approach from Hartsop (near Patterdale) is relatively dull.
- BLENCATHRA (Saddleback) – the giant of the north-easternmost corner of the Lake District.

Sights

Houses

- DALEMAIN – highly distinguished architecturally, all the more interesting for its amalgam of Georgian and Elizabethan styles. Fine grounds.

- HUTTON-IN-THE-FOREST is outside the Lake District proper, but worth seeking out: a peel tower with later additions; fine period furniture and an attractive eighteenth-century walled garden.

Castles

- BROUGHAM is the most impressive of the ruined castles in and around the Lake District, in a quiet setting by the River Eamont.
- LOWTHER (not open, nor medieval) is an eye-catching ruin (and just a bit spooky) in fine parkland. Easily seen from the road, or more close up from a public footpath.

Museums

- STEAM MUSEUM, Penrith – traction engines, old foundry works, a fairground organ: an interesting mixture.

Family attractions

- LOWTHER PARK: an amusement park with children's activities.

Best churches

- TORPENHOW, the region's most striking Norman church.
- BOLTONGATE is unique in England for possessing a stone-vaulted nave.
- KELD CHAPEL and MARTINDALE (St Martin's) – both tiny churches in remote locations; each has simple charm.
- ST SWITHIN'S CHAPEL, Brougham – built at the time of Cromwell, and so a rarity; exceptional screen.
- DACRE – restored inside, but worth a visit for its carved cross-shafts and for the stone bears in the churchyard. Good view of Dacre Castle from outside.
- SHAP ABBEY, though ruined, with not much to see apart from the tower, is in a pleasant, tucked-away setting, and is worth a look if you are planning to visit nearby Keld chapel.

Best villages
- ASKHAM has a green throughout the length of its long, sloping main street, flanked by attractive cottages, and there's not a jarring note anywhere.
- HESKET NEWMARKET is a smaller version of Askham, and equally unspoilt.
- CALDBECK – John Peel's grave, plus relics of the village's milling and mining heritage. A nicely set waterfall is nearby.

Towns
- PENRITH is the only town in this area, and is just outside the National Park. A few fairly attractive streets, and quite a good shopping centre, but it's not really a place to seek out because of the traffic. Its best sight is the Steam Museum.

South of the A66, north of Ullswater

Travelling westwards along the A66 from Penrith to Keswick, you won't find much to grab your attention in the first few miles. On either side of the road the scenery undulates only slightly; the A66 actually forms the National Park boundary for a couple of miles at one stage, but the really interesting countryside is some way to the south. **Dacre** is a village on a hillside in quiet farming country between the A66 and Ullswater. Somewhat hidden away at the northern end of the village is the church, thought to have been built on the site of a Saxon monastery, which was recorded in the eighth century in the writings of the Venerable Bede.

Scattered around the churchyard are four stone bears, very little about which is known. They are probably medieval and tell some story (not necessarily a religious one), perhaps a fable of *one* bear in four stages; one theory is that the bear is first shown asleep, then a wild cat jumps on to its back which the bear tries to capture and finally eats. The church itself is impressively large for such a small village, but restoration in the last century has not left a wealth of interesting features with the notable exception of two pre-Norman stone

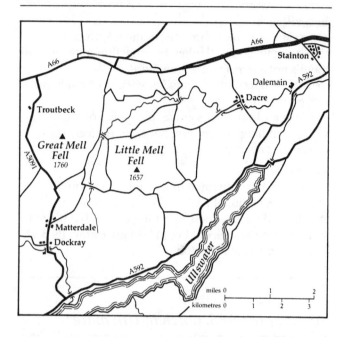

cross-shafts; the finer of the two, beautifully carved with a mythical creature resembling a winged lion, is probably Anglian dating from around 800, while the other is a much cruder work of the Viking period, depicting Adam and Eve and two men (supposedly King Athelstan of England and King Constantine of Scotland – they met at this village in 926). There is quite a good view from the churchyard of Dacre Castle (not open), an imposing early-fourteenth-century fortified sandstone building with a peel tower, occupied over many centuries by the Dacre family, and still used as a home.

At **Matterdale**, on the A5091 between the A66 and Ullswater, a diminutive church steeple peeps over a wall, with the rest of the building below the level of the road. The interior is typical of a plain Cumbrian country church of the humbler kind, dating from the sixteenth or seventeenth century, with nave and chancel in one in the simplest rectangular plan; two massive cross-beams support the roof.

The A592 runs south-west from the A66 west of Penrith to Ullswater and on past Glenridding. Three miles or so from Penrith is **Dalemain**, a fine country house on the right (west)

side of the road (open Easter to mid-Oct, Sun to Thurs, 11.15
to 5). From outside it looks a formal, neat Georgian mansion,
and all of a piece, and that is the impression you get from the
hall and reception rooms downstairs; the real surprise starts
at the Norman peel tower, where one ascends into the
Elizabethan part of the house, which contains a warren of
small rooms including the panelled Old Oak Room and the
Nursery; there's even a priest's hole, not rediscovered until
1851. The Hassell family have been here since 1679, and the
house benefits from having a genuine lived-in feel in spite of
the rarity of the period furnishings. Portraits of Hassells past
and present look down from every other wall; included
among these are pictures by Van Dyck and Zoffany. There
are two only moderately interesting displays: a very small
one on regimental history is at the foot of the tower, while
outside across the yard is a slightly haphazard collection of
agricultural bygones housed in an old barn. Better are the
landscaped gardens laid out in the seventeenth and
eighteenth centuries. Dalemain has the distinction of
possessing one of the Lake District's most architecturally
remarkable tea-rooms; it is housed in the medieval Old Hall:
antique long tables and bare, rough stone walls. Snacks, light
lunches and home-made cakes are served all day, and you
don't have to pay admission to the house if you come here
only to enjoy the tea-room.

Ullswater

Two miles south-west of Dalemain is the head of **Ullswater**.
To many this is quintessential Lakeland scenery, a
captivating blend of the snaking lake itself, the tree-fringed
pastures around it and the diverse outlines of fells above the
pastures. Its sinuous shape makes Ullswater tantalisingly
difficult to see in its entirety. Wordsworth pronounced the
lake as being 'the happiest combination of beauty and
grandeur, which any of the Lakes affords'.

   From the north, first impressions may not be very positive,
however; the beauty of Ullswater is very much concentrated
around its southern half. **Pooley Bridge**, at the northern end,
is a disappointing village, ranged around a dog-leg of road
just off the A592, with a trippery air to it; its saving grace, a
pretty stone road-bridge, does not compensate for the rest.
The village is of note only as being one of the terminals for

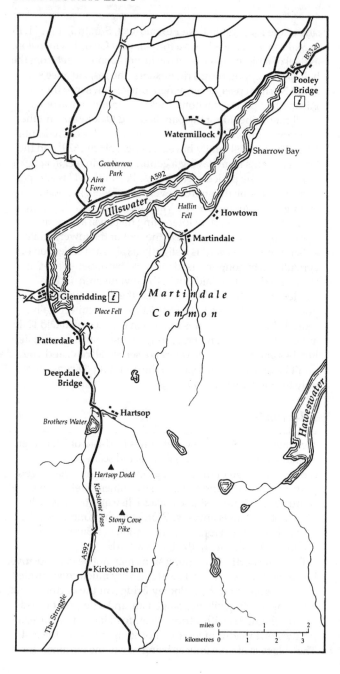

the lake steamers; the pier is at the west end of Pooley
Bridge. The converted nineteenth-century steamers operate
from Easter to the end of October, three times daily from
Glenridding to here and back, via Howtown (on the eastern
side). There is a small tourist **information centre** in the
village.

The west side of the lake

The A592 follows the entire western side of the lake, and
gives excellent views after the lake has made its first bend as
you travel south-westwards. Traffic crawls along this twisty
road in summer, so to get anything from it prepare to stop at
the small car-parks as soon as you spot them. Apart from a
footpath from Watermillock northwards there is no
waterside walking on this side of the lake.

   Aira Force is the one stop-off point which really deserves
some time. The force, or waterfall, is the finest of a series of
falls set in a superb wooded chasm spanned by a stone
bridge. From a large car-park just north of the main road and
immediately east of the junction with the A5091, a path leads
into the woods and over the Aira Beck; it takes about 20
minutes to explore the site (don't miss the view of the falls
from the higher of the two bridges), but if you want to escape
from the coachloads of crowds it is more rewarding to walk
around **Gowbarrow Park** (see walk on p. 232), a lowish fell
immediately to the east where William and Dorothy
Wordsworth saw that famous host of golden daffodils.
Views over Ullswater open out as soon as you step outside
the woods, and the rising path soon gets a panorama of all
the lake bar its southern end. Below, nestling in the woods,
is Lyulph's Tower, an ancient hunting-lodge of triangular
plan. Close to the car-park is a tastefully got up National
Trust cafe with a verandah and terrace. There is another
car-park for Aira Force on the A5091, just north of the
junction with the A592.

   South of here, the A592 runs alongside the lake towards
Glenridding, an ex-mining village now totally geared to
tourism. Glenridding has a National Park **information centre**
in its car-park; inside is a re-created mine shaft of the
Glenridding mines. The village's blackest hour was in 1929
when a nearby reservoir at Kepple Cove burst and a quarter
of a million gallons of water swept down, battering and

flooding Glenridding; fortunately there were no casualties, but the damage was great.

Patterdale, further south, takes its name from St Patrick; St Patrick's Well, reputed to have healing properties, is by the roadside north of the village in a stone recess. Both Glenridding and Patterdale are curiously charmless considering their natural advantages. Much less spoilt than either village is **Hartsop**, a hamlet just east of the main road at the entrance to Hayeswater valley, a pleasing scene of Lakeland vernacular which includes two houses with spinning galleries.

The main road continues southwards up the **Kirkstone Pass**, which is the highest, though not the most dramatic, pass in the Lake District; views are more impressive if travelling northwards towards Ullswater.

The road runs almost alongside **Brothers Water**, generally regarded as a lake though there are several tarns in the Lake District which exceed it in size; it was named after two brothers who drowned in it while skating. Further south, where the pass starts to rise, on the opposite side of the valley to the road, an artificial terrace is visible; this is thought to be a Roman road linking Whitbarrow (where there was another road) to the north with Galava fort near Ambleside. Other pointers reinforcing this theory are a fragment of road and ditches at Matterdale (near Dockray) and a line of large kerbstones near Ullswater.

The pass reaches 1489 feet by the Kirkstone Inn, where a road runs south-westwards towards Ambleside. This used to be the main road but is now unclassified; it is aptly named The Struggle. An annual pram-pushing race from Ambleside and up The Struggle to the Kirkstone Inn takes place in summer. The A592 continues southwards into the Trout Beck Valley (see p. 173).

The east side of the lake

This is the unspoilt side of the lake. From Pooley Bridge follow the signs for Howtown and Martindale; the minor road gets some lakeside views early on, but then there are too many hedges in the way. Soon, on the lake side of the road, is **Sharrow Bay**, one of Britain's most celebrated hotels (see p. 113), where elegant afternoon tea, which is available to non-residents, is an unforgettable experience – both for the gargantuan quantities and the sumptuous surroundings.

Howtown is just a hotel (a very good one; this is also open to non-residents) and a pier for the steamer service. The lakeshore walk from here to Glenridding somehow has the edge over all other such waterside walks in the Lake District, with the possible exception of Derwent Water. Its quality has something to do with the constantly changing vistas, the alternations of mixed woodlands and open pasture, and the slight rises and falls in the path itself which give the walk its third dimension. See walks on pp. 233, 234 and 237.

South-west of Howtown, beyond a cattle-grid the road zigzags over the shoulder of **Hallin Fell**, a small but steep-sided hill which provides one of the most pleasing views of Ullswater. At the top of the rise are two car-parks by the 'new' church of St Peter's where you can make the 15-minute ascent to the summit.

The next left turn after these car-parks leads past **Martindale**'s old church, the Elizabethan church of St Martin. Not much adorns its interior: very unchurchy rectangular windows, a flagstoned floor and simple whitewashed walls. It still has its seventeenth-century pews and a pulpit dated 1634 which bears the maker's initials. By the altar is an old font which is thought to have been originally a shrine used by the Romans on the nearby High Street route a mile or so to the east; the scratches on it were made by local dalesmen who used it for sharpening tools. St Martin's became derelict in the nineteenth century and St Peter's was built; the roof on the former has since been restored. South of here is a series of narrow valleys collectively termed **Martindale Common** – mainly walkers' country, since all the roads are dead-ends.

Helvellyn and Fairfield

This range of fells, roughly 13 miles long, stretches from just above Ambleside to the A66 at the foot of Blencathra, and is bounded to the east by the Kirkstone Pass and the southernmost reach of Ullswater and to the west by St John's in the Vale, Thirlmere and the A591. No road perforates this great upland area, though it is crossed by many paths and bridleways.

Helvellyn (3116 feet) is one of the Lakeland giants – the highest peak after Scafell Pike and Scafell. Its west and east sides present strikingly different faces: above Thirlmere (to the west), the mountain appears as a steep and even slope, wooded at its base, while from Glenridding it's rugged and highly dramatic, including as it does two knife-edge ridges of Striding Edge and Swirral Edge, which together form a huge corrie – gouged out by glacial action in the Ice Age. The summit is grassy and remarkably flat and friendly: so level, in fact, that an aeroplane landed on it in 1926. There's a memorial to this on the summit as well as the Gough Memorial, commemorating the spot where in 1805 a dog guarded his master's body for three months after a fatal accident – an event that inspired both Wordsworth ('Fidelity') and Scott ('The Faithful Dog'). The trig point and stone shelter are the highest point of a succession of peaks along the ridge, which goes up and down very gently; Dollywaggon Pike (2810 feet) is the southernmost of these, while the northern end effectively culminates at Great Dodd (2807 feet) six miles away. Allow at least five hours to climb it; if the views are clear on top you will certainly be enticed to walk along the ridge and take it all in.

The easiest route is from Wythburn church (where there is a car-park) on Thirlmere, which isn't a very eventful ascent but has the advantage of the surprise you get when you look down upon Striding Edge, Red Tarn and the rest from the top (provided you can see anything at all). Much more interesting (but requiring a head for heights) is the eastern approach up Striding Edge: it looks quite scary end-on, and there is a short section where you have to use your hands to haul yourself up, but in sensible footwear and in all but the direst weather it is not particularly hazardous when you are ascending (it is, however, harder to find your footing when descending), and there is an alternative path a few feet below the edge itself which you can use if the wind turns strong. In summer there can be hundreds of people on Helvellyn; it's not unknown for people to carry their dogs up Striding Edge. Once up, it's quite easy to devise round routes using the ridge – for example, to Dollywaggon Pike and Grisedale Tarn, or north to Raise and the Sticks Pass. Remains of lead-mining activity are in evidence close to Glenridding – notably in Greenside and the Sticks Pass (so named because of the sticks that used to mark the line of the track used by packhorses carrying lead ore from Greenside Mine to smelters at Stonycroft and Brigham). Red Tarn, superbly sited between Striding and Swirral Edges, was deepened by

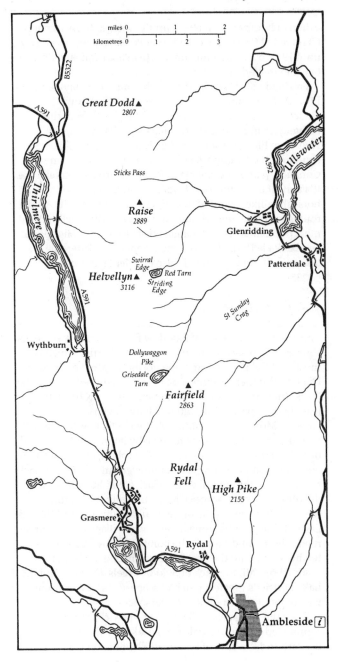

a dam of boulders in 1860 to supply water to these mines. Greenside Mine was worked from the seventeenth century until 1962; by 1875 £1 million-worth of lead and silver ore was being extracted annually.

Fairfield (2863 feet) lies just to the south of Dollywaggon Pike. A drop from each mountain of 1000 feet down to Grisedale Tarn makes Fairfield quite separate from the Helvellyn range, and worth climbing in its own right: Helvellyn blots out some of the views north, but this is compensated by a spectacular panorama of Windermere, Coniston Water and the main fell group around Scafell Pike. It's almost made for round walks, thanks to the horseshoe-like layout of the ridges that lead up to it. All the routes are quite long (though not particularly gruelling); the most popular is also the longest from Rydal, via High Pike and back via Rydal Fell, but the ascent from Patterdale, taking in St Sunday Crag, is also excellent (see walk on p. 235).

Back o' Skiddaw

The huge upland mass of Skiddaw Forest, roughly six miles square and crossed by no road, creates a barrier which is most visitors' perception of the northern extent of the Lake District. But there is quite a lot of interest tucked around the 'back' (northern side) of this massif. This is probably the least-known part of the National Park – even on a Bank Holiday Monday the odds are that you will have much of it to yourself. While it's easy to see why it tends to get missed out – the smooth, expansive tracts of rolling moorland, the quiet farmland and long, rather uneventful side valleys lack the drama of the central lakes – Back o' Skiddaw has its devotees. It's very peaceful and, strangely, feels more remote than some of the more mountainous parts of the Lake District. Many of its stone hamlets and villages have simple rustic charm, and there is the bonus of some huge views further north into the Scottish Lowlands, even from the road. Above all, the back of Skiddaw feels *different* – not the Lake District's greatest patch of scenery, but a worthwhile way of getting the region into perspective.

From the A66 seven miles east of Keswick, a minor road signposted to Mungrisdale can be taken as the start of a road tour around the back of Skiddaw. The turn-off is immediately next to the slopes of **Blencathra**, shown on OS maps as 'Saddleback or Blencathra', but usually referred to by the latter. Viewed from the west or east, it is unmistakable, owing to its strange scooped-out southern escarpment, a complex of deep hollows joined on to a sagging, saddle-shaped ridge. It gives its name to the Blencathra Foxhounds, one of Lakeland's most famous packs.

Mungrisdale has a pub and a humble, chapel-like eighteenth-century church, with a harmonium instead of an organ. North of here, the road hugs the fellside closely until **Bowscale**, the next hamlet. This is the starting-point for the walk to Bowscale Tarn, just about the most tucked-away of all the Lakeland tarns, hidden between a grassy hillock to the north and the 500-foot curved natural wall (a glacial feature) of Bowscale Fell to the south. Tourists in the early nineteenth century used to make a special point of coming here, egged on by the legend that two giant trout that lived in the tarn were immortal and by a rumour that the tarn is so deep and dark that stars could be seen reflected on its surface even on the sunniest of days. The walk takes 30 minutes each way, and the track is very clearly defined and easy to walk, although it becomes a rather fainter grassy path later on. Look for a signpost to the tarn, leaving the road by the first house in the hamlet. The track rises gently above the broad valley of the River Caldew, the northern side of which is occupied by **Carrock Fell**, the only fell in Skiddaw Forest to be composed of volcanic rock; it even has an outcrop of gabbro, a rock found in the Cuillins on Skye. Geologists home in on this odd fell, where over 20 types of minerals can be found; mining for tungsten ores (wolfram and scheelite) took place in the valley from 1854 to the early 1970s. Carrock Fell's summit is ringed by the remains of the wall of what was the largest hill fort in Cumbria. A burial cairn inside the fort has the appearance of an early Bronze Age cairn, and the fort itself is thought to be of the same date.

Coffee, tea and good cakes (plus the odd shelf of second-hand books) are sometimes on offer at the Friends' Meeting House at **Mosedale** (look out for signs). North of here, the moors flatten and become desolate and just a shade eerie. **Hesket Newmarket** comes as something of a relief – a picture-book village of attractive houses flanking a long, sloping green. In the centre is a roofed market cross, put up

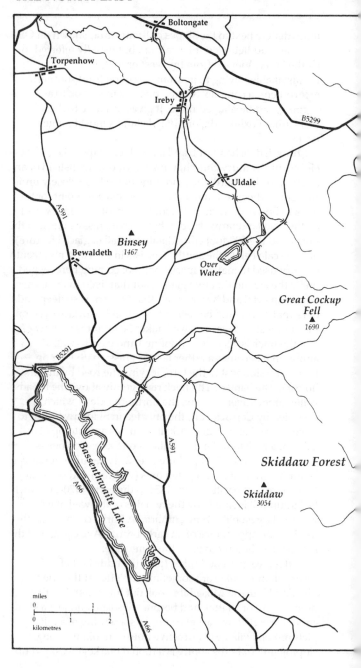

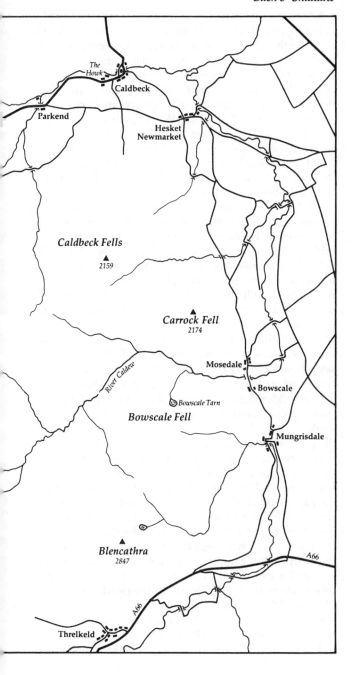

in the eighteenth century at the time when 'Newmarket' was added to the village name and nearly all the houses were built. Until then the village comprised little more than Hesket Hall, the cruciform, gable-winged seventeenth-century farmhouse at the top of its street – said to have been designed as a giant sundial, its 12 corners providing the shadows. Charles Dickens and Wilkie Collins passed through Hesket Newmarket and Caldbeck in 1857, and recorded their travels in *The Lazy Tour of Two Idle Apprentices*.

Caldbeck, where the road from Hesket Newmarket meets the B5299, is the most northerly village in the National Park – in fact, the boundary's northernmost point is at a corner of the B5299 just a mile from here. The village, once a flourishing milling and mining centre, has an oddly diffuse shape: rows of cottages are interrupted by open green spaces and a bridged stream runs along one broad side street. A few of the village's eight mills survive, though none is working. A former fulling-mill is now The Old Smithy (a gift shop), while Priest's Mill retains its waterwheel (which you can get to turn round by putting 10p in the slot) and houses a craft shop, second-hand bookshop, another gift shop and a civilised tea-room adorned with country bygones. For lunch, there's **Parkend** (a mile or so west on the B5299), a seventeenth-century farmhouse now a restaurant-with-rooms, where the food is deliciously fresh and home made.

Caldbeck's most intriguing place is a miniature limestone chasm with a waterfall known as **The Howk**; however, this is easily missed. The approach to it is through a wooded dingle, past the atmospheric ruins of Bobbin Mill (to which used to be attached a 42-foot waterwheel nicknamed Red Rover; this was dismantled in 1940 when scrap metal was in short supply). The waterfall tumbles into a cauldron called the Fairy Kettle, polished and scooped out by the passage of the water. Nearby is the Fairy Kirk, a small cavern. To reach The Howk from the church, start with the church on your right, take the road through the village, and take the first right turn after the turn signposted to the car-park; a restored corn-mill is soon passed, then as soon as you cross the river take a gate on the left signposted to The Howk – the path is obvious all the way from here.

Caldbeck owed its prosperity as a mining centre to the rich mineral resources, especially lead and copper, of the Caldbeck Fells to the south. Mining was at its peak from the time of the Napoleonic Wars until the closure of Roughton Gill mine in 1878, although wolfram and barytes were mined locally as late as the 1960s.

To the left of the churchyard path, as you approach the porch, and decorated with hunting-horn motifs is the prominent white tombstone of John Peel – of 'Do ye ken, John Peel' fame. Peel was a huntsman (and drinker) extraordinary, born in 1776 – reputedly at Parkend. He eloped to Gretna Green with a local girl, but his mother-in-law later softened towards him and the marriage was solemnised in Caldbeck in 1797. The famous song immortalising him was written by a woollen manufacturer, John Woodcock Graves, who produced the wool for John Peel's 'coat so grey'; the tune was rewritten by William Metcalfe, conductor of Carlisle Choral Society, in 1869.

Also buried in Caldbeck churchyard is Mary Robinson, the 'beauty of Buttermere' (see p. 57). The spacious church, like many others in north Lakeland, is dedicated to St Kentigern (alias St Mungo), who preached here en route for Wales from his bishopric in Glasgow.

For the best views from the car, keep to the B5299 west of Caldbeck. Two prominent features of the view over the Solway Firth to the Scottish Lowlands are the pointed peak of Criffel and four white cooling towers near Annan. **Boltongate** is as far as you need go along this road, but it's worth taking this small village in: inside its externally unassuming church is a stone-vaulted nave, a feature otherwise found only in Scottish church architecture. This vaulting technique was originally from Burgundy, being first used in Scotland at the Cistercian abbey at Melrose. Local tradition asserts that the church was built in a single night by Michael Scott, a thirteenth-century Scottish wizard; other sources have claimed that it was the work of specially imported French builders. In the nineteenth century, a baffled Bishop Goodwin remarked 'mathematically it ought to have fallen down, because the weight of the massive stone roof should have forced the walls out'.

A minor road is signposted from Boltongate for **Ireby**, a pleasant largish village, presumably much sleepier now than when a thriving market used to operate here. Remains of the market cross are just behind the central square, which itself is abutted by the former Moot Hall (long since converted into cottages). Ireby's former church lies on the narrow lane signposted to Torpenhow. A good mile clear of the village itself, and approachable only through a field and then via a careful leap over the churchyard wall, this feels as if it's been forgotten for ever. Only the Norman chancel remains, surrounded by sandstone tombstones and (in summer) waist-high cow parsley. No services are held here, and the key is with the Redundant Churches Fund.

Torpenhow, two miles west of Ireby, is just a long street of houses, but at its western end is a minor gem of a church: Norman, with a fine chancel arch (look out for the three figures linking arms on one capital and the heads of people and beasts on the other), a painted wooden seventeenth-century nave ceiling (said to come from the headquarters of a livery company), and a crude arch around the door.

A minor road south-east from Ireby leads through Uldale (not much to speak of: just a remote hamlet built around a crossroads) and on to **Over Water**, a pretty tarn which, viewed from its northern side, makes a fine scene with the unforgettably named Great Cockup Fell as a backdrop. Unfortunately, since Over Water is used as a reservoir there is no access to it. Westwards, between here and Bewaldeth (which is just off the A591) are the farm and cottages at Fell End, the most convenient point for ascending Binsey (see walk on p. 228).

North of the A66, east of the National Park boundary

The fells fizzle out quite suddenly north of Ullswater, while further north, on the other side of the A66, the scenery has not a hint of Lakeland character: it's predominantly gently rolling farming country, where the contour lines just get up over 1000 feet.

A series of minor roads, including the B5288, is signposted to **Greystoke** from the A66. If heading for Penrith, it is worth making a diversion here, since you can then follow the B5288 into town; otherwise there is not enough to merit a major detour. Greystoke does have a briefly interesting village centre, where sandstone cottages surround a triangular green, at the centre of which stands an old stone cross. Greystoke Castle stands beyond, and its huge estate spreads to the north and west of the village; the castle is not open, and is concealed from view. St Andrew's Church, at the end

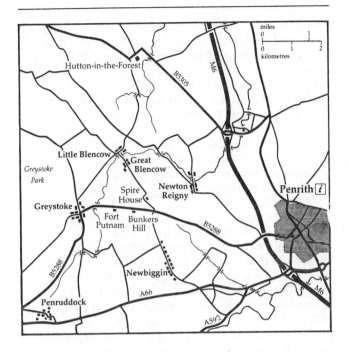

of a lane of cottages (turn off by the post office), possesses a spacious though much-restored interior – worth a quick look for its carved misericords, a fragment of medieval stained glass depicting the devil being trampled on by a saint (a rare instance of the devil making an appearance in a church window), and two effigies to barons of Greystoke. On a path leading north from the church, about 100 yards away, is a plague stone, used in medieval times for cleaning coins when the village was hit hard by plague to reduce the risk of transmitting the disease.

East of Greystoke, the B5288 passes close by three folly farms, built by the eleventh Duke of Norfolk as eye-catchers in the late eighteenth century and two of which were named after American battles. First, on the right, is Fort Putnam – massive, castle-like and highly eccentric. Half a mile further on, on the same side of the road, stands the smaller polygonal Bunkers Hill. Almost immediately, across fields to the left, you can then see Spire House, with its church-like spire projecting out of the top of a polygonal tower; to get a closer view, take the next left, by a pub.

Hutton-in-the-Forest is an imposing country house (open May to mid-Sept, Thurs to Sat, 1 to 4; gardens open all year, daily), which was one of the three main manors of the Royal Forest of Inglewood (and is still the home of Lord Inglewood). It is a little off the beaten track – some four miles north-west of Penrith, and just off the B5305 – but worth a visit. At the centre of the building is a fourteenth-century peel tower built by the Hutton family. Three hundred years later the Fletchers, wealthy Cockermouth merchants, became owners of the castle and converted it from a fortress to a country house, adding the baroque façade. Much of the castellated parts are nineteenth-century embellishments and additions.

Inside, the highlight is the gallery, adorned with panelling somehow acquired from Torpenhow church (see p. 100) and containing some very fine carved wooden furniture. The atmosphere of the house is quite dark and cluttered, though not oppressive, and there is antique china, tapestries and furniture, plus some Arts and Crafts touches from its nineteenth-century owner (a cousin of Gladstone and friend of William Morris), including a fabric and two wallpapers personally designed for the owner by Morris. A number of outstanding specimen trees are in the grounds, where there is also a woodland walk. The tea-room is a pleasant long room in one of the older parts of the house.

Penrith

Penrith dates from pre-Roman times as a market town, sited in an important bridging position and on a long-established major route to Scotland. Border skirmishes troubled the town over many centuries, and the street plan reflects the town's former role as a place of refuge, with narrow streets leading into large open spaces such as Great Dockray, into which livestock could be brought in times of danger. Several street names act as mementoes of the town's once numerous gates (none of which survives) – Middlegate, Stricklandgate, Castlegate, Friargate, Sandgate and Burrowgate.

The centre of Penrith has some quite dignified buildings but most of the time the heavy traffic is its dominant feature. It has a fairly comprehensive range of shops – a pedestrianised area leads off the cobbled market place. But for architecture alone, only the Georgian close surrounding

St Andrew's Church is pleasant enough to be really worth walking around. Take a quick look inside the church – quite a grand design of 1720. In the churchyard are two eroded upright stones enclosing two pairs of crescent-shaped 'hogback' stones: this curious arrangement is thought to be a tenth- or eleventh-century tomb to an officer of the church, though traditionally it has been held to be that of a giant who was a king of Cumbria.

Penrith's tourist **information centre**, with a little museum attached, is housed in one of the town's most ancient buildings, the former Robinson's school (dated 1670) in Middlegate. The school opened as a charitable institution for the education of girls; it closed in 1970.

Penrith **Steam Museum** (open Easter to Sept, Mon to Fri, 10 to 5) in Castlegate is in the former Castlegate Foundry, which was operated by the Stalker family from 1859 to 1959 for the manufacture of agricultural machinery. It looks unassuming from the outside, but inside is an array of goodies which should hold your interest even if you are only moderately intrigued by traction engines and foundries. A large hall contains a collection of nineteenth- and early twentieth-century traction engines and steamrollers, plus a steam organ (converted to electricity) which is regularly performed. Surrounding the yard at the back are the old works, whose blacksmith's shop, mill, foundry and office look as if nothing has been touched since they closed down: an ancient ledger open on a desk, and shelves and shelves of gently rusting ironmongery. There are also a few bits and pieces which are somewhat tangential to the main theme: some antique motorcycles and an old cottage (a humble reminder of the pre-electric era). Annoyingly, labelling of exhibits is at the best merely perfunctory and often almost non-existent, and the museum does not publish a guidebook.

At the top of Castlegate, opposite the railway station, are the fragments of the fourteenth- and fifteenth-century **castle** (open all year, daily). Licences to crenellate, or to fortify, were granted in 1397 and 1399 to William Strickland (who became Bishop of Carlisle) after the town was burned down by the Scots in 1345; later the castle fell into the hands of the Neville family. By 1550 the structure was in ruins; one substantial L-shaped portion of wall stands, plus sundry smaller lumps. There is just about enough left to give you an idea of what it looked like, though its noisy and not very inviting present-day setting does not make it worth going out of your way to see.

Penrith is larger than any of the towns inside the National Park boundary, and has quite a full range of shops and eating-places. One of the most prominent shops in the centre is James and John Graham, an old-fashioned grocer's with a high ceiling and walls adorned with antlers on shields; it has a big selection of cheeses, many of which are made locally.

The Cumbrian Kitchen in Market Square is a licensed eatery with an all-day menu of pizzas, pasta and salads plus good home baking. For lunch, try In Clover (Poets Walk) where the daily menu is home cooked and mostly vegetarian, with lush desserts; and at teatime you can find wholefood goodies in the little Bluebell Bookshop (Three Crowns Yard). Little Passepartout in Castlegate is a relaxed and friendly place for a well-cooked dinner, strong on local produce.

Wordsworth spent much of his childhood in Penrith, though there are no Wordsworthian sights as such. He and his sister Dorothy attended Dame Birkett's school (near St Andrew's Church), where they made friends with Mary Hutchinson, William's future wife. William and Dorothy used to enjoy climbing up Penrith Beacon, the wooded hill just to the north of the town, which is still a very good viewpoint. A monument on top commemorates the 1745 rebellion; bonfires used to be lit here as part of a chain of beacon fires warning of Scottish invasions.

South of Penrith

To the south of Penrith is a landscape very much like the Yorkshire Dales: limestone scars, the broad and lush Lowther Valley, and stone villages with long greens. The good scenery starts close to the north-eastern corner of the National Park, but before it is reached there is a concentration of antiquities close to the A6, just south of the A66 roundabout, which is worth taking in. At **Eamont Bridge** the B5320 heads west from the A6. Immediately on the left (south) side of the road is Arthur's Round Table, a sizeable prehistoric earthwork of unknown date and purpose, but probably a meeting-place constructed in 2000–1000 BC. The next right turn is signposted to Mayburgh

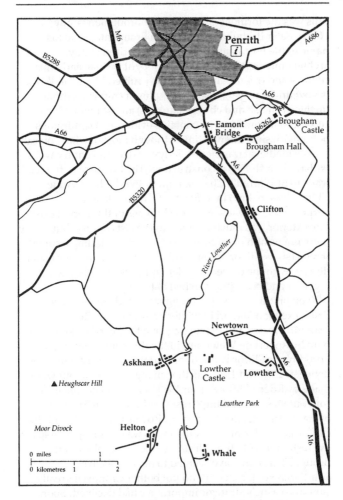

Henge: park on the verge 100 yards before the first house (the Henge is not signposted again). In the field on the right is a raised bank, concealing a large artificial crater with a nine-foot-high standing stone in the middle; in the last century there were three stones next to it and two pairs of stones by an eastern entrance to the Henge, but these were taken for use as building material.

Immediately south of Eamont Bridge, take the B6262 east from the A6. As soon as the road passes under a stone bridge, the massive curtain walls of **Brougham Hall** appear.

This was the former residence of the Brougham family; Henry Peter Brougham, first Baron Brougham, gave his name to the brougham carriage. The Carlton family, arch-enemies of the Broughams, bought the hall early this century and (reputedly) deliberately ruined it in 1934. Work is now under way to create a complex of craft workshops (including a fish and cheese smokery) and student accommodation. The site contains evidence of continuous occupation since Roman times, though most of what you can see are medieval fragments, early-nineteenth-century walls and modern (1980s) reconstruction. The bridge over the road leads to St Wilfred's Chapel, built in 1658 by Lady Anne Clifford (see below) in defiance of Cromwell; not surprisingly, very few English churches of this period exist. The exterior was much restored in the last century, but inside there is a wealth of imported woodwork, including a superb screen (sixteenth or seventeenth century) of a most unusual design, with the carved wooden uprights placed closely together and beautifully arched at the top.

Keep on this B-road for **Brougham Castle** (open all year, daily, exc Mon and Fri in winter), a ruin by the River Eamont, erected as a defence against the Scots. Its keep was built by Robert de Viewpoint in the thirteenth century, and Lord Robert Clifford added the curtain wall and gatehouses between 1290 and 1314. Further changes to the layout were made by Roger Clifford from 1360 to 1389. It later fell into ruin but was painstakingly restored between 1651 and 1662 by Lady Anne Clifford, a fervent Royalist and the last of the Cliffords, a determined woman who was also responsible for the restoration of other Clifford castles at Appleby and Brough. This may have seemed to be provocatively anti-Parliamentarian, but did not bother Cromwell greatly since the castle's strategic importance had declined. Soon after Lady Anne's death, parts of the building were demolished. Enough survives, however, to make it possible to imagine how the castle looked after its final restoration.

Continuing south on the A6, the long and straggly village of **Clifton** is reached. At the northern end, on the right of the road as you approach from Penrith, is Clifton Hall (open all year, daily). This three-storey peel tower is all that remains of the hall, the rest of which was demolished in the early nineteenth century and replaced by the present-day farm. The tower dates from around 1500, although the windows

are seventeenth and eighteenth century. You can go inside:
the walls, roof and floor joists are intact, and the staircase
takes you up to the second floor.

The southern end of the village was the site of the 1745
Battle of Clifton Moor: the Jacobeans, who had taken
Carlisle, advanced to Derby but then retreated to Clifton
Moor, where the battle took place with the Duke of
Cumberland's Hanoverian troops; the Scots fled, but by then
Cumberland's men were too fatigued to follow.

The A6 crosses over the motorway, after which take the
third turning on the right for **Lowther**, one of the estate
villages for Lowther Castle. The eighteenth-century 'village'
is tiny, but memorable and all of a piece: two crescents of
cottages plus a rectangular close. The other estate village, a
few hundred yards beyond, is **Newtown**, a grand name for
just one row of cottages. Lowther Castle is a spectacularly
sinister-looking ruin set in magnificent rolling parkland; two
fine avenues, mainly of mature oaks, lead from it. The castle,
home of the Lowther family, was built in 1806–11 to replace
an earlier mansion which burned down in 1720; the present
structure was abandoned when it proved too costly to
maintain. Its architect was Robert Smirke, and this was his
first commission, at the age of 25; he later designed the
British Museum. The Lowther estate is private (the castle is
not open to the public), and the only access to the parkland is
from a few not very well signposted public footpaths,
although this is certainly extremely pleasant walking country
(see walk on p. 230). In August the Lowther Horse Trials are
held here – a big event which also includes a country fair.
Lowther Park, a family outing, is two miles south of the
castle and signposted from the A6 near Clifton: adventure
playgrounds, jousts, a circus, 'fun for everyone' (open June
to mid-Sept, daily, 10 to 6, plus Easter and weekends rest of
year).

Continue on the unclassified road towards Askham;
Lowther church, opposite the main castle driveway, has a
large nineteenth-century mausoleum for the Lowther family
in the churchyard.

Askham is an outstandingly attractive village with a long,
broad main street sloping from west to east, lined for its
entire length on either side by swathes of grass dotted with
mature trees, constituting what is in effect the village green.
No houses stand out particularly, but the composition is very

pleasing. Both Askham's pubs are good for lunch: conventional pub food at the Queens Head and a lighter, imaginative range of dishes in Jack Horner's at the Punch Bowl Inn. Opposite the latter, at the bottom of the village, is the entrance to Askham Hall (home of the Earl of Lonsdale), which is private and screened by a wall; an adjacent bridleway leading off the street gives a rear view of this late-fourteenth- and late-seventeenth-century house with a tower. Further down still is the nineteenth-century church, in a secluded spot among trees by the river.

South of Askham is where the landscape resembles the Yorkshire Dales most strongly. Two limestone scars run north to south along the top of low hills east of the River Lowther. **Helton** and **Whale** are both hamlets of stone cottages with a green at the centre – another typical Dales feature – and surrounded by dry-stone walled pastures. West of here is a mournful landscape of gently rising moorland hills, boggy and generally inhospitable, with **Moor Divock** at the centre. These moors are studded with antiquities, including a five-foot-high monolith called the Cop Stone (once part of a stone circle), and a 65-stone circle (64 of which lie low in the heather) on **Heughscar Hill**.

Haweswater and Shap

For Haweswater, turn off the unclassified road from Askham at **Bampton**, a village in two parts: Bampton and Bampton Grange. There is an attractive scene at the latter, with a sandstone bridge over the River Lowther and an eighteenth-century church adjacent. After a mile and a half along the road to Haweswater, the road crosses a small stone bridge; from here, a signposted footpath to Park Bridge leads past **Thornthwaite Force** (about 100 yards from the road), a waterfall with a pleasant sylvan setting amid small crags.

In 1940 the Manchester Water Corporation enlarged **Haweswater** from two and a half to four miles in length to form one of the largest reservoirs in northern England; a 120-foot-high dam was built at its eastern end. The lake was favoured as a reservoir partly because of its height: at 694 feet above sea-level, it is the highest of all the lakes in the area, and this altitude made transportation of water down to towns some 80 or 90 miles distant relatively simple.

Those who knew the valley rue the loss of Mardale, by all

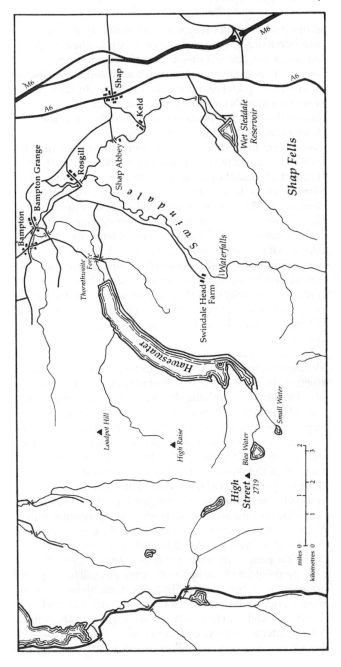

accounts a charming valley with a remote sheep-farming village containing a seventeenth-century pub (the Dun Bull Inn) and a tiny church (after construction work on the reservoir began, the graves were exhumed and the bodies reburied in a special cemetery annexed to the churchyard at Shap; the church's Jacobean pulpit was removed to Rosthwaite church in Borrowdale). A picture of Mardale church hangs in the church at Bampton.

Writing in the early twentieth century, the travel writer Bradley described the place as 'a hamlet unforgettable for the charm of its romantic beauty and seclusion from the world'. Mardale's most famous moment in recent years was in the drought of 1984 when the water level dropped so low that the drowned village was revealed. TV crews came, bringing with them former inhabitants who could remember the village as it was, and hordes of sightseers followed. It became possible to walk over an old stone bridge and around ruined walls which had been under water for nearly half a century. Eventually the valley became so crowded that the road was closed, but this didn't stop people walking over the fells from Patterdale and Kentmere to get a glimpse of the scene.

Haweswater does not otherwise attract visitors in anything like the numbers as do many of the other major lakes, owing chiefly to its inaccessibility. It does not have the visual appeal of Ullswater, say – with the slopes rising steeply from both sides, Haweswater has an unchanging, corridor-like appearance as you drive along it from the east, and when the water level is low the neat white scar above the water's edge makes it impossible to forget that this is a reservoir. But views from the south-west end of the road are more stirring: there is a panorama of Haweswater's one island, close by a wooded promontory, with the craggy hills of the High Street range looming up to the west. Haweswater is popular with birdwatchers anxious to catch a glimpse of the golden eagle, which has been re-introduced to the Lake District.

The car-park at the south-western end of the lake is the starting-point for all the best walks from this valley. The chief attraction is the ascent on to **High Street**, the highest point of the long ridge which stretches 10 miles from just above the Trout Beck Valley in the south to the north end of Ullswater. Named after a pre-Roman trackway which became a major Roman road connecting the Roman fort at Galava near

Ambleside with that at Brocavum near Penrith, it is no coincidence that the route has some of the most extensive views in eastern Lakeland; the Romans in particular were nervous of attacks from the Britons and thus chose a ridge which would enable them to keep watch over the valleys below. On a clear day it is possible to see a long way to the south, including Heysham nuclear power station and Blackpool Tower. See walk on p. 238.

Easy walks from Haweswater are limited to there-and-back strolls along the lakeside or up to one of two tarns, both of which are in dramatic and rugged settings below the High Street ridge. To reach either, take the gate at the end of the road and proceed 50 yards to a signpost. For **Small Water**, keep forward (signposted Kentmere) and follow the path for just under a mile; for **Blea Water** (the deepest Lakeland tarn – 207 feet deep; in fact, even among the lakes in the Lake District only Wastwater and Windermere are deeper), turn right, follow the path until it crosses a stream (Mardale Beck), then turn left and proceed for a mile.

East of Haweswater is an area of lonely and generally bleak moorland hills, and only lusher **Swindale** stands out scenically. It is approached by a drive over featureless moorland from near the hamlet of Rosgill, but suddenly the steep-sided dale begins – one of the Lake District's best-kept secrets, with a large natural amphitheatre and a series of waterfalls and pools cascading down a ravine at its far end. After the unfenced road reaches a cattle-grid it becomes gated; parking at Swindale Head, the farm at the end of the road, is not always possible (the farmer puts a No Parking sign out when he needs to use the yard), so it is usually best to park by the cattle-grid and walk the remaining mile and a half. Keep straight on at Swindale Head (signposted Mosedale) and follow the track ahead to reach the falls, which are at the left end of the valley; as soon as you reach the stream, make your own way alongside it up to the flight of falls.

From Bampton the drive to Shap has some good views to the west of the High Street range and of the hills around Swindale. **Shap Abbey**, signposted to the right of this road, is a Premonstratensian foundation of 1180 (the last abbey to be founded, and the last to be dissolved, in 1540, possibly getting a stay of execution because of its use as a shelter for travellers crossing the Shap Fells). The best-preserved part is the sixteenth-century tower, although the bases of the other walls give a rough idea of its layout and size. From here it is a short and pleasant walk across fields (see p. 228) to **Keld** to make a pilgrimage to its minute sixteenth/seventeenth-century chapel (to reach it by car, continue along the road towards Shap village and take the next turning right). Inside this barn-like building all is touchingly plain – bare, rough stone walls, the most basic of wooden benches and no electricity. Its partition wall and fireplace survive as relics of its days when it was used as a cottage. Surprisingly for such a sleepy and out-of-the-way hamlet, Keld has the bonus of possessing a tea and craft shop.

Shap village is dominated by the noisy A6 and by a large granite quarry, the stone from which has been used for numerous public buildings, including St Pancras Station and the Albert Memorial.

Where to stay

For a key to prices, see p. 10

Barton
Old Vicarage, Barton, Tirril, near Penrith, Cumbria CA10 2LR.
Tel Pooley Bridge (076 84) 86307
A detached house, occupied by a music teacher, his wife and young children, with three rooms to let; comfortably furnished, in keeping with the Victorian style of the house, which occupies a quiet position on a cul-de-sac, with views towards the High Street range. £

Caldbeck
High Greenrigg House, Caldbeck, Wigton, Cumbria CA7 8HD.
Tel Caldbeck (069 98) 430
An imaginatively modernised farmhouse in remote moors near the northernmost point of the National Park boundary. The hall indicates what kind of hotel this is: a collection of local maps available for guests'

consultation, the day's weather forecast displayed, and usually a row of walking boots. The atmosphere is informal (with guests sharing tables) and will appeal to lovers of the great outdoors. The owners have published their own booklet of walks starting from the hotel. Food is wholesome and served in ample quantities. There's a games-room (table tennis and snooker), plus quantities of books and board games in case you're snowed in. £

Mungrisdale
The Mill Hotel, Mungrisdale, Penrith, Cumbria CA11 0XR.
Tel Threlkeld (076 87) 79659
A simple but civilised guest-house: a seventeenth-century mill cottage with a trout stream in its grounds, well placed for the northern fells (and it has a

drying room). Well-planned bedrooms, cosy lounges. The food is ambitious and the atmosphere sociable, with a touch of country-house. ££

Ullswater

Sharrow Bay, Ullswater, Penrith, Cumbria CA10 2LZ. Tel Pooley Bridge (076 84) 86301 A totally relaxing country-house hotel on the east bank of the lake, Sharrow Bay is renowned for the prodigal luxury of its breakfasts, lunches, teas and dinners. It's a Victorian house (with cottage and farmhouse annexes) full of antiques, objets d'art, flowers and thoughtful details, where guests feel supremely pampered. No children under 13. £££££

Watermillock

The Old Church, Watermillock, Penrith, Cumbria CA11 0JN. Tel Pooley Bridge (076 84) 86204 Well off the A592, this is a very peaceful eighteenth-century house (on the site of a twelfth-century church) with gardens down to the western shore of Ullswater and a boat for guests' use. It's a place of impeccable décor and considerable style – the hostess has a flair for soft furnishings – and most of the bedrooms have the lake view. ££££

Bed and breakfast

Best bets are around Ullswater. Unfortunately, none of the lake's villages is attractive, but there are numerous possibilities near the A592; the other side of the lake is lovely but there is little B&B accommodation. The area bounded by the A592 to the south, the A66 to the north and the A5091 has some peaceful hamlets and hilly landscape, and would make a good base, though there's not a lot of accommodation here either. Less frequented still is the road around Back o' Skiddaw, from Mungrisdale to Caldbeck; quite a lot of farmhouse and guest-house accommodation here, and good if you want to get away from the bustle of the popular parts of the Lakes – but some will find it too remote and lacking true Lakeland drama.

THE SOUTH-WEST

Langdale · The Wrynose and Hardknott Passes:
from Langdale to Eskdale · Eskdale ·
Gosforth to Wast Water · Ravenglass to
Broughton-in-Furness · The Duddon Valley ·
Ulverston · The Furness peninsula · Skelwith
Bridge to Coniston Water · WHERE TO STAY

Scenery

The highest peak in England, plus a concentration of
rugged mountains that make up the wildest part of the
National Park; also some superb scenic roads and
deep, remote dales.

Scenic highlights
- WAST WATER and the fells close to it – majesty and awe:
  can't fail to impress.
- LANGDALE – more and more exciting as you drive
  down it, lured by the magnetic presence of Langdale
  Pikes and Bow Fell.
- The WRYNOSE and HARDKNOTT PASSES – the most
  spectacular drive in the Lakes.

Also worth seeing
- ESKDALE – refreshing and delightful mixture of
  lowland and fells; broad, varied and subtle landscape.
  Lots of interesting sights too. You can take it in by
  miniature railway.
- The DUDDON VALLEY – narrow and partly wooded,
  pretty rather than dramatic.
- Roads leading into the Duddon Valley from the west
  via CORNEY FELL and BIRK FELL, and from the east from
  BROUGHTON MILLS.
- CONISTON WATER – see it from the east side, or better
  still take a trip on the National Trust's steam yacht.
- Parts of the FURNESS PENINSULA: an unspoilt beach at
  Sandscale Haws; views of Morecambe Bay from the
  road from Ulverston to Roa Island.

Best walks

Easy walks

- Several possibilities in ESKDALE, mostly using the railway for the return route.
- Forestry or non-forestry rambles in the DUDDON VALLEY.
- Lowland walks in GREAT and LITTLE LANGDALE, taking in woods, pastures and waterfalls.
- CHURCH BECK (near Coniston) – interesting for relics of the copper-mining industry.
- TILBERTHWAITE GILL – pleasant views.
- Low fells with good views: IRTON PIKE (near Eskdale) and BEACON (near Blawith).
- COLWITH FORCE, SKELWITH FORCE and DUNGEON GHYLL – three waterfalls within a few yards of the road.

Fell walks

Fell walkers are spoilt for choice: large tracts of unpopulated, untamed mountain scenery, offering the most challenging walking and rock-climbing in England. Obvious objectives are SCAFELL PIKE, GREAT GABLE, LANGDALE PIKES, BOW FELL, CRINKLE CRAGS, PILLAR, HARTER FELL and THE OLD MAN OF CONISTON. BLACK COMBE has the view of views on a really clear day.

Sights

Houses

- BRANTWOOD – Ruskin's home, full of his personal touches.
- MUNCASTER CASTLE – a peel tower, altered in the last century; numerous family-type attractions in addition to the tour of the house.
- SWARTHMOOR HALL – an Elizabethan house with important Quaker connections.
- CONISHEAD PRIORY – a nineteenth-century Gothic mansion, being restored.

Water-mills

- Mills at BOOT and MUNCASTER (near Ravenglass), the latter producing flour for sale.

Railways

- RAVENGLASS AND ESKDALE RAILWAY – seven miles of miniature railway leading in from the coast to the heart of Eskdale.
- BR'S CUMBRIAN COAST LINE from Barrow northwards gives good coastal views.

Museums

- RUSKIN MUSEUM, Coniston – lots of Ruskin sketches; a moderately interesting supplement to Brantwood.
- FOLK MUSEUM, Millom – packed with local history; a far from formal atmosphere.
- RAILWAY MUSEUM, Ravenglass – the history of the Ravenglass and Eskdale Railway.
- LAUREL AND HARDY MUSEUM, Ulverston – an enthusiast's eccentric shrine to the comic duo.

Archaeology

- SWINSIDE STONE CIRCLE – in a remote field, but worth seeking out.
- HARDKNOTT CASTLE – a strategically placed Roman fort; remains are scant but nevertheless impressive. Magnificent location.
- WALLS CASTLE – a Roman bath-house, intact to a surprising degree, tucked away at the edge of woods.

Best churches

- FURNESS ABBEY – Cistercian abbey ruins of great beauty, in its time the greatest abbey in the north-west.
- GOSFORTH and IRTON CHURCHES both have stunning ancient stone crosses. Gosforth has interesting Norse hogback tombstones inside the church, too.
- WABERTHWAITE – plain and ancient, nicely hidden away on the Esk estuary.
- WASDALE HEAD – sobering climbers' graves in the churchyard. Superb location under the shadow of Great Gable and Scafell Pike.

Castles

- PIEL CASTLE – a fourteenth-century ruin on its own island guarding Barrow harbour. Off the beaten track, but worth seeing for its magnificent site.

Best villages

- ELTERWATER – a little village with a tiny green and a good pub, by the river in Great Langdale.
- BOOT – just one street, with a stone bridge at one end near the water-mill.
- BROUGHTON-IN-FURNESS – a handsome ex-market town with a fine central square, so sleepy it's really more of a village than a town.

Towns

- MILLOM, an industrial nineteenth-century town, is worth visiting for its museum.
- BARROW-IN-FURNESS, an industrial port, is pretty grim, though has curiosity value.
- ULVERSTON – a market town which has made few obvious concessions to tourism.

Langdale

This valley, almost at the geographical heart of the Lake District, can be reached by taking the B5343 from Skelwith Bridge, which is on the A593 three miles west of Ambleside. Little and Great Langdale together make up the dale.

Great Langdale acts like a magnet for visitors, drawn by the wonderful outline of Langdale Pikes, with even higher mountains at the head of the valley. **Little Langdale,** to the south, is a separate valley joined to Great Langdale by **Colwith Force,** the more impressive by far of the two Brathay waterfalls (the other being Skelwith Force at Skelwith Bridge). The force is a succession of mini-rapids ending at a 15-foot fall and dropping a total of 50 feet. Little Langdale was a major route for the Romans coming from Galava (see p. 173) at Ambleside en route for the coast via the Hardknott Pass, and later became a packhorse route. The hamlet of **Little Langdale** comprises a handful of cottages, plus a

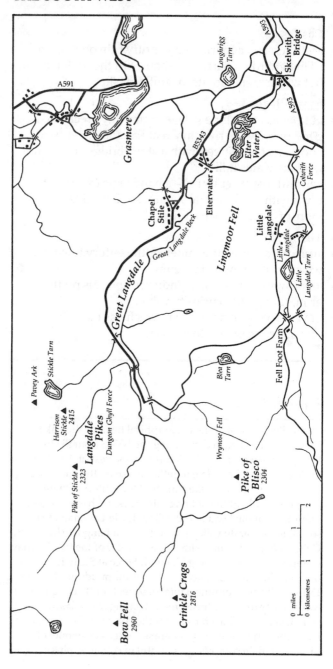

chapel and a good pub, the Three Shires Inn. Lying south-west of the hamlet is **Little Langdale Tarn**, a haunt of wild geese.

Elterwater village, at the east end of the two valleys and just south of the B5343, used to be an important centre of the Lake District's gunpowder industry which grew up in conjunction with the area's mining and quarrying activities. The gunpowder-mill to the west of the village has been replaced by a large timeshare complex (unobtrusive but controversial), but one slate quarry south of Elterwater village still functions. The village itself is pleasingly straightforward, with a pocket-handkerchief of a village green (just large enough to accommodate one tree) flanked by the commendable Britannia Inn (see p. 149) and the village shop. From the car-park a path leads through meadows alongside **Great Langdale Beck** towards the east end of **Elter Water** itself: a difficult lake to see, as it's privately owned, but there is one fine view from this path looking over the water towards Langdale Pikes. **Chapel Stile**, a mile west of Elterwater village, has an informal jumble of houses ranged along two sloping lanes which lead down to the B5343, and a development of modern houses along the main road itself.

Continuing westwards along the B5343, **Great Langdale** proper begins – one of the real pearls of Lakeland, with the brooding presence of the knuckle-shaped twin summits of the Langdale Pikes (2415 feet), probably the best-known mountain shape in the Lake District, stealing the show. Sealing in the valley is a crescent of fells – left to right, Pike of Blisco (2304 feet), Crinkle Crags (2816 feet) and Bow Fell (2960 feet). Crinkle Crags, with its five pinnacles and deep incisions, is rated as one of the best ridge walks in the District, and shapely Bow Fell is a rewarding ascent (see walks on p. 249). Langdale Pikes (the left-hand summit is Pike of Stickle, the other, slightly taller, is Harrison Stickle) is very popular with walkers, and there is often a constant procession of visitors on its slopes. Close to Harrison Stickle, a great cliff known as Pavey Ark soars above Stickle Tarn and creates a fine and sombre scene. Some bad footpath erosion has occurred on Pavey Ark, due to the sheer numbers of visitors who come here, and it is necessary to descend with great care.

Close to the foot of Langdale Pikes is **Dungeon Ghyll Force**, not a grand waterfall, but fetching in a small-scale way, and delightfully sited. Below Pike of Stickle, Langdale's stone axe 'factory' has attracted hordes of souvenir-seekers, anxious to take home a piece of hand-worked flint, though the National Trust would rather they could resist the temptation. Five thousand years ago 'tuffs' of volcanic rock were cut here with granite hammers and taken to the coast for polishing with sandstone before being shipped for export.

Beyond the Old Dungeon Ghyll Hotel (see p. 149) the B5343 makes a sudden left turn and becomes an unclassified lane, climbing steeply towards the start of the Wrynose Pass. On the way it passes within a few hundred yards of **Blea Tarn**, which nestles close to a small plantation in a fine setting under the shadow of Wrynose Fell, and is one of the finest tarns in the Lake District to be so easily accessible. A path leads from a car-park down to Blea Tarn.

Just west of the junction of this unclassified road with the road from Little Langdale is **Fell Foot Farm**, a low white farmhouse surrounded by yews. The terraced mound at the rear is thought to be a 'thing-mound', a Viking meeting-place where leaders held an annual parliament (Tynwald Hill on the Isle of Man is a similar feature, and still in use).

The Wrynose and Hardknott Passes: from Langdale to Eskdale

The **Wrynose Pass** and the **Hardknott Pass** perforate the western fells of the Lake District east to west, providing the most direct, and a quite thrilling, road link from the centre of the National Park to Eskdale and the west coast. It is a remarkable drive either way, though the Hardknott Pass is the major climax and so perhaps the westerly direction has the edge. Dramatic drops (particularly on the Wrynose Pass) and gradients of up to 1 in 3, together with views westwards of the coast and the Isle of Man, make this arguably England's most scenic drive. Not surprisingly, in summer the road fills up with a procession of cars, and the steepest and narrowest parts can be bottlenecks with vehicles waiting to squeeze past each other; in wintry conditions the road is often closed.

As a route, the Passes date from Roman times, forming a link from Ambleside to the coast, although the modern road follows a slightly different course for most of the way (the

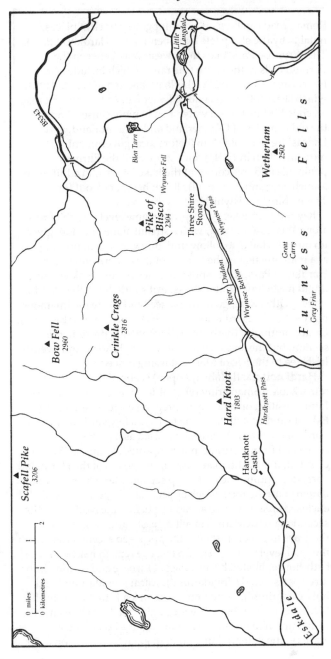

Roman road can be seen as a faint grassy track in places,
notably by the sharp left-hand bend in the Hardknott Pass).
The Wrynose Pass takes the lowest route between the
Furness Fells to the south (the range which includes Grey
Friar, Great Carrs and Wetherlam), and the fells to the north
which seal off the west end of Langdale. At the top, the road
reaches 1281 feet. It's a watershed in more senses than one –
the old counties of Cumberland and Westmorland, and
Lancashire in its old form (before local government
reorganisation in 1974, which lopped off the Furness
peninsula and this corner of the Lake District, in addition to
Manchester and Liverpool) all met here. Look out for the
Three Shire Stone which marks the point.

Beyond Wrynose, a deceptively tame level stretch of road
along Wrynose Bottom, with a stream alone one side, gives
no hint of what is to follow until dire warning notices appear
at a road junction at the bottom of the eastern end of the
Hardknott Pass. If it is snowing or icy or you think your car
might misbehave under stress, exit south down the Duddon
Valley. Otherwise, go into first gear and tackle the infamous
hairpin bends; Hard Knott is the fell immediately to the north.
Disappointingly, there are no breathtaking drops in this
section, but the sudden view down into Eskdale and over the
Irish Sea to the Isle of Man is startling indeed.

Hardknott Castle (always open) is one of the most
remarkable Roman army remains in Great Britain, not least
for its position on a nearly impregnable spur overlooking
Eskdale and Scafell Pike. The fort lies a few yards to the
north of the road, but is easily missed as it is almost
concealed from view and not signposted. From the Wrynose
direction follow the road down from the top of the Hardknott
Pass, descending the first steep section after which the road
flattens out; the fort, which appears as a large stone-walled
enclosed area, is visible ahead just before the road makes its
second major descent. Travelling eastwards from Eskdale,
the place to park is just after the *first* steep ascent, after which
the road levels a little. The first visible remain reached is the
bath-house, heated by an adjacent furnace and divided into
three parts – cold ('frigidarium'), warm ('tepidarium') and
hot ('caldarium'). From here the path leads to the fort itself,
Mediobogdum, where three-foot-high walls enclose an area
containing remains of the commandant's house and a
granary, the latter holding enough grain for a garrison of 500

for two years. A short distance to the north-east, towards Hard Knott, is a level area which may have served as the parade-ground. The fort was built between AD 117 and 138 and finished under Hadrian; it was probably evacuated in the reign of Antoninus Pius, reoccupied in around 160 under governor Sextus Calpurnius Agricola, and sacked in 197, after which it was not occupied again. Mediobogdum thus operated for only a short period, and there are pointers, notably in the small sizes of the bath-house and of the commandant's house, that it was not fully garrisoned for long even when it was occupied.

Eskdale

After the rugged exhilaration of the Wrynose and Hardknott Passes, the mellowness of Eskdale makes a welcome change. This dale assumes several characters: at the eastern end, pyramidal Harter Fell rises up graciously and dominates the valley; the valley floor is almost true lowland in character, with the meandering River Esk leading westwards through pastures and mixed woodlands, yet Eskdale is bounded to the north and south by desolate, windswept moorland plateaux. At the foot of the Hardknott Pass, just to the north of the road, is **Brotherilkeld Farm** (not open), one of the earliest dalehead farms; its origins are thought to date from Saxon times, though the present building is seventeenth century. Furness Abbey bought its vast estate (some 14,000 acres of rough grazing) in 1242, and permission to enclose the land was granted by the lord of the manor of Millom to the monks towards the end of the thirteenth century. The land was acquired by the Forestry Commission in 1935, though opposition, including that from the National Trust, was such that no planting took place. The Eskdale Fair is held at the farm on the last Saturday in September.

Boot is a little village built along a short cul-de-sac just north of the valley road; parking is almost impossible, so nearly everyone walks up from the car-park at Dalegarth Station a few yards down the road. Beyond a line of cottages, the pub and an old stone bridge, in fact at the very end of the road, is **Eskdale Mill** (open Easter to Sept, daily exc Sat, but open Bank Hol Sat, 11 to 5), an ancient corn-mill on the Whillan Beck which operated from at least the sixteenth century until the 1920s. It was restored by Cumberland

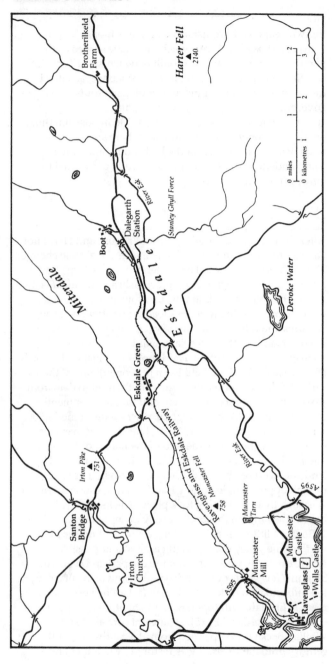

County Council in 1972 to working order, although corn is not ground here. Inside is a quite informative exhibition with display stands and old photographs, and the atmosphere is well re-created, even to the point of cobwebs and a motheaten bowler hat on a chair. Nearby is the Burnmoor, a welcoming pub for lunch. At the entrance to Boot village is Brook House, which makes a pleasant stop for teas and light meals.

Boot is in fact a railway terminus, though of the quaintest kind. The **Ravenglass and Eskdale Railway** (alias 'Ratty') winds its way from Ravenglass on the coast to Dalegarth Station close by Boot, a seven-mile journey completed in 40 minutes by miniature trains. The line opened in 1875 to serve the Nab Gill iron-ore mines which were on the slopes of the north side of the valley above Boot, but just two years later the railway company went bankrupt. The Whitehaven Iron Mines Company, which worked the mines, managed to get the railway company placed in the hands of the official receiver, but with the steady decline of the Cumbrian iron industry under way increasing reliance was placed on the tourist trade. The line became a major attraction, but after a series of accidents and the flooding of the mines, the line closed in 1913. A model railway engineer purchased it in 1915 and converted it to narrow gauge, and seven years later Beckfoot granite quarry opened in Eskdale, creating a new demand for transport in the valley. After the demise of the quarry in 1953, the railway was again closed, but just before its auction in 1960 a local band of enthusiasts managed to scrape together the required money to save the line, probably for posterity.

Services on the line operate all year round, and explorer tickets (giving unlimited travel for the day) are available. The best easy walks in Eskdale are of the linear rather than the circular type, so the railway provides the ideal way to return to your starting-point (see walk on p. 241). Only some of the trains are hauled by steam engines, the oldest of which was built in 1894 (the other engines are diesel); carriages are a mixture of open-topped and enclosed, and are all modern.

A mile south of Dalegarth Station, and set amid mature woodland and luxuriant ferns, is **Stanley Ghyll Force** (or Dalegarth Falls as it is also known), approached by a footpath (see walk on p. 239) which crosses a series of footbridges before the waterfall itself finally comes into view.

West of Dalegarth Station and Boot, at the scattered village of **Eskdale Green**, the dale broadens and splits, divided by **Muncaster Fell**, an isolated ridge which gives lovely views down Eskdale without climbing very much (see walk on p. 241); features of it include a three-storey stone tower with an octagonal spire (built to commemorate a meeting of Henry VI and a shepherd in 1461) and Muncaster Tarn, hidden in woods and enhanced by three islands.

Eskdale proper goes off to the left at Eskdale Green, but the principal road and the railway keep north of Muncaster Fell. A cul-de-sac leading north-east from Eskdale Green ends at **Miterdale**, a quiet valley with some Forestry Commission plantations; beyond the head of the valley, and easily approached by footpath from here, is Burnmoor Tarn, half a mile long. Half a mile west of the village, the Bower House Inn has bar meals and a garden.

The only upstanding hill west of Eskdale Green is **Irton Pike**, 751 feet high and easily ascended by a steepish but short path (see walk on p. 245). By virtue of its isolated position, you can see both Wastwater and Eskdale (as well as the coast) from the top.

West of Irton Pike, a pub worth visiting is the Bridge Inn at **Santon Bridge**. A minor road running south-west from Santon Bridge to the A595 passes the turning for **Irton Church** (signposted), whose churchyard has an extremely fine ninth-century cross-shaft carved with interlacing patterns (of Irish origin).

Muncaster Castle and Muncaster Mill are both close to the A595 near Ravenglass. **Muncaster Castle** (open Good Friday to 30 Sept, daily exc Mon, but open Bank Hol Mon, castle 1.30 to 4.30, grounds 12 to 5) is signposted off the main road a mile or so east of the village. The Penningtons, a family which has been here since the thirteenth century, have very much opened up the house and grounds as a tourist attraction, resulting in a slightly odd overall mixture – an adventure playground, a gift shop, a garden centre, a menagerie of bears and a craft shop are all around; there is also an owlery, as the house is the headquarters of the British Owl Breeding and Release Scheme which runs a rescue service for owls. More conventional country-house pleasures are here too, though: an eye-catching peel tower substantially enlarged and altered by the fourth Lord Muncaster, who in 1862 employed Anthony Salvin as architect. Its glory is the view of Eskdale and the fells from the terrace, described by Ruskin as 'Heaven's Gate'. Inside it is richly furnished in mostly heavy décor, much of it quite flamboyant, including an octagonal galleried library and an airier drawing-room with a barrel-vaulted ceiling. Among the works of art are four portraits by Reynolds, a marble entitled 'The Dancing Hours' by Canova and a copy of a Titian by Gainsborough, done for a bet to see if he could obtain the colours of the original using crayon instead of paint (Gainsborough won). Muncaster Castle is famous for its gardens; when planted, the rhododendrons were reputedly the most extensive collection in Europe, and there are some very fine azaleas and tree specimens. A nature trail leaflet is available, giving an extended walk around the grounds.

Muncaster Mill (open Apr, May and Sept, daily exc Sat, 11 to 5; June to Aug, daily, 10 to 6), north-east of Ravenglass, is a water-mill next to the Ravenglass and Eskdale Railway, and has a station to itself. Milling took place here pretty much continuously from 1470 or even earlier to 1961, though in its last years only animal feed was crushed. After the railway company bought it in 1975, painstaking restoration has been carried out – in addition to re-cutting ('dressing') the millstones and rebuilding the machinery, the ¾-mile-long mill-race that supplied water to the mill had to be cleared out. It is now back to working order, and flour is produced and sold here. Milling does not take place continuously, however: for much of the time the machinery just freewheels. Contact the mill (tel Ravenglass (0229) 717232) if you want to time your visit to coincide with the milling process.

Ravenglass has the distinction of being the only true coastal village in the National Park. There's nothing quite adding up to the level of picturesque, though the tapering-out street of mainly eighteenth- and nineteenth-century buildings has an obviously different flavour from anywhere else in the Lake District. Sleepy though it now is, Ravenglass was once a thriving port and market town, which obtained a market charter in 1209 and was a key centre for trade with Ireland; it also had its fair share of smuggling. Decline set in at the end of the seventeenth century, and the village was thoroughly run down a hundred years later. The harbour silted up and an attempted revival of the market in 1796 petered out.

The street ends at a sandy beach overlooking the estuaries of the Esk, Irt and Mite, and the harbour is bound to the west by sand-dunes which support Europe's largest colony of black-headed gulls. A port was established here in Roman times, bringing in imported grain for transportation to Hardknott and to serve Glanoventa Fort which was sited on the coast some half a mile south of modern Ravenglass; the railway company which built the Cumbrian coast line demolished what was left of the fort in the 1850s. Still very much visible, however, is the shell of its bath-house, known today as **Walls Castle** (always open), of which the doorways, room divisions and niches survive. It can be reached by a track signposted from the road on the east edge of the village (see also walk on p. 241). Excavations were made in 1881; the walls stand up to 12 feet high, the tallest remains of a Roman building in northern Britain.

Most visitors come to the village because of the Ravenglass and Eskdale Railway, which has its headquarters here, plus a small and well-laid-out museum display about the history of the line. If you plan to take the train from here, it is worth looking at the museum before you set off. There is a free coach link service from Ravenglass Station to Sellafield (see p. 71).

Ravenglass' port days are over, though there are usually plenty of small leisure vessels in the harbour. Once a year, in late June, the gruelling Three Peaks Race comes this way: contestants have to sail and walk a route taking in three British peaks – Snowdon, Scafell Pike and Ben Nevis.

Gosforth to Wast Water

Gosforth, which lies just east of the A595 and five miles south-east of Egremont, is a pleasant if unassuming large village of compact terraces of cottages lining a long and narrow sloping main street. Its one pride and joy is the celebrated Gosforth Cross in the churchyard at the east end of the village on the Wasdale road. Breathtakingly slender, and carved with mysterious Viking figures and dragons, together with an image of Christ, this almost miraculously preserved tenth-century monument is one of the finest of its kind in the country. It stands 15 feet tall, and is of soft sandstone. Theories exist that the scenes depicted on it tell of

Nordic sagas, but no one has yet come up with a universally accepted explanation. One panel may depict Vidar fighting a double-headed dragon, while another may show Heimdal the hornblower guarding the rainbow bridge leading to the realm of the gods. Inside the church is more Saxon masonry, including two Norse hogback stones, tenth-century memorials to chieftains; one memorial is in the shape of a thatched cottage, while the other depicts a battle scene.

At a fork in the centre of Gosforth, the road signposted to Wasdale runs eastwards through agricultural landscapes for three miles until reaching **Nether Wasdale**, a tiny hamlet at the brink of the sudden transition into the mountain scenery of Wasdale. The hamlet has a little church built as a chapel of ease for St Bees Priory, containing seventeenth-century panelling and a pulpit of the same period; its aisle was added in 1830.

From Nether Wasdale, the road runs towards **Wast Water**, where it continues along the north-west side of the lake. The road itself doesn't detract appreciably from Wast Water's stunningly severe and barren scenery. The Screes, a dark wall of a ridge, has a stern and foreboding presence on the south-east (non-road) side of the lake; this, plus the delightful whaleback shape of Yewbarrow on the road side, all contribute to frame the vista of Great Gable, the pyramidal and shapely fell whose outline is used on the National Park logo; the fell's adjacent twin is Kirk Fell, similar in outline though less craggy and not as high. Visible ahead and to the right as you drive along towards Wasdale Head is the massive irregular form of Scafell and Scafell Pike, a great chink in the skyline separating the two.

Wast Water is the deepest lake in England at 258 feet; it even *looks* deep, the plunging slopes of The Screes continuing under water at the same angle for an appreciable way. Wast Water supplies water to Sellafield, though you wouldn't know this just by looking at the lake. In the interests of conservation, no boating is allowed.

Wasdale Head is the valley's one hamlet, little more than the inn of the same name (which serves meals and snacks in the bar; there's a separate restaurant; see p. 150), an outdoor equipment shop (which also sells soft drinks and sweets) and a couple of scattered farmsteads; it is so remote that mains electricity did not arrive until 1979. Yet the hamlet's fame lives on as being the birthplace of British rock-climbing,

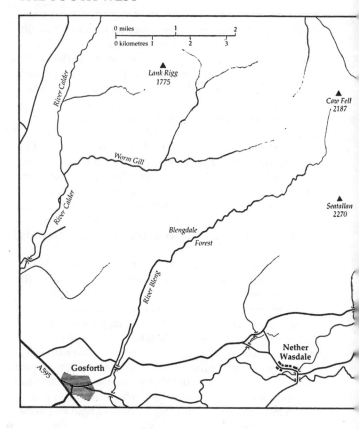

which occurred at the end of the last century, when climbers, incredibly sparsely equipped by today's standards, poured into the area as the passion took off for the conquest of hitherto unclimbed routes. In 1886 Haskett-Smith, one of the great pioneer rock-climbers, conquered Napes Needle; this and the Needle ridge, on Great Gable, constitute one of Britain's most celebrated rock features. A big boom at the beginning of this century followed, with climbers heading in particular for Napes Needle, Pillar Rock and the crags associated with the Scafell group. Many rock-climbing routes are more difficult today because of changes to rock surfaces which have occurred since thousands of climbers have scaled the slopes, although safer techniques and improvements in the standard of equipment have accompanied these changes.

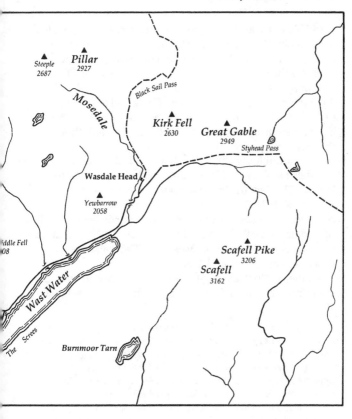

Standing in a group of yew trees a few hundred yards east of the inn is Wasdale Head's tiny church, built in the eighteenth century but not licensed for burials until the following century; in the intervening years, coffins were carried along a corpse road over the moors past Burnmoor Tarn to Boot in Eskdale. In the cemetery are several graves of climbers killed on the nearby fells.

Wasdale Head has a show, which takes place on the second Saturday in October (sheepdog trials, Cumberland sports, shepherds' crook displays) – surely the finest setting for such an event in the district.

There is very little in the way of easy walks from here – even the footpath that runs along the south-east side of Wast Water is quite tough-going underfoot. The slopes of the area are all big ones, and the scale of the scenery is large too; the obvious objectives are summits, and all of these are high – there's nothing involving an ascent of less than 1700 feet. Probably the best bets are to go up to the top of the Styhead Pass or the Black Sail Pass, with a view into Ennerdale from the former and close-ups of Great Gable and the Sty Head valley, which runs down towards Borrowdale, from the latter (even these involve over 1000 feet of ascent, though they are well graded).

It is undoubtedly as a fell-walking and climbing centre that Wasdale excels, with Great Gable an obvious lure. Scafell Pike, at 3206 feet the highest mountain in England, and its partner Scafell (3162 feet) have harsh magnificence and complicated forms. The other major attraction is the so-called Mosedale Horseshoe, which takes in a peak called Pillar and circles around the valley of Mosedale. The walks are described on pp. 246 and 248.

Samuel Taylor Coleridge was the first person to write a letter from the top of Scafell Pike, on Thursday, 5 August 1802:

. . . on a nice Stone Table am I now at this moment writing to you – between 2 and 3 o'clock as I guess – surely the first letter ever written from the Top of Sca' Fell! But O! what a look down just under my feet! The frightfullest Cove that might ever be seen, Huge perpendicular Precipices, and one Sheep upon its only Ledge, that surely must be crag! . . . I have no shadow of hesitation in saying that the Coves and Precipices of Helvellyn are nothing to these! From this sweet lounding Place I see directly thro' Borrowdale, the Castle Crag, the whole of Derwent Water, and but for the haziness of the Air I could see my own House.

Ravenglass to Broughton-in-Furness

The A595 around the base of the south-westernmost fells in the Lake District takes in a strip of low-lying and scarcely fascinating farmland and coast. It must be the dullest scenery in the National Park; all the interest of the road is derived from views of the hills which rise steadily from just above sea-level. The coast south of Ravenglass is marred for some miles by firing-ranges and characteristic Ministry of Defence security fencing.

Two miles south-east of Ravenglass is a signposted turning off the A595 for **Waberthwaite Church**, which stands on the Esk estuary in the hamlet of Hall Waberthwaite. Rectangular

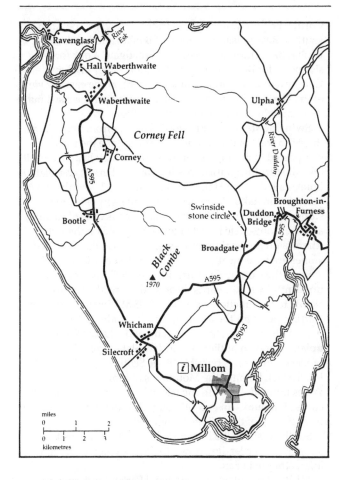

in form, and with whitewashed, uneven walls, this is a refreshingly untampered-with, genuinely rustic-feeling church. Its two treasures are a carved oak pulpit dated 1630 and an eight-foot-high cross-shaft outside (probably ninth or tenth century) with an intricate pattern that appears to incorporate a horse and human figures. The font is a sandstone monolith, curiously squeezed into a corner; it is thought to have been carved in Norman times, although it may have its origins as a capital on a Roman pillar.

From here, the most interesting route to Broughton-in-Furness and the Duddon Valley is via the

Corney Fell road, which rises from Corney (off the A595 south of Ravenglass and north of Bootle) and heads for Ulpha, Broughton-in-Furness or Broadgate. Look for signposts for Bootle (from the Duddon Valley end) and Corney and Broughton (from the A595). Huge easterly views of the Duddon Valley and westerly ones over the coast make this a memorable drive in either direction.

Swinside stone circle is worth a detour from here. From the A595 west of Broughton-in-Furness take the road signposted to Broadgate, or from the Corney Fell road itself take the turning southwards for Millom. Park at an isolated house called Cragg Hall and follow the road downhill for 100 yards before taking a track on the right signposted to the stone circle. An easy 15-minute stroll leads towards a farm, and the stone circle is just before it in a field on the right (there is no public right of way into the field itself). Fifty-five stones are here, neatly arranged in a 90-foot-diameter circle.

From the Corney Fell turn-off, the A595 leads swiftly but uneventfully southwards through the largish village of **Bootle** to the junction with the A5093 at **Whicham**, the best starting-point for the ascent of **Black Combe** (see walk on p. 249), the very south-western tip of the Lake District's uplands, and an outlier of Skiddaw Slate. From the summit of Black Combe it is possible to see Scotland (Criffel and the Lowlands), Ireland (the Mountains of Morne), England, Wales (Snowdonia) and the Isle of Man (Snaefell), though of course it requires an exceptionally clear day to get this view from the top of the 1970-foot-high fell.

South-west of Whicham and the A5093 is **Silecroft**, a straggly village leading down to the sea where there is a long, straight beach.

Millom lies outside the National Park boundary, on a peninsula separated from the rest of non-National Park southern Cumbria by the Duddon Estuary. This stark industrial town grew up in the late nineteenth century with the development of the nearby Hodbarrow Mines, the world's largest iron-mines. The initial entrepreneurs were Nathaniel Caine from Liverpool and John Barratt (who owned mines in Cornwall and later at Coniston), who together formed the Hodbarrow Mining Company. In 1868 they discovered thick pockets of exceptionally high-quality ore, and the New Mine was opened, yielding 300,000–400,000 tons per year until 1918; by 1968 the mine

had become uneconomic and was closed. A brief renaissance
of Millom as a steel-making town in the 1970s fizzled out
abruptly. A mile-long sea wall from Haverigg to Hodbarrow
Point, built in 1905 to protect the mine from flooding, still
exists; it encloses a lagoon which is now an RSPB reserve.

Millom Folk Museum (open Easter, early May to mid-Sept,
daily exc Sun (but open Bank Hol Sun), 10 to 5), in the town
centre, is packed with local history – lots of artefacts and
memorabilia connected with the mines, a reconstruction of a
section of the mine complete with a cage from Moorbank
Shaft, a reconstructed room from a miner's cottage giving an
idea of living conditions at the mine's heyday, and some
relics of agricultural industries; there is also a small case
commemorating the poet Norman Nicholson (1914–87), who
spent his life in Millom. The museum allows visitors to pick
up and handle most objects on display.

Pre-industrial Millom (such as it is) lies ¾ mile north of the
town on the A5093. Here are the remains of a substantial peel
tower with a still-lived-in house built into it, and a restored
Norman and thirteenth-century church containing some fine
monuments to the Hudleston family who lived in the castle.

Broughton-in-Furness lies just off the A595 amid quiet,
rolling countryside. Endowed with the pleasantly sleepy feel
of a large village, yet at the same time with a hint of urban
character around its neatly rectangular market place,
Broughton could be classified as both town and village, but
ultimately its size puts it in the latter category. Its facilities
are limited to a handful of small shops and a couple of pubs;
the Square Cafe is a good bet for tea and snacks. Around the
old market square are mostly eighteenth-century houses,
with the town hall on one side. Markets are no longer held,
but the slabs on which fish used to be put are still here; also
at the centre of the square is an obelisk erected to
commemorate the golden jubilee of George III in 1810, with
the town stocks alongside.

The Duddon Valley (also called Dunnerdale)

A narrow, winding river valley dotted with unspoilt hamlets,
and offering a delicious blend of sheep-farming country and
wild fells, the Duddon Valley possesses no sights apart from
natural ones and is a little off the beaten track (which means
it does not fill up with visitors in the same way as some other

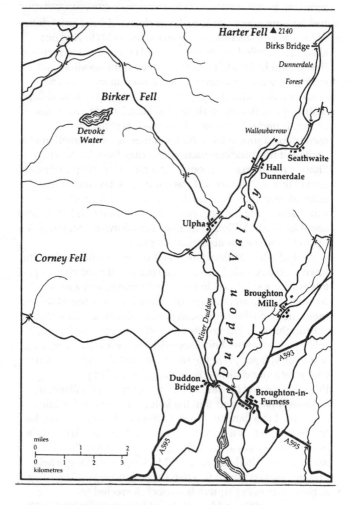

parts of the Lake District). Wordsworth paid tribute to the beauty of the valley in his Duddon sonnets.

In its entirety the valley stretches from Wrynose Bottom (between the Wrynose and Hardknott Passes) to the Duddon Estuary just south of Broughton-in-Furness, but its finest section is between Birks Bridge (two miles south of the Wrynose–Hardknott road) and Ulpha (some five miles further down). Access from the southern end is off the A595 at Duddon Bridge, where there is a signpost for Ulpha.

Drivers taking in the Duddon Valley need not travel the

entire route along the unclassified valley road; the most
scenic options are to take in one or more of the fell roads that
enter the valley from its sides.

The narrow and charming part of the Duddon Valley
starts, at the southern end, at **Ulpha**, where there is a
photogenic stone bridge; from here there are two fell roads,
leading westwards over high ground. The **Corney Fell** road
(see p. 134) heads south-west and then west before reaching
the A595 near Bootle. The **Birker Fell** road from Eskdale
Green to Ulpha is not quite in the same league as the Corney
Fell road, though there is a good view north for a short
section over Eskdale and Hardknott; most of the rest is
featureless moorland. At a signpost pointing north to Stanley
Ghyll (unsuitable for cars) you can walk along a track on the
opposite side of the road to **Devoke Water**, the only tarn of
any significance on this south-western massif. It is enclosed
by low, green slopes and boasts one very small island, so it is
probably worth a look only for curiosity value, although as it
is only a five-minute walk it makes a feasible picnic place.

The valley road continues north-east to **Hall Dunnerdale**,
a hamlet where there is a junction with another unclassified
road leading south-east to Broughton Mills. This road is
gated and narrow, but after a sharp climb there is a parking
area at the top from where a fine view of the Duddon Valley
and its surrounding landscape of knobbly crags and hillocks
can be taken in.

Proceeding along the valley, the northernmost hamlet is
Seathwaite, where there is a pub. The road loses sight of the
river, which passes through a wooded gorge and half
encircles **Wallowbarrow**, a soaring volcanic crag, a favourite
with rock-climbers and which dominates the central part of
the valley. Walking along this stretch of the Duddon and
around the uplands that surround it is particularly delightful
(see walk on p. 242), and there is a path that follows the river
from here to Birks Bridge. North of Wallowbarrow, the
scenery on the west bank soon gives way to Forestry
Commission conifer plantations, though the road itself
continues through hummocky moorland. A car-park with a
picnic site at **Birks Bridge** is the starting-point for
waymarked forest walks in Dunnerdale Forest; for easy
walking, Seathwaite is more rewarding and varied, but Birks
Bridge is a good place to begin for the ascent of Harter Fell,
which commands both this valley and Eskdale. At Birks

Bridge itself a stone bridge spans the Duddon, which at this point rushes through a miniature chasm and over rapids; the road reaches a T-junction with the Wrynose–Hardknott road (see p. 120).

Ulverston

The northernmost town on the Furness peninsula, Ulverston is a bustling market town of no great pretensions. It has ancient origins but grew mainly in the eighteenth century after the opening of a canal to the Leven estuary 1¼ miles east of the town and the building of a turnpike road to Kendal in 1763. Its centre is still very much of eighteenth- and nineteenth-century appearance, with a cobbled main street, dominated at one end by a handsome Italianate building (now the Trustee Savings Bank), leading through the heart of the town; a lively market is held here on Thursdays, and there is a daily covered market.

The Bay Horse bistro-style restaurant serves lunch and dinner with flair and fresh ingredients. For tea and coffee, try Renaissance in Fountain Street.

Visible from every other street in town, steep-sided **Hoad Hill** is capped by a mock-up of Eddystone Lighthouse built in 1850 in memory of Sir John Barrow, geographer and Secretary to the Admiralty. You can climb up the monument when an orange flag (visible from the town) is flying at its base, but even if the monument is closed the view from the hill of Morecambe Bay and the southern Lakeland fells is worth seeing.

The best indoor visit in Ulverston is on the town's southern periphery (first find the road to the railway station then follow the signs). **Swarthmoor Hall** (open mid-Mar to mid-Oct, Mon to Weds and Sat, 10 to 12, 2 to 5) is an Elizabethan manor house owned by the Society of Friends (Quakers). George Fox, founder of the Quaker movement, first came here in 1652 when the house was owned by Thomas Fell and his wife Margaret. Fell, a judge, was sympathetic and allowed meetings to be held at the house. Because of his standing, the Quakers were immune from persecution until his death in 1658, after which Margaret and many guests were arrested. However, the movement by then was too strong to be stamped out.

Writing of the many trials of Quakers at the time, Fox

wrote: 'Justice Bennet, of Derby, was the first to call us Quakers, because I bade him quake and tremble at the work of the Lord.' The Hall features a carved oak chest in which Fox's celebrated *Journal* had been stored.

When the Quakers took possession of the house in the early years of this century, much had to be done to restore the fabric of the building, particularly the Great Hall. Nevertheless, it retains some fine panelling and furniture, and has a gracious atmosphere. The newel staircase, centred around a kind of wooden cage, is an architectural rarity, and one of the steps is deliberately higher than the others so that intruders would stumble and the occupants would be alerted.

Ulverston's main crowd-puller is **Cumbria Crystal** in Lightburn Road (open all year, exc Christmas, last week in July, first week in Aug, Bank Hols, Mon to Fri, 9 to 4), a crystal glass factory opened in 1975 where you can see traditional glass-blowing and cutting techniques in operation. A shop selling seconds adjoins it. Plans are afoot to open a new visitors' centre at Canal Head.

In a yard off Upper Brook Street, a central shopping street, is the **Laurel and Hardy Museum** (open Easter to Oct, daily exc Weds and Sun, 10 to 5) – the world's largest collection of Laurel and Hardy memorabilia. Stan Laurel was born on the other side of the town centre at 3 Argyle Street (look for the plaque). The collection is all stashed away in a not very big room (you can just tell that it is someone's house as there are a few pieces of homely furniture peeping through all the exhibits). Ephemera lines not only the walls but the ceilings as well, and that which is not glued on is fixed by drawing-pins or yellowing adhesive tape; there is an array of Laurel and Hardy books and oddities displayed haphazardly. The next room is filled with old cinema seats which originally served a cinema in Accrington; non-stop videos of the comic duo are shown here.

The Furness peninsula

To the south of the Lake District, bounded to the west by the Duddon Estuary and to the east by Morecambe Bay, the Furness peninsula is scenically a mixed bag: much of the industrial southern tip verges on the hideous, while further north are some tolerably unspoilt villages, a number of

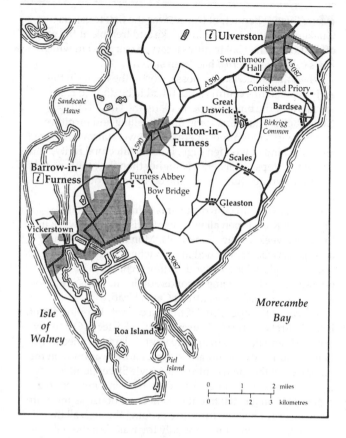

interesting sights, and remarkable estuary and sea views –
certainly enough to justify a day's touring.

South of Ulverston, the scenic route is the A5087, where
there are sweeping views across the vast sands and mudflats
of Morecambe Bay. Just before the first coastal stretch, and
on the Morecambe Bay side of the road, is the entrance drive
for **Conishead Priory** (open Easter to Sept, Sat, Sun and Bank
Hol Mon, plus Weds and Thurs in July, 2 to 5; house can be
viewed by guided tours only, 2.30 and 3.45). The 'priory' is
an early-nineteenth-century Gothic extravaganza built as a
country house on the site of an earlier house, which in turn
replaced a twelfth-century Augustinian priory. After the
owner, a Colonel Braddyll, went bankrupt, the house had a
chequered history – a period as a hydropathic hotel, then as a

TRY WHICH? MAGAZINES FREE!

As well as books and Action Packs, Consumers' Association also publishes magazines: Which?, Gardening from Which?, Which? way to Health and Which? Wine Monthly.

If you'd like a free trial of any of these magazines, simply complete and return this card to us, post free, and we'll send you details.

☐ Which?

☐ Gardening from Which?

☐ Which? way to Health

☐ Which? Wine Monthly

(tick those that interest you)

Name (Mr/Mrs/Miss/Ms)_____

Address_____

_____

_____

_____Postcode_____

DETACH HERE

BFL1

NO
STAMP
REQUIRED

Consumers' Association
FREEPOST
Hertford X
SG14 1YB

convalescent home for miners; it later fell into disuse while an unsuccessful attempt was made at turning the site into a holiday camp. It has deteriorated alarmingly, though the Manjushri Institute for Buddhist Studies, which now owns it, is making valiant efforts at restoration. Nevertheless, if you can put up with the chunks of decaying masonry and the obvious institutional feel of the place, it makes quite an interesting if unconventional country house to visit, full of vaulted cloisters and wedding-cake ceilings.

A very good viewpoint over Morecambe Bay – just that bit more elevated than the main road itself and much quicker to walk up than Hoad Hill in Ulverston – is **Birkrigg Common**, an area of open land next to the minor road that runs from Bardsea to Great Urswick. Also on a minor road parallel to the A5087, between Scales and Gleaston, are the ruins of fourteenth-century **Gleaston Castle**, which encompass a farm.

At a roundabout on the A5087 at the south-east end of the peninsula, continue on an unclassified road to **Roa Island**, an unattractive village of nineteenth-century terraces at the end of a causeway, but in an amazing position at the mouth of the huge harbour enclosed to the south by the Isle of Walney; usually the scene is dominated by multitudes of small craft and sea-birds. Ferries leave from here (Easter to Sept) to **Piel Island**, half a mile to the south, on which stand the ruins of Piel Castle, thought to have been built in the thirteenth century but rebuilt in 1327. The castle belonged to Furness Abbey and commanded a crucial position in the harbour, which played an important role in the abbey's trade with Ireland and the Isle of Man.

Barrow-in-Furness occupies the prime position in this harbour, an ideal one for major shipping. The town grew up in the nineteenth century with the advent of the south Cumbria iron industry; a planned town was built, whose broad, straight and (partially) tree-lined streets still characterise the town's present form. But for all that, Barrow is quite memorably ugly, with a whiff of impoverishment normally associated with inner cities. The great Vickers dockyards are the feature of much of the town centre; recently vast sheds housing the construction works for Trident submarines have been erected. Stark tenements line the wide streets of Barrow Island, just south of the town centre. Barrow's main street is a shade more cheerful, with statues of the town's nineteenth-century magnates at either end, and an imposing Gothic town hall of 1887 in the centre. There is a small museum attached to the main library.

South of the town is the **Isle of Walney**, 11 miles long and a mile wide at its widest point, joined to the mainland by a road bridge. Much of it is covered with unprepossessing residential development. The suburb of **Vickerstown** lies close to the point where the road links the island to Barrow. Most of Vickerstown is ordinary, but its oldest part contains a garden village built at the turn of the century for employees at the Vickers shipyards. In concept and execution, the development owes much to Lord Leverhulme's utopian model for housing factory employees pioneered a few years earlier at Port Sunlight in the Wirral, Cheshire. A trail around Vickerstown is available from the tourist **information centre** in Barrow.

At the island's north and south extremes are nature reserves, excellent for watching eider ducks and other nesting sea-birds; day permits are on sale at the sites.

Just beyond the northern fringes of Barrow, and signposted from the A590, is **Furness Abbey** (open all year, daily exc Sun morning), one of England's great abbey ruins. In 1124 Stephen, Count of Boulogne (later king of England), gave a site at Tulketh, near Preston, to monks of the Order of Savigny; three years later they moved to Furness and building commenced. The Savigny monks later amalgamated with the Cistercians, and by 1537 Furness Abbey, which owned large estates in Lancashire, Cumberland, Westmorland and the Pennines, was the second richest Cistercian house in England after Fountains in Yorkshire. Of the sandstone ruins, much of beauty remains, particularly the twelfth-century north transept (which stands just about to its original height), the five round-headed arches in the cloister and the sedilia in the presbytery. Half a mile from the abbey, and well signposted, is **Bow Bridge**, a three-arched sandstone fifteenth-century packhorse bridge which served one of the abbey granges.

Dalton-in-Furness can be taken in virtually at a single glance. The main A590 goes through its triangular market place; markets were held here from 1239 until recent times. By it is Dalton Castle, a fourteenth-century peel tower erected to defend the approaches to Furness Abbey (particularly from marauding Scots); its prison was used until

1774. A key is available from a house across the road, but
there is very little to see inside. Also in the market place is a
quaint cast-iron fountain, put up in 1897 and high-Victorian
in spirit; a motto, Keep the Pavement Dry, is inscribed on it,
though it is unclear whether this is an instruction to users or
a boast on the part of the manufacturer. Just above the
market place is a striking nineteenth-century church
designed by Paley and Austin, eminent architects of the day.

At the end of a minor road off the A595 just north-west of
Dalton-in-Furness (signposted Roanhead) is **Sandscale
Haws**, a National Trust-owned area of beach and
sand-dunes, one of the loveliest stretches of the Cumbrian
coast, with views across the Duddon Estuary of Black Combe
and other southern Lakeland fells. In all it's possible to
follow the coast around for about 1½ miles.

Skelwith Bridge to Coniston Water

Skelwith Bridge is really just a hotel and a handful of houses
by a road junction – where the B5343 to Langdale branches
off the A593. A few yards off the A-road here are the
Kirkstone Galleries, the showroom for slate products made
from stone quarried near the Kirkstone Pass; annexed to it is
a coffee shop, restaurant and gift shop. A path signposted
through the yard of the slate workshops leads to the river
and to **Skelwith Force**, not the tallest Lakeland waterfall at a
mere 20 feet but the fall bearing the greatest volume of water.

The A593 south from here passes through pleasantly
varied scenery of woods and rough pasture, though with no
distant views to speak of. **Yew Tree Tarn** is right next to the
road, surrounded by heavily wooded hills; a footpath leads
around the far side of the tarn. Just south of here are
car-parks for the start of the walk to Tarn Hows. **Tilberthwaite Gill** is a mile north of the A593, on a cul-de-sac in
a secretive valley; rather surprisingly, two parallel roads
somehow squeeze their way in (take the western one for
Tilberthwaite). The Yewdale Beck tumbles down from a
ravine (Tilberthwaite Gill); from the car-park it is an easy
walk up to the footbridge at the bottom of the ravine and
only marginally more demanding to continue around the
top. But the distant views of Langdale and close-ups of wild
scenery around Furness Fells and Wetherlam make it a
rewarding short outing (see walk on p. 244). A few paces

further along the road from the car-park is an ancient cottage with a good example of a spinning gallery (a raised verandah where spinning used to be done). Another farmhouse with a spinning gallery is visible from the A593: look out for **Yew Tree Farm**, one mile north of Coniston.

Coniston is an ex-mining village turned resort, sited under craggy foothills of The Old Man of Coniston, the mountain that dominates the western side of the lake. It has less charm than one might expect for its position, though it is not exactly ugly: a Y-shaped arrangement of streets with sombre grey-stone nineteenth-century buildings, plus the odd terrace of cottages up on the hillside as a memento of the village's former importance as a mining centre. A National Park tourist **information centre**, a couple of walking equipment shops and antique shops are in the middle of the village. Try the traditional bar of the Sun Hotel for a good pub lunch; and a mile or two south-west, near Torver, the Wheelgate guest-house (unobtrusive outside but attractive within) serves memorable teas.

John Ruskin, who lived at Brantwood (see p. 147) on the opposite side of Coniston Water, is buried in Coniston churchyard – preferring burial here to Westminster Abbey. His memorial cross (at the far left end of the churchyard from the entrance) has a kind of pictorial biography of him. The east side depicts an artist with the sun and a mountain behind (the mountain is Mont Blanc, and the sunrise motif was used on the cover of *The Modern Painter*), a winged lion (*The Winged Lion of St Mark*), a seven-branched candlestick (*The Seven Lamps of Architecture*) and a tabernacle (*The Stones of Venice*); on the west side his late work is represented, including the angel of destiny (*Fors Clavigera*), the Guild of St George which features in the same book, and a depiction of *Sesame and Lilies*; the north side is merely interlaced pattern, but the south one bears a floral scroll with animals (Ruskin's interest in natural history). A small museum (open Easter to Oct, daily, 10 to 5.30) about Ruskin's life and works is opposite the tourist information centre; it's rather specialist in taste and not very self-explanatory, but makes a fairly interesting supplement to a visit to Brantwood. The bulk of the exhibition is taken up with Ruskin's sketches, but there are also displays of his mineral specimens and some lacework made by the local lace industry Ruskin set up, along with some general paraphernalia (Ruskin's umbrella

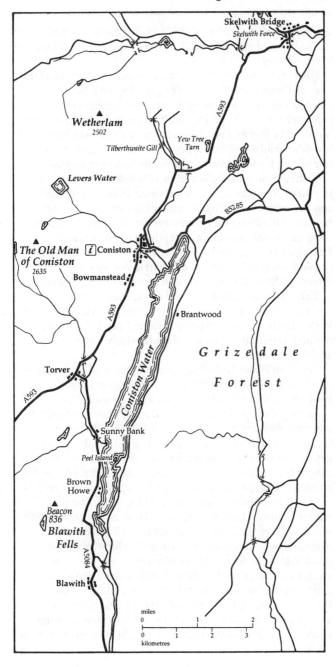

and paintbox and, rather oddly, a case of mementoes of
Donald Campbell (see p. 147), to whom there is a memorial
in the village).

The best walks from Coniston are associated with **The Old
Man of Coniston** (2635 feet). The popular climb to the top
takes in some rugged and quite impressive mountain scenery
(see walk on p. 249), giving excellent views southwards over
Morecambe Bay and north into the main fell group. Easier
low-level walks up Church Beck towards Levers Water are
interesting for the remains of Coniston's copper-mining
industry; mining took place from 1599 to 1942, employing
imported Austrian and German miners in the seventeenth
century when tunnelling became necessary. The mining
peaked in the last century, when several hundred miners
were employed, operating at depths of up to 1230 feet.
Remains of old engine houses, inclines and wheel shafts still
abound, though it takes imagination to re-create the scene of
intense industrial activity in what is now such a wild and
solitary place. In early times, ore was carried north to
Dunmail Raise for smelting, then shipped from Greenodd to
Wales. In the nineteenth century the railway to Coniston
opened, providing a link to the south which survived until
1958.

Coniston Water is virtually invisible from Coniston village
and from much of the A593. Its best vantage-points from
land are the minor road that runs along its east side; a
sequence of car-parks in the woods enables you to stop and
admire a lovely view across the lake to The Old Man of
Coniston. The A5084 from Torver to Blawith and beyond
gets a brief west lakeside section, and there are a couple of
car-parks. The lake's only proper waterside footpath runs for
about three miles from near Sunny Bank guest-house on this
road to Bowmanstead (just south of Coniston). The path
passes Coniston Hall (whose grounds are now a camp-site),
which was originally built as a peel tower in 1250 and
extended over the centuries; its massive chimneys make
it unmistakable. Brown Howe picnic-site near the south-
western corner of the lake has lakeside access, and is the
starting-point for walks into the Blawith Fells to the west of
the road; of these, Beacon (836 feet) is a particularly good
viewpoint for the lake (see walk on p. 245), its name being
derived from the beacon that used to be lit to warn of Scottish
raids.

At 5½ miles in length, Coniston Water is the third longest lake in the Lake District. Its really striking attribute is its straightness: apart from a trivial kink near its southernmost point it is possible to steer a dead straight course right down it. This makes it ideal for speedboats – Donald Campbell, who set the world water speed record at 260.35 mph in 1959, used to race *Bluebird* along this stretch of water until his tragic crash here in 1967.

One way to experience this lake is by the rather more sedate steam yacht *Gondola*, a near-silent craft which operates from the pier at Coniston and stops at Park-a-Moor near the south-east corner of the lake and at Brantwood. There were originally two steam yachts, the *Gondola* itself and the *Lady of the Lake*, both built in 1859 by Jones and Quiggan of Liverpool for the Furness Rail Company. The *Gondola* ceased operating before the last war as trade slackened off, and the *Lady of the Lake* was broken up in the 1950s. Fortunately, the *Gondola* was kept as a houseboat, though its machinery was removed and the boat was damaged in a gale. The National Trust acquired it in 1976 and immaculately restored it, and it was back in service in 1980. No other public craft in the Lakes has such opulent period décor, complete with plush upholstery and polished wood. In earlier days it was described as 'a cross between a submarine and a cucumber, with suspicions of vast steam canoe', although the *Illustrated London News* was kinder in acclaiming it to have the graceful gliding motion of a Venetian gondola together with the elegance and speed of an English speed yacht. The round trip takes an hour; there are four sailings daily in spring and autumn, and five in summer (it does not run from November to Easter).

Two writers have strong associations with Coniston Water. Ruskin (see above) lived at Brantwood, and Arthur Ransome had a house near Coniston and used the lake for settings in his children's novel *Swallows and Amazons* (notably **Peel Island** near the southern end, which appeared as Wildcat Island).

Brantwood (open mid-Mar to mid-Nov, daily, 11 to 5.30; mid-Nov to mid-Mar, Weds to Sun, 11 to 4), in an enviable position on the east side of the lake and overlooking The Old Man of Coniston and its associated fells, was Ruskin's home from 1872 until his death in 1900. He had happy childhood memories of the Lake District, and knew of the existence of

Brantwood; William Linton, a wood engraver, and his novelist wife Eliza Lynn sold the property to Ruskin. Shortly after he moved in, Ruskin set about adapting Brantwood from a derelict building to a comfortable home, adding the turret, constructing paths in the grounds and filling the house with paintings and books; the dining-room, added in about 1878, has seven lancet windows which may represent *The Seven Lamps of Architecture*. After his death, his priceless collection of pictures, books, geological specimens and manuscripts was auctioned off. Fortunately, many of the items were purchased by John Howard Whitehouse, a dedicated follower of Ruskin and founder of Bembridge School on the Isle of Wight, where Ruskin's educational theories were put into practice. Whitehouse also purchased the house itself, with the intention of creating a national memorial to Ruskin. Today, Ruskin's personality still pervades the character of the house, which contains a large collection of Ruskin watercolours, his books and furniture, and many art treasures. There are also some informative displays giving helpful summaries of his philosophy, schemes for social and educational reform, his art and writings on art and architecture, and his associates.

In the grounds – notable for rhododendrons, azaleas and daffodils in spring – is a three-mile nature trail (the best available opportunity for walking on the east shore of Coniston Water) and a stone seat built for Ruskin.

Just down the slope from the entrance to the house a gallery has been set up dedicated to the works of Alfred Wainwright, author of what has become the definitive series of guidebooks on walking the Lakeland fells. In addition to a few Wainwright drawings, the original *Westmorland Gazette* printing-press, and the great man's socks, tweed jacket, camera and pipe are here, along with maps he drew at the age of 10. There's also an apt quote in reminiscence of his days as treasurer in Kendal Borough Council, where he was told that every page of his ledgers should be fit for framing; sure enough, a framed ledger is hung over the quote.

Jumping Jenny, a tea-shop named after Ruskin's rowing-boat, is adjacent to the Wainwright gallery and is open to non-visitors, serving home-made cakes in Brantwood's former stables, now hung with Pre-Raphaelite reproductions. Around the back of the building, and up a staircase, is the Lakeland Guild Craft Gallery, a small craft shop selling pottery, patchwork, knitwear and jewellery.

Where to stay

For a key to prices, see p. 10

Coniston

Sun Hotel, Coniston, Cumbria
LA21 8HQ. Tel Coniston
(053 94) 41248
On the outskirts of the village
at the foot of The Old Man of
Coniston, the Sun is a
family-run hotel attached to a
traditional inn. Thomas De
Quincey and Hartley Coleridge
once lived here, and it's more
recently remembered as
Donald Campbell's base. Now
it's colourfully refurbished,
with pretty floral fabrics, and
the cooking is well-varied
English traditional. Bedroom
views are the crags, the forest
or the car-park – four-poster
beds compensate for the
latter. £££

Elterwater

Britannia Inn, Elterwater,
Ambleside, Cumbria
LA22 9HP. Tel Langdale
(096 67) 210
This rambling old inn has an
excellent central position and is
particularly well placed for
walks, notably up Langdale
and towards Grasmere. It
commands the pocket
handkerchief of a village green,
and not surprisingly acts as a
magnet for visitors, especially
in summer. The bar and
residents' lounge are warmly
old-fashioned, with low
ceilings and cosy corners. The
rooms are adequate (with
tea-making and TV), though on
the small side; there are no
private baths. ££

Great Langdale

The Old Dungeon Ghyll Hotel,
Great Langdale, Ambleside,
Cumbria LA22 9JY. Tel
Langdale (096 67) 272
This isolated traditional inn
with great views of the crags is
popular with walkers and
climbers, and is also a good bet
for families – except perhaps on
a lively Saturday night. It's
inexpensive, informal and
relaxed, and food comes in
generous helpings. The lounge
and dining-room are big and
comfortable, bedrooms simple
(duvets and stripped pine). £

Spark Bridge

Bridgefield House, Spark Bridge,
Ulverston, Cumbria
LA12 8DA.
Tel Lowick Bridge (022 985) 239
Well off the beaten track, in
rolling hills beyond the
southern end of Coniston
Water (an area with scenically
much going for it, though it's
not in the fells), this gracious
Victorian house is run
competently as a small
country-house-style hotel, with
the emphasis more on country
house than hotel. The back
garden is a feature of the view
from the lounge and
dining-room. Décor is
restrained and rooms
uncluttered, with high ceilings,
period features, dark wooden
furniture and a fair scattering of
antiques – overall, quite a
formal effect; there is no
television. Dinner is at 7.30 for
8; the standard of cooking is
accomplished, and care is taken

to balance the sequence of six courses. ££

Torver
Sunny Bank Mill, Torver, Coniston, Cumbria LA21 8BL. Tel Coniston (053 94) 41300
The original mill holds self-catering units, and the Victorian-extended mill-house is a quiet and civilised guest-house, comfortably modernised, in pretty lakeside gardens. No children under 10. ££

Wasdale Head
Wasdale Head Inn, Wasdale Head, Gosforth, Cumbria CA20 1EX. Tel Wasdale (094 06) 229
Well known to walkers and climbers, this is the old inn with the incomparable setting below the fells at the head of Wast Water. It has simple pine-panelled bedrooms, a rather smart lounge, friendly bars for yarn-swapping and copious amounts of good filling food. £££

Bed and breakfast
Good bets are Eskdale, the Duddon Valley, Langdale and the Coniston area, but with the exception of the last of these there is only a smattering of accommodation. All of these have lovely scenery, and are close to the main fells; they also tend to be much quieter than the traditional resorty parts of the Lake District. Eskdale is a particularly attractive proposition, not only for the quality of landscape in the immediate vicinity but also for its easy access to Wasdale.

THE SOUTH-EAST

*Windermere · Windermere town ·
Bowness-on-Windermere · Ambleside · The
Trout Beck Valley · Rydal Water and Grasmere ·
Tarn Hows and Hawkshead · Grizedale to Force
Falls · Grange-over-Sands and Cartmel · The
Winster Valley · The Lyth Valley · South of the
Kent estuary · Kendal · Kentmere and
Longsleddale ·* WHERE TO STAY

Scenery

Green and undulating country for the most part,
predominantly a mixture of Silurian rocks and
limestone, heavily wooded in places, with the
occasional view into the fells. Mild and gentle,
particularly in comparison with all that upland
bravado further north and west.

Scenic highlights

- GRASMERE and RYDAL WATER – two smallish lakes
  whose magical setting becomes apparent as soon as
  you join paths along their southern sides.
- WINDERMERE – England's longest lake, the most
  popular place in the Lakes for boating, and very busy
  in season. Not perhaps the place to come just to relax,
  but there is usually plenty happening. Hard to make
  much of from the car, so a boat trip is the way to see it
  in its full glory. Some shore walks on the western side,
  plus panoramic views from hills surrounding the lake.

Also worth seeing

- KENTMERE and LONGSLEDDALE – two long valleys
  north of Kendal; not often visited and strikingly
  remote.
- GRIZEDALE – the largest forestry plantation in the
  Lakes, filling a deep valley west of Windermere.

- TARN HOWS – a tarn created by enlarging two natural tarns to make a large one, and further enhanced by tree planting. Can get horribly overrun with visitors; aim to see it very early or late in the day.
- MORECAMBE BAY – vast area of sands and mudflats, with one of the fastest incoming tides in Britain, and a huge population of waders. Best seen from the train or one of the low wooded hills that surround it.

Best walks

Easy walks
- The shores of GRASMERE and RYDAL WATER, best seen from Loughrigg Terrace.
- Lakeside strolls on the west shore of WINDERMERE.
- SCOUT SCAR, a level-topped limestone ridge edging the Lyth Valley, easily reached from the road, with views all around.
- HAMPSFIELD FELL – one of the finest views from the hills abutting Morecambe Bay.
- ARNSIDE KNOTT – another lovely vantage-point of Morecambe Bay, with a good coastal walk nearby.
- HUMPHREY HEAD POINT, a pleasant coastal cliff walk.
- Waymarked forest walks in GRIZEDALE.
- STOCK GHYLL FORCE, a waterfall near Ambleside.
- Easy hill walks with good views include GUMMER'S HOW, LATTERBARROW, ORREST HEAD and WHITBARROW SCAR.

Fell walks
- WANSFELL PIKE, near Ambleside, has grand views of Windermere, but is much less demanding than a fully fledged fell walk.
- LONGSLEDDALE and KENTMERE VALLEYS.
- HELM CRAG, a natural vantage-point over Easedale.

Sights

Houses
- SIZERGH CASTLE – a peel tower with an Elizabethan house and fine gardens.

- LEVENS HALL – largely Elizabethan in character; more of a family afternoon out affair than Sizergh. Famous topiary.
- TOWN END – an evocative seventeenth-century yeoman's farmhouse.
- HILL TOP, Beatrix Potter's sweet sanctuary: small rooms, and too many visitors. Worth coming if you are a Beatrix Potter fan; if not, skip it and visit Town End for an example of an old-fashioned Cumbrian farmhouse.
- HOLKER HALL – spectacular mock-Elizabethan mansion in high-Victorian spirit.
- RYDAL MOUNT – Wordsworth's last and grandest house, full of memorabilia; charming views.
- LEIGHTON HALL – the Gillows' Gothic mansion overlooking Morecambe Bay.

Castles
- KENDAL: there are two; the 'new' one (built by William Rufus) is the more impressive, and its ruins stand on a grassy hill overlooking the town and its surroundings.

Gardens
- HOLEHIRD and LAKELAND HORTICULTURAL SOCIETY: two gardens on the same site, with a particularly wide array of specimens.
- STAGSHAW – native plants and exotica on a hillside overlooking Windermere.
- RYDAL HALL – a trail leads through gardens to a grotto and cascade; close to Rydal Mount.
- GRAYTHWAITE – azaleas and rhododendrons in the grounds of an Elizabethan house, in the woodlands to the west of Windermere.

Best churches
- CARTMEL PRIORY – justly dubbed the 'cathedral of the Lakes'.
- CARTMEL FELL (nowhere near Cartmel) has a remote country church with unusual box pews.
- GRASMERE and HAWKSHEAD: both large, rustic Lakeland churches.

- Interesting stained glass at BOWNESS, STAVELEY and TROUTBECK.

Museums

- ABBOT HALL, Kendal. In three parts: the Museum of Lakeland Life and Industry (the museum to see above all others in the Lakes), the art gallery (displayed in the classical magnificence of Abbot Hall) and a natural history and archaeology collection (on the other side of town).
- WORDSWORTH MUSEUM and DOVE COTTAGE, Grasmere. Good and professionally set-out museum about the Lake Poets sets the stage for a visit to what was Wordsworth's home before he moved to Rydal Mount.
- LAKELAND EXPERIENCE: a Lake District audio-visual show.
- WINDERMERE STEAMBOAT MUSEUM: restored steamboats in a boat-house on Windermere, plus a potted history of boating on the lake.
- HOLKER HALL LAKELAND MOTOR MUSEUM is a minor visual treat of vintage cars, cycles, motorbikes and automobilia. Open to people not visiting the house.
- STOTT PARK BOBBIN-MILL: closed in 1971, but rescued and now back as a working museum. Informative guided tours and demonstrations help make it a very good short visit.
- HAWKSHEAD GRAMMAR SCHOOL. Famous as Wordsworth's school, complete with his name carved on the desk. Ancient classroom, used into this century, is a sight in itself.
- The BEATRIX POTTER GALLERY, Hawkshead: original paintings for her children's books, hung in the house of the solicitor she married.
- Windermere AQUARIUM has freshwater British fish.
- STEAMTOWN, Carnforth: a substantial collection of locomotives and a few other railway relics.

Water-mills

- HERON CORN-MILL – one of the largest in the north of England, restored to working order and producing flour again.

Railways

- LAKESIDE AND HAVERTHWAITE RAILWAY: steam engines pull relatively modern (ex-BR) carriages four miles along the wooded Leven Valley to the ferry station at the southern end of Windermere.
- ULVERSTON to ARNSIDE. Part of the BR line from Barrow to Lancaster, so the trains are perfectly ordinary, but for views (and for feats of engineering) this stretch must be one of the most remarkable on the whole rail network, public or private, as trains trundle over viaducts and along the coastal extremities around the north side of Morecambe Bay.

Archaeology

- GALAVA ROMAN FORT: the remains are very scant, though at least they are labelled. Hard for the layman to make much sense of it.

Best villages

- CARTMEL – remains unspoilt, probably because of its peripheral position to the National Park. Attractive central square, second-hand bookshops, medieval gatehouse and the priory church.
- HAWKSHEAD – a Lakeland showpiece, whose quaintness brims over: lots of cobbled alleys, whitewashed cottages and pretty corners, plus tea-rooms and craft shops.
- TROUTBECK still feels like an agricultural village: typical Lakeland vernacular farm architecture, roadside wells, pleasant views.
- GRASMERE is a large village with Wordsworth stamped all over it: lots of Wordsworth and other literary connections, and some interesting gift-type shops, though in season the volume of visitors can be overwhelming.

Towns

- KENDAL – historic town made rich on the wool trade. Much to see in addition to its excellent museums and arts centre: two castle sites, ancient streets, old yards and ginnels, and a pleasant stretch of the River Kent.

- AMBLESIDE: the old village on the hillside is worth a short exploration. The centre is often traffic-ridden and very busy. Excellent for outdoor shops.
- WINDERMERE and BOWNESS are two largely nineteenth-century resorts which have almost grown into one. The busiest part of the Lakes in summer, and can be a traffic bottleneck. A few sights at Bowness, plus the lake itself, and lots of eating-places.
- GRANGE-OVER-SANDS is in a lovely position on the north side of Morecambe Bay, with one or two good short walks nearby; the town itself is a sleepy resort-cum-retirement place, not in itself exceptionally interesting.

Windermere

England's longest lake stretches north to south 10½ miles from Waterhead near Ambleside to Lakeside at its narrow southern end. Wooded slopes dotted with villas line its shores, while the water itself is nearly always busy with ferries, yachts, speed-boats and water-skiers – it's the only lake in the Lake District which has no speed-limit for water traffic. Its opposing shores offer strong contrasts: the west one is the quieter, enveloped in dense woods and virtually free from road traffic, while the east shore is more developed, with three resort towns and a main road. The north end of the lake looks out towards Crinkle Crags (the westernmost major summit), Bow Fell, Langdale Pikes (the prominent, double-knuckle form), Fairfield and Wansfell. From the surrounding hills are a number of good viewpoints of the lake; the best of these are Wansfell Pike and Jenkin Crag near Ambleside, Orrest Head and Queen Adelaide's Hill near Windermere, Biskey Howe and Brant Fell near Bowness, Gummer's How towards the south end of the lake, and Latterbarrow near Hawkshead. Lakeside strolls are mostly confined to the west shore – the longest uninterrupted stretch of lakeside path is between the chain ferry terminal (the cross-lake route for the B5285) and Wray Castle to the north – but there is a briefly delightful path

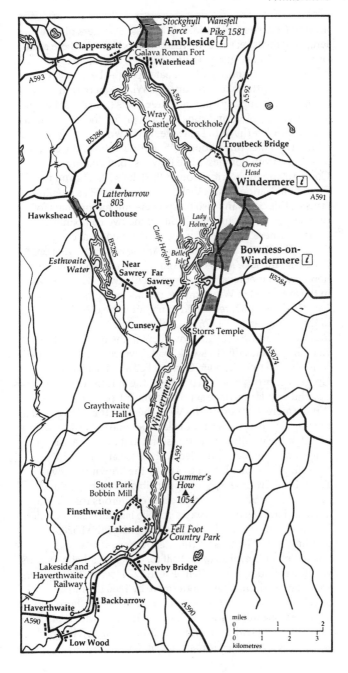

around Cockshott Point from Bowness. Steamers ply the length of the lake: since the roads around Windermere offer only fragmentary glimpses of the water, and there is no continuous lakeshore path, a boat trip is the best way of experiencing the lake close up. The Windermere Iron Steamboat Company operates three boats (the oldest being *Tern*, built in 1891), and runs services plying the length of the lake from Waterhead to Lakeside, via Bowness (the full round trip takes three hours); 45-minute tours of the central lake leave from Bowness. The Bowness Bay Boating Company operates trips around the lake's islands and to Brockhole National Park Visitor Centre, as well as evening cruises; this company also has power- and motor-boats for hire. See p. 268 for further details of the two companies.

Windermere's shores have been occupied from early times. The Romans built a fort at Ambleside and a villa on Belle Isle, the lake's largest island. Norse settlers colonised here, and in medieval times Furness Abbey had large estates in the area west of Windermere; monks built a chapel on Lady Holme which remained in use after the dissolution of the monasteries. In 1761 a local turnpike trust was founded, leading to an improvement in the quality of the Kendal–Ambleside–Keswick road. Two years later the road from Kendal to Dalton via Cartmel Fell and Backbarrow Gorge was turnpiked. Accordingly, the volume of traffic shot up, and regular carriage services came into being. Windermere's opportunities were there for the taking, and in the late eighteenth century the lake became the fashionable haunt of the wealthy, who transformed it into an Arcadian landscape of woods sprinkled with classical villas. Much tree-planting took place at this time: the Browne family of Town End, Troutbeck, was responsible for many of the plantations of Scots pines and other coniferous trees in the area, and in 1798 the Curwens of Belle Isle afforested Claife Heights on the east side of the lake (north of the B5285), planting 30,000 larches on this steep slope.

The first of the villas to be built for purely aesthetic reasons was the round house on Belle Isle in 1774 (see p. 170). Others soon followed, making Windermere by 1800 the most developed of all the lakes. Croft Lodge at the northern end of the lake was built by Joseph Brancker in 1830, who replaced a classical villa with something in as different a style as was possible, an eclectic marriage of Renaissance with

Strawberry Hill Gothic, complete with castellations and wrought-ironwork. Hartley Coleridge declared it 'a style which neither Vitruvius, Palladio, Inigo Jones, Piranesi nor Sir Jeffry Wyatville ever dream'd of, even in a nightmare, or under the influence of opium'. On the east shore a mile south of Belle Isle is Storrs Temple (1804), an octagonal garden house for Storrs Hall, built at the end of a short stone causeway. A romanticising feature of the lake, it was erected in honour of Admirals Nelson, Duncan, Howe and St Vincent, and complements the other octagon, the original Claife Station, across the water by the west shore. These two, together with Belle Isle, constituted a classical group in the central area of the lake. Colonel Bolton, a wealthy slave trader, later lived at Storrs Hall, and this became a centre of Windermere festivals and regattas, notably the regatta of 1825 where the day after a great champagne dinner 50 oared barges proceeded down the lake; among the guests were Wordsworth, Sir Walter Scott, Christopher North and George Canning (the future Prime Minister).

In 1847 the Windermere Railway opened, and the towns of Windermere, Bowness and Ambleside grew rapidly. At the southern end of the lake, the Furness Railway Company extended its existing line in 1868 from Barrow to Greenodd up to Lakeside via the Backbarrow Gorge. A new ferry terminus was thus created, complete with refreshment pavilion.

The west side of the lake

Haverthwaite is a small and unremarkable hamlet lying just south of the A590. A quarter of a mile south-east of it, and signposted immediately after crossing the River Leven, is **Low Wood**, at the centre of which stands a tall tower. This was a gunpowder-mill until 1937, one of seven in the Lake District. Now it and the ex-gunpowder workers' cottages function as a craft centre, with a glass-cutting gallery as well as a shop selling paintings and sculpture.

Just north of the A590 is the southern terminus for the **Lakeside and Haverthwaite Railway**. From here, trains trundle along four miles of reopened track, giving you 18 minutes' worth of the flavour of how Victorian trippers used to arrive by train and pick up the steamer at Lakeside, the railway's northern terminus. The engines are powered by steam, although the carriages are familiar BR rolling stock painted a different colour. Beware of huge crowds in season: this is one of the most popular tourist attractions in the Lake District.

The ride takes you through wooded Backbarrow Gorge – more a valley than a true gorge. **Backbarrow** itself had a flourishing iron industry from the early eighteenth century to the 1960s, with charcoal being used for smelting as late as 1920; industrial blue used for laundering was also manufactured here. Today the Lakeland Village, a time-share development, stands on the site of this vanished industrial complex.

Lakeside is just a ferry and train terminus building plus a hotel. Apart from the railway, there is not enough to merit a long stopover if you are making the tour of the lake by ferry from Bowness or Waterhead. The ferry terminus used to have a large tower, used as a beacon at night for boats, and a palm court band used to perform in the cafe here. At least the cafe survives, externally something of a period-piece, raised by cast-iron columns to get the views of the southern end of the lake.

At a triangle of roads near Finsthwaite, just west of Lakeside, is **Stott Park Bobbin-Mill** (open Easter to Oct, daily, 9.30 (2 Sun) to 6.30), English Heritage's one and only working museum. The last bobbin-mills in the country were in the Lake District; this one closed as late as 1971, and one at Spark Bridge (a few miles to the west) was the very last to go, in 1983. The mill opened in 1835, and its appearance is very much of a nineteenth-century mill; at first water power was used, then water, steam and electric turbines were installed at later dates (the steam engine is still in working order). It was owned by the Coward family from 1855 until its demise; by 1971 it had become something of an anachronism, as bobbins were mostly made from synthetic materials by then. When the mill's last handful of clients switched to synthetics, Stott Park's days were ended. Saved from demolition and redevelopment, the mill has survived remarkably intact – so much so that guides who used to work at the mill will show you how the lathes operate and bobbins are created out of the raw material. They will also tell you horror stories about working conditions – accident rates were alarming, and it comes as something of a surprise that only one bobbin mill in the area burnt down (that was at Force Mills near Satterthwaite). There is a display about the mill's past, and a small shop sells various bobbin products (not just cotton reels; handles and toys are also made by the bobbin process) and sometimes second-hand industrial wooden bobbins are on sale.

North of Stott Park, the minor road runs through dense forest (a not very prominent signpost on the east side of the road indicates the path to the lakeshore about 1½ miles north of Stott Park), reaching a junction by the entrance to **Graythwaite Hall**. The house, Elizabethan but remodelled in Victorian times, is not open to the public but its grounds are (early Apr to June, daily, 10 to 6). The grcunds were landscaped in the nineteenth century and contain superb azaleas and rhododendrons: hence at their peak in late spring. There are also Dutch and rose gardens.

By keeping to the north-east fork by Graythwaite Hall, you can pick up two sections of lakeshore path (both are signposted, but there is only limited parking space). Both are delightful lakeshore strolls, and (probably because the paths are so hard to find) are never crowded; the traffic queues and hordes of Bowness certainly seem more than a short crow's flight away. The first path is a quarter of a mile from the junction; it follows the shore for nearly a mile. The other is a little easier to spot, and leaves the road by an isolated house in the woods just north of the Cunsey Village sign (which faces south); a very attractive path follows the shore past a wooded knoll called Rawlinson Nab, and re-emerges into the open, reaching the road near High Cunsey, in all about a mile. If you are driving southwards from the ferry and the B5285, take the Cunsey turn; the path is signposted after three-quarters of a mile, just before the road leaves the woods.

The most obvious starting-point for walks on the west side of the lake is near the ferry terminal on the B5285. Easiest of all is the walk north along the unclassified road (open to the public as a path only) close to a weight restriction roadsign (referring to the ferry), from where there are glorious views of the central lake before the road enters forest. Good round walks taking in Claife Heights, the wooded slopes that dominate this central west side of the lake, can easily be devised, though route-finding along the labyrinth of forest paths can be a little involved.

Close by the ferry terminal are some reminders of **Claife Station** ('station' in its sense as a viewing-point), a mansion built in 1799. Cockin's *A Guide to the Lakes* went as far as recommending specific sites and architectural forms to promote the development of Arcadian villas and summerhouses, and this was one of them put into practice. A two-storey octagonal structure was later enclosed by the Curwens of Belle Isle within a castellated rectangular wall (which can still be seen near the ferry terminal on the west side of the lake); the ruin of Claife Station itself can be reached by taking a footpath from the car-park, signposted to Claife Heights.

At **Far Sawrey** the landscape becomes more open: small scale and intimate, hedge-fringed green fields, with Far Sawrey's Victorian church standing alone by one of them. **Near Sawrey** is the slightly larger of the two villages, with an attractive grouping of mostly white-rendered cottages around a V-shape of lanes opposite the Tower Bank Arms, a traditionally furnished pub owned by the National Trust, plus a scattering of farmsteads and guest-houses a little further east.

Hill Top in Near Sawrey (open Apr to Oct, daily, 10 (2 Sun) to 5.30) was the beloved home of Beatrix Potter, her haven from the stifling routine of her middle-class parents and Kensington home. After a series of family holidays in the Lakes, first at Wray Castle (see p. 164) then in 1896 at Lakefield (now Ees Wyke, a hotel) in Near Sawrey, she discovered that Hill Top was for sale. Using the royalties from her first book *Peter Rabbit*, she purchased the house. Her parents would most certainly have objected had they known she had intended to move in here, so she made them believe she was simply buying the place as an investment. Slowly she increased the length of her stays until she was spending most of the year at the house. For the first time in her life she was truly happy, despite her total solitude, thoroughly immersed in the house and countryside which was to become her favourite home. Six of her classic children's books centred on Near Sawrey and Hill Top; the latter became Jemima Puddleduck's farm and Tom Kitten's house, and many parts of the house are instantly recognisable from her illustrations. After her marriage at the age of 47, Potter could not bear to make alterations to Hill Top, so she and her husband moved into Castle Cottage in the same village, keeping the farm as her own little sanctuary.

Beatrix Potter spent the last 30 years of her life devoted to the rescue of the Lake District by buying up farms and land to give to the National Trust, which she felt was the only way of safeguarding the future of the landscape she loved. She wanted Hill Top preserved as an example of Lakeland vernacular, and it has survived exactly as it was in her lifetime. Inevitably perhaps, it has also become a shrine to her own life and works, and 75,000 visitors a year walking through its low-ceilinged rooms have raised a few alarm bells in the National Trust. Accordingly, further visitors are not positively encouraged (though not actually discouraged either); information centres do not make a point of leaving around leaflets about the house, the house itself is very discreetly signposted in the village, and the standard blue flash used for highlighting tourist sights on OS maps is missing for Hill Top.

Just west of Near Sawrey lies **Esthwaite Water**, 1½ miles long, with reedy shores and partly wooded promontories sheltering under low hills. Roads encircle it, though none of them runs close to the shore for more than a few yards: the best road view is from the car-park in the south-western corner. Boats can be hired from the adjacent farm. The only footpath is at the northern end of the lake, leaving the road at a junction close to the north-west corner, but it follows the shore for only a very short distance. Hence it is no longer possible to do as Wordsworth used to and circuit the lake on foot except along tarmacked roads:

My morning walks
Were early; oft before the hours of school
I travell'd round our little lake, five miles
Of pleasant wandering, happy time! ('The Prelude')

Just north of Esthwaite Water is a minor turn north for **Colthouse,** one well worth taking in preference to the B5286, as there are very pretty views over an intricate landscape of pasture and woods, with Langdale Pikes looming in the distance. Colthouse is a mere hamlet; in 1913 Beatrix Potter discovered an ancient account book in a barn which showed that Wordsworth lodged with the Tysons of Colthouse, though it is not known whether he lodged here or at the Tysons' other house in Hawkshead. Potter also recorded an early visit to the Friends' Meeting House, an unassuming rough-cast building of cottagey appearance with the plainest of interiors, built in 1688 at the time of Quaker persecutions. Half a mile north, just after a road junction and a National Trust sign for Loanthwaite, a path signposted on the east side of the road is the most convenient way of ascending **Latterbarrow** (all 15 to 20 minutes and 500 feet of it), the only significantly elevated ground in the vicinity that isn't covered with woodland. Despite the brevity and ease of the climb, this summit gives a good panorama of Windermere, The Old Man of Coniston, Bow Fell, Langdale Pikes, Fairfield, Dollywaggon Pike and Ill Bell.

Further north along this road is the gatehouse for **Wray Castle**, a wildly indulgent mansion-cum-folly built in the form of a medieval fortress for Dr James Dawson, a retired Liverpool surgeon, in 1840–7. It is almost too bold close up, and must primarily have been intended to be viewed in the context and proportionately grand scale of its setting. Wordsworth came here and found the house 'dignified', and planted a mulberry tree. Beatrix Potter had her first Lake District holiday here at the age of 16, when her parents rented the castle for the summer. Among the friends they made was Canon Rawnsley, later to become one of the founders of the National Trust, who suggested to Beatrix that she should submit *The Tale of Peter Rabbit* to Frederick Warne, the company that was to publish all her children's books. The National Trust have leased the house to a training college for the merchant navy, and the house is not open to the public, but you are allowed to use its car-park and take a path to the lakeshore, which can be followed southwards for 3½ miles to the ferry and the B5285.

Soon the minor road joins the B5286; a mile down the first left turn is the Drunken Duck, a remote but attractive pub for lunch. The B-road winds its way through woodland before joining the A593 at **Clappersgate**, effectively an outskirt of Ambleside. Close by is Brathay Hall (not open), bought by a Jamaica merchant, George Law, in around 1784 and rebuilt and painted white to become the most noticeable feature of the northern end of Windermere. Coleridge jotted down a passing thought: 'Mr Law's white Palace – a bitch'. The hall is now a school.

The east side of the lake

The drive along the A591 and A592 is a poor way of seeing Windermere. For the most part, trees screen the view, and in summer the roads are often very busy – worst in Bowness, which can be a bottleneck. Apart from the attractions at Ambleside (see p. 171), Windermere town (see p. 166) and Bowness (see p. 168), there is a handful of features worth taking in on the east side of the lake.

Brockhole (open Mar to Sept, daily, 10 to dusk), two miles south-east of Ambleside on the west side of the A591, is the headquarters of the National Park, and houses a National Park **visitor centre**. Brockhole is a beautifully set nineteenth-century mansion (the former home of a cotton magnate), with grounds sloping down to the lakeshore and lots of mature trees; picnic tables are scattered about invitingly. In addition to the shop and information desk, there is a display covering about 5000 years of the Lake District, and a side show featuring lifesize mock-ups of scenes from Beatrix Potter's stories. It is worth timing a visit to coincide with one of the centre's many lectures and events, which are held on most days throughout the season; for details check in the Brockhole broadsheet *What's On*, available at visitor centres. In season Brockhole fills up almost to capacity on rainy days; drier ones, and Saturdays, are less busy.

Queen Adelaide's Hill, a low hillock immediately west of the A592 (just south of the junction of the A592 and A591) and just beyond the western outskirts of Windermere, is a good place for viewing the lake; there is a picnic site here too.

The **Windermere Steamboat Museum** (open Easter to Oct, daily, 10 to 5), on the A592 just north of Bowness, is a collection of nearly 30 antique boats, gathered appropriately enough into a boat-house by the lake. Exhibits include *Dolly*, the world's oldest mechanically powered boat (built in about 1850 and submerged for 67 years in Ullswater), Beatrix Potter's rowing-boat, and *Esperance*, the first twin-screw steam yacht, used by H. W. Schneider to commute to Lakeside from his house – now the Belsfield Hotel; see p. 169 – in Bowness (he took a special train from Lakeside to his office in Barrow) and immortalised as Captain Flint's houseboat in Arthur Ransome's *Swallows and Amazons*. The steam launch *Osprey* periodically takes visitors for 45-minute cruises on the lake.

Near the southern end of the lake is **Gummer's How**, one of the few hills around Windermere to rise above 1000 feet (its summit is actually 1054 feet), and whose conical form gives it the character of a genuine summit. It is reached in 20 minutes by an easy path leading from a minor road running north-east from the A592 from Fell Foot Country Park. Start from the car-park and picnic site near the top of the road, walk uphill and take the second gate on the left just before the forest begins. The path is obvious all the way to the top, from which there are excellent views over the lake, the Winster Valley and Morecambe Bay.

Fell Foot Country Park (open daily, 10 to dusk) is an area of parkland formerly occupied by Fell Foot House and now sensitively converted into a National Trust country park with opportunities for picnicking, bathing and strolling by the water's edge. The park has a cafe in a folly boat-house (resembling an outsized toy fort, complete with portcullis), a launching-stage for boats of five horsepower and under, rowing-boat hire and an adventure playground. It is particularly suitable for families with small children – much better than anything Bowness has to offer. A caravan site and chalet development is adjacent, well screened from the country park itself.

Windermere town

Confusingly, Windermere the town is a little way from Windermere the lake. The town grew up around a hamlet called Birthwaite, where Windermere station opened in 1847. The railway authorities wanted to build it closer to the lake, but wealthy landowners opposed this: the railway would have cut off many villas from the lakeshore; views would have been spoilt by viaducts and the landowners' Arcadian peace shattered. One of the first buildings to be constructed close by the station was Rigg's Windermere Hotel. This was followed by rows of stone villas, ranged along broad residential streets. In the 1850s rapid development took place towards Bowness and the lakeshore, as Windermere village expanded westwards and southwards from the station. By the 1880s it had become the size of a town, with some 40 lodging-houses, two churches, several parades of shops and a school.

Wordsworth feared the worst, and vehemently opposed the railway, which he felt would bring artisans and labourers and other 'uneducated persons' who would fail to understand how to appreciate the Lakeland scenery, and that the transportation of masses of people into the heart of the Lakes would destroy the very amenity they came to enjoy. In their defence the railway company answered that the crowds would be concentrated around the terminus and the rest of the district would retain its character of retirement and seclusion. In a sonnet Wordsworth sent to the *Morning Post* he pronounced:

Is then no nook of English ground secure
From rash assault? Schemes of retirement sown
In youth, and 'mid the busy world kept pure
As when their earliest flowers of hope were blown
Must perish; – how can they this blight endure?
And must he too the ruthless change bemoan
Who scorns a false utilitarian lure
'Mid his paternal fields at random thrown?
Baffle the threat, bright Scene, from Orrest-head
Given to the pausing traveller's rapturous glance:
Plead for thy peace, thou beautiful romance
Of nature; and, if human hearts be dead,
Speak, passing winds; ye torrents, with your strong
And constant voice, protest against the wrong.

Proposals to extend the line, to Wordsworth's further horror, along the lake and up to Ambleside and Keswick were mooted by the railway company but came to nothing. A cutting was constructed and attempts were made to extend the line in 1875 and 1877, but John Ruskin and Canon Rawnsley successfully opposed the scheme.

Windermere today retains much of its Victorian character, with lots of suburban-looking streets of stone-built houses (many functioning as guest-houses), adorned by the occasional mock-Tudor gable or rustic wooden eaves. But the town is remarkably short on things to do; there are two only moderately interesting shopping streets (both dominated by heavy traffic in summer), and no sights. Notable among the shops is The Fellsman, a long-established shop selling walking and climbing equipment, and the Windermere and Bowness Dollmaking Co. (at the corner of College Road and Elleray Road), an antique shop which also does a trade in repairing antique dolls. One of the town's best places for light lunches and teas is the Miller Howe Kaff (run by the Miller Howe Hotel), set in an unlikely location in a household store called Lakeland Plastics, just behind the station. Also near the station is the Village Restaurant, serving simple filling lunches, more ambitious dinners, and memorable baking. In the High Street, Roger's has pretty décor and imaginative cooking; you must book for the good-value lunches.

The best walk from Windermere is the 20-minute ascent of **Orrest Head**, signposted opposite the National Westminster Bank near the station: a leisurely climb along a well-graded path (where it ceases to be surfaced, by a house, take any fork – they rejoin) through woods to a limestone hillock with a very fine view over the lake and central fells, as well as the Pennines; a view indicator identifies all the summits.

In Lake Road (the A5074) at the south end of Windermere, just as it merges into Bowness, is a clock tower erected in 1907 in memory of John Byrde Baddeley, Victorian travel writer and author of the *Thorough Guides*. After it first appeared, the guidebook in this series to the Lake District became the definitive guide to the fells.

Bowness-on-Windermere

Bowness is effectively an extension of Windermere town, and it's not immediately obvious where the dividing-line between the two is. After the railway opened at Windermere, development crept towards the lake, soon reaching Bowness and engulfing its old village centre. Development really took off in the 1850s–80s. The earliest housing was along Elim Grove and Helm Road, then by the 1870s expansion was taking place along Lake Road. Compared with Windermere, Bowness was several rungs down the social ladder, and was increasingly the preserve of the tradesman rather than the Lakeland gentry. It had great reliance on passing trade. In 1881 the Windermere Hydropathic Hotel opened as the fashion peaked for the taking of spa remedies.

A substantial part of the old village survives today, concentrated in a tight network of lanes known collectively as Lowside behind the parish church, St Martin's, and remains as the least-spoilt part of the town. In one of the lanes is the **Lakeland Experience** (open all year, daily), where an audio-visual show about the Lake District is given. **St Martin's** church dates from the fifteenth century but has been heavily Victorianised, and its white walls covered with verses and painted decoration. The east window probably came from Cartmel Priory church. A seventeenth-century wooden sculpture of St Martin and the Beggar stands towards the rear of the church.

Lake Road forms the central axis of the town, a long sloping main shopping street leading down to the lakeside and piers. It gets very busy in summer with crowds spilling out over the pavement and on to the road, and is the nearest the Lake District gets to the commercialism of a seaside resort – a sample of what might well have happened to the Lake District without the National Trust or the National Park. Apart from the tourist shops, the street is notable for the Royalty cinema (an independent film house with cheerful psychedelic décor; the programmes are mainly new releases suitable for family viewing) and a concentration of restaurants. Notable among the latter are the Hedgerow Vegetarian (good value, friendly service, informal atmosphere) and Rastelli (excellent pizzas and pasta; cramped, bustling, cheerful). Other good places to eat at are Jackson's Bistro (West End), with a short interesting menu, changing frequently, and the Porthole Eating House (Ash Street), where food and wine are more up-market than the informal décor suggests.

The **promenade** area around the steamer piers is where all the crowds, coaches and cars seem to converge – a parade of ice-cream stands, the pervasive smell of chips and the insensitive Shepherd's Aquarius building (a modern disco/cafe/gift shop complex) by the water's edge provide the tackier elements. Visually, the saving grace of this corner apart from the lake itself is the Belsfield Hotel (begun in 1840), an Italianate mansion with banked lawns dropping to the level of the road. It was built as a home for the Baroness de Sternberg, and much extended throughout the nineteenth century.

There is, however, scope for some pleasant short strolls from here. **Biskey Howe** is a viewpoint over the lake, reached by taking Helm Road and following it up to its highest point; the viewpoint is a couple of yards off to the left of the road, and it is possible to park at the top. Another good viewpoint, requiring a longer walk, is **Brant Fell**, reached via Brantfell Road. The most popular walk from Bowness is along the lakeside southwards to **Cockshott Point**: take Glebe Road (the road between the tourist **information centre** and the Shepherd's Aquarius) until it bends left, then keep straight on following the path along the lakeshore. Views down the lake open up immediately; this is a good vantage-point for seeing **Belle Isle**, at 38 acres the lake's largest island. On it is a domed cylindrical house with a portico, built in 1774 for Thomas English, a wealthy Nottingham merchant. John Plaw's remarkable design (no one before in this country had devised a domestic building of a perfectly round plan; he had ingenious solutions to the problem of sewage disposal, involving planting the building in a sunken area; and he hid the chimney flues in the centre of the dome) heralded the first house on Windermere to be sited purely for aesthetic purposes. Not surprisingly, considering its position as the focal-point of the centre of the lake, the house became a subject for landscape artists of the period. The house was sold to the Curwens (who still own it) in 1781. William Cockin (1736–1807), Kendal schoolmaster and early travel writer, found the circular house and its accompaniments to be

a considerable accession to the beauties of the lake. And could one with a wish throw a bridge from shore to shore, and place the uncommon row of houses near Shap across the island, or even conjure a city upon it . . . [it] might then become a rival to the celebrated lake of Geneva, which owes its principal superiority over all other lakes to its having a city at one end and being surrounded with palaces.

The tourist **information centre**, opposite Shepherd's Aquarius, has the Countryside Theatre attached to it, where regular evening slide shows and lectures are held. Inside the centre itself is a stuffed specimen of the rare Tizzy Whizzie, a grotesque winged hedgehog with a squirrel's tail and closely related to the red herring; a sober label on the glass case records the last sighting of the beast under a Windermere pier before the war.

Along Glebe Road, opposite the car-park, is the **Lake Windermere Aquarium** (open Mar to Oct, daily, 10 to 6.30), a collection of about 20 types of British fish, including species found in Windermere, housed in a dark and rather poky room. The fishtanks are labelled, but that's the extent of the information. Nearby is Windermere Aquatic, a boat shop with a big stock.

Ambleside

First impressions of Ambleside tend to be that the town is one giant one-way system, with houses and shops built around it. This isn't totally fair, as the old part of the town (known as Above Stock) is unspoilt and clear of through traffic. For the most part, however, Ambleside is a major resort with a Victorian face and twentieth-century traffic conditions. Sights tend to be around the peripheries of the town – Stock Ghyll Force, Galava Roman Fort and Stagshaw Gardens. The town's intrinsic attraction is as a shopping and entertainment centre, with an excellent range of outdoor shops and a cinema. The Lake District Summer Music Festival features a programme of classical concerts held at Charlotte Mason College. The Ambleside Sports are held in early August in Rydal Park, just north of the town, and include traditional Cumbrian sports events.

The opening of the ferry terminus at Waterhead in 1845, near the north end of the lake, sparked off an expansion of Ambleside, which got its new Gothic church in 1854 and a new market hall in 1863; terraces of guest-houses appeared along Church Street, Rothay Road and Compston Road towards the end of the nineteenth and at the beginning of the twentieth centuries. Among its most distinguished nineteenth-century residents was writer Harriette Martineau, who in 1846 built The Knoll, an Italianate villa, and lived there for 30 years; visitors to the house included Charlotte Brontë, Ralph Waldo Emerson and George Eliot.

The **town centre** consists of a rectangle of one-way roads of no special character, the eastern side being the twisty principal shopping street, which is lined with nineteenth-century grey-stone buildings, the odd large hotel among them. The overall effect is not distinguished, but the shape helps give it personality, and it has quite an animated feel. Among the shops are a bookshop, a concentration of shops selling walking and climbing equipment and a couple of woollen shops, plus a fair range of general shops. Almost opposite the town hall, a little further down the slope, is an alley (The Slack) leading to Sheila's Kitchen, one of the Lake District's best inexpensive tea-room/restaurants (not open in the evening): local ingredients and a Swiss flavour, particularly in the puddings.

Compston Road looks straight and uninviting, but has two

good eateries: Harvest Vegetarian, which does very
reasonable and quite imaginative vegetarian food
(particularly good fruit crumbles) in the daytime and
evenings, and Zefferelli's, a comfortable pizzeria with
stylised Japanese bold décor. The latter is housed in a small,
trendy complex with an independent cinema (more oriental
décor here; refreshingly modern with a touch of fantasy) and
an indoor shopping mall with a craft shop, a wholefood shop
and a wholefood bakery.

Situated in Vicarage Road, off Compston Road, **St Mary's
church**, with its soaring 180-foot spire, was built in 1854 by
George Gilbert Scott. A rush-bearing ceremony takes place
here on the first Saturday in July; a mural, depicting this
event, was added to the interior in 1944. One window is
dedicated to Wordsworth; after his death Mary Wordsworth
donated a bible and lectern to the church. Wordsworth
himself, as Distributor of Stamps for Westmorland, had an
office in a building now called the Old Stamp House (next to
a bakery on the corner of Church Street and Lake Road).

Lake Road makes a poor walk southwards towards
Waterhead, with snarling traffic and little to look at. Five
minutes along here stands the Hayes Garden Centre,
unmistakable for its Kew-style hot-house, a huge store
selling a wide range of garden products. Skelghyll Lane, off
Old Lake Road opposite the garden centre, is the
starting-point for walks up to Jenkin Crag, a viewpoint over
Windermere, and for an excellent round walk up Wansfell
Pike via Troutbeck, perhaps the most satisfying round walk
associated with Windermere.

Just outside the main car-park, Ambleside's famous **Bridge
House** straddles a brook. The comically minute two-storey
structure, now a National Trust **information centre**, was a
summerhouse for Ambleside Hall (now demolished), but a
satirical legend is in circulation to the effect that a Scotsman
lived here with his family to avoid paying land tax.

Above Stock, the old name for the village now engulfed by
Ambleside, lies on the steep slope roughly opposite the
entrance to the main car-park, on and around the road
signposted to Kirkstone. Early settlers developed the village
up here as this was out of reach of floodwater yet had a
supply of fast-flowing water to power the complex of mills
which grew up; these included mills producing bobbins,
corn and paper. The old corn-mill, built in the fourteenth

century and functioning into this century, is still there, though the 16-foot wheel itself is a modern reproduction. Peggy Hill, Fairview Road and other crisscrossing old lanes and alleys harbour some attractive corners.

Waterhead comprises just the northern ferry terminal for Windermere, with a few large hotels and a summer horse-and-trap service to the centre of Ambleside. A little further south along the A591, and lying just to the east of the road, **Stagshaw Garden** (open Apr to June, daily, 10 to 6.30; and July to Oct by appointment only) has exotic trees and shrubs, as well as rhododendrons, magnolias and azaleas and native flowers, on an eight-acre hillside site. In summer there are roses and in early autumn hydrangeas, but the garden is at its best in spring.

Not a great deal remains of **Galava Roman Fort**, sited next to Borrans Park (reached by following the A5075 from Waterhead until turning left into the park, then immediately taking a gate on the right into a field) apart from grassy lumps and the bases of its stone foundations. The first fort on the site was a wooden one built by Agricola in about AD 70 on a Roman road that ran from Watercrook, near Kendal, to the port of Ravenglass via the Hardknott Pass. Galava was a strategically sited vantage-point from where the Romans could keep check on the routes over High Street to the north and Wrynose to the west. The wooden structure was replaced by a stone one in AD 122. It is probable that there was a quay at Galava, and there may have been one near Fell Foot at the southern end of the lake.

Stock Ghyll Force is a romantically set waterfall in a lush setting among ferns and trees, with the cascades dropping about 70 feet in two drops. This was a favourite spot for Victorian tourists; the old metal turnstile gate and the woodland paths to the fall date from then. To reach it, take the lane from the centre of Ambleside between Barclays Bank and the town hall; the gate leading to the fall is on the left of the road, after half a mile (cars can be taken to this point).

The Trout Beck Valley

This marks the beginning of the hill country north of Windermere, not yet dramatic but certainly with some upland character. The valley road rises up between the bases of smooth green fells and up on to the Kirkstone Pass (see p. 90).

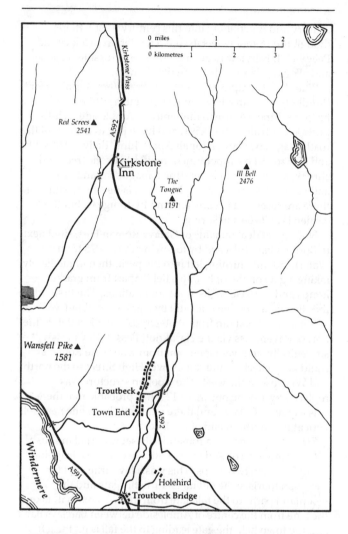

Holehird Gardens and **Lakeland Horticultural Society Gardens** (open at all reasonable times), just to the east of the A592 and near Troutbeck Bridge, has a wide range of horticultural specimens, including Alpine plants and a rock garden, situated in the extensive grounds of Holehird, now a Cheshire Home; a fine view extends westwards from the Alpine garden. The house was built in 1869 for M. M. Dunlop, who petitioned against the extension of the railway to Ambleside, since the 50-foot embankment would have cut his grounds in two. Beatrix Potter came here with her parents for summer holidays in 1889.

Troutbeck lies off the main road and consists of a mile-long string of hamlets, each with its own roadside well. There is no centre as such, and although Troutbeck has a post office and church it does not feel like a conventional village. It has over a dozen 'statesman-plan' farms dating from the seventeenth and eighteenth centuries, in varying degrees of restoration. Opposite a handsome bank barn (a barn-type unique to the Lakes and the Yorkshire Dales) at the south end of the 'village' is **Town End** (open Apr to Oct, Tue to Fri and Sun, 2 to 6 or dusk if earlier; last admission 5.30), a statesman farmhouse which has survived miraculously untampered with. The Browne family built it in 1626 and lived here until 1944, when the National Trust took it over. This fascinating house, still without electricity, retains the Brownes' hand-carved furniture and domestic implements – the accumulated belongings of a family that kept everything and modernised nothing. The building's statesman plan consists of two sections: the downhouse, for washing, cooking, pickling and brewing, and the firehouse, which constituted the living-quarters.

Troutbeck has two pubs. The Mortal Man has a famous jingle on its inn-sign, painted by Julius Caesar Ibbetson who lived close by in the early years of the nineteenth century:

O mortal man that lives by bread
What is it makes thy nose so red?
Thou silly fool that looks so pale,
'Tis drinking Sally Birkett's ale.

The eighteenth- and nineteenth-century church on the main road has an east window with stained glass by Burne-Jones, William Morris and Ford Madox Brown.

Rydal Water and Grasmere

North of Windermere is one of the most renowned showpiece areas of the Lakes, with the dual attraction of its literary associations and the magical composition of craggy fells encompassing the two lakes – Grasmere and Rydal Water.

The area teems with Wordsworth associations: there's

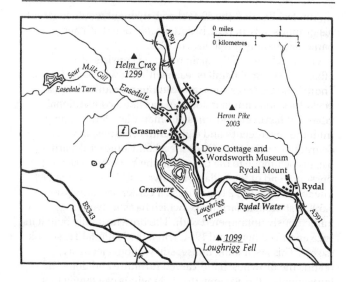

scarcely a hillside or dale which isn't mentioned somewhere
in his or Dorothy's writings. It also harbours some excellent
walks of varying degrees of difficulty. The one real black
mark is the busy A591, whose traffic's echoes fill the valley
and can be quite difficult to ignore.

Rydal, lying a few yards north of the A591, is a small
hamlet with a handful of large houses, among them Rydal
Mount (open Apr to Oct, daily, 9.30 to 5; Nov to Mar, daily,
10 to 12.30, 2 to 4), the sixteenth-century farmhouse (altered
in later years) where Wordsworth lived from 1813 until his
death in 1850, the most opulent of Wordsworth's homes in
the Rothay Valley. He was by then a famous man – hordes of
sightseers used to come with the hope of catching sight of
him – and a wealthy one, with a substantial income, as well
as being Poet Laureate and Distributor of Stamps for
Westmorland. The Rydal years were not all happy ones:
Dorothy suffered a prolonged mental illness and William's
daughter Dora died here. They weren't all productive ones
as far as poetry was concerned; in the years as Poet Laureate,
William wrote no poetry. He lavished most of his attention
on the 4½-acre garden, which became one of his great joys,
the focus of his passionate interest in landscape arts; its
views of Rydal Water and Windermere must have been the
catalyst to his inspiration. Parts of the garden's features were

inherited: the first of its two terraces, the Mount and Pelter bridge. Wordsworth elaborated the theme of the picturesque, creating one of the most significant new designs of the time.

Rydal Mount itself was leased from a Lady Fleming; its condition when Wordsworth started living here was far from satisfactory, and he purchased a plot of land below the house, known today as Dora's Field, with the intention of building another house should he have to leave Rydal Mount. In spring Dora's Field is spectacularly carpeted with daffodils (these were not the inspiration for his famous poem; the site of the original Wordsworth daffodils is Gowbarrow Park on the shores of Ullswater).

Today Rydal Mount survives much as Wordsworth knew it, although some pieces of furniture have been moved to Dove Cottage. Family portraits, Wordsworth's possessions, his study, and a collection of his first editions are here.

Opposite Rydal Mount is **Rydal Hall**, a predominantly eighteenth-century house owned by the diocese of Carlisle and used for retreats and conferences. The grounds are open to the public (open all year, Weds and Sat, 9 to dusk); these include formal gardens, the Rydal Torrent (a series of waterfalls) and the Grotto, a summerhouse which Wordsworth used to like to visit. A leaflet giving details of a self-guided trail is available. The church by the main road was built in 1824 as a chapel for Rydal Hall; Wordsworth's pew was the one situated in front of the pulpit.

Rydal Water and **Grasmere**, its slightly larger partner half a mile to the west, are the valley's two gleaming jewels, glacial lakes with drumlins (hillocks made of glacial deposits) forming little islands, nestling in the midst of intimate fells and deciduous woodlands. The scenery is far from grand or intimidating – much of its charm lies in its small scale: Grasmere itself is less than a mile long, surrounded by steep-sided though not particularly tall fells. This topography lends itself admirably to easy walks (see p. 255), the most popular being the much-trodden path along the southern shores of both lakes. A good starting-point if you are keen to avoid the crowds at Grasmere village is by an obscure car-park reached by taking a south turn off the A591 just east of Rydal (marked by a weight restriction sign, and immediately crossing a stone bridge), then taking the first turning on the right, which can be followed on foot beyond the car-park to Rydal Water. Loughrigg Terrace, the slope above the southern end of Grasmere, is one of the classic Lakeland views, showing the valley off from its best angle. Rydal is the start of a much more ambitious walk, the Fairfield Horseshoe, which goes up Heron Pike, on to Great Rigg, then along the Fairfield ridge before returning south via High Pike and Low Pike.

Grasmere village is very self-conscious and trippery, but to miss out Grasmere would be like going to Egypt and skipping the Pyramids. Wordsworth and his family lived in four places in the Grasmere neighbourhood: Dove Cottage, Allan Bank, the Old Parsonage and Rydal Mount.

The village is probably the most visited village in the Lakes, and feels like it (parking in summer can be impossible, despite the existence of two large car-parks). The main part of the village is lined along the B5287 plus one or two offshoots: gift shops, Victorian hotels and cafes abound, but on the whole it's all quite well behaved. It has medieval origins, with an ancient church and a few older cottages, but most of it is of nineteenth-century appearance, the legacy of wealthy magnates who built villas here after the railway reached Windermere in 1847.

Grasmere has a rectangular green at its centre, surrounded by shops (some quite up-market, though inevitably there is some tat) aimed very much at the tourist trade, including The Heaton Cooper Studio (a gallery selling contemporary Lake District landscape pictures), a perfumery, a bookshop, a walkers' outdoor shop and a confectioner's. There are lots of places to eat; two of the best are Rowan Tree and Baldry's, both with a vegetarian slant, and both are good for inexpensive light snacks. You can eat more ambitiously in the restaurants of two hotels, Michael's Nook (lunch and dinner) and White Moss House (dinner only; see p. 207). In winter the village virtually closes up.

Dove Cottage (open all year exc mid-Jan to mid-Feb, daily, 9 to 5.30), Wordsworth's home between 1799 and 1808, is the major literary pilgrimage spot in the Lake District. It stands at the south end of Grasmere village, in the hamlet of Town End (with the church on your left, follow the road to the A591, and Dove Cottage is just opposite; usually it's just a matter of following the crowds). Here William spent the happiest years of his life, his first home of his own (previously he had always stayed with friends or relatives), where he spent the first six years of his married life and where the first three of his children were born (John in 1803, Dora in 1804 and Thomas in 1806). Most significantly, this was where he wrote much of his finest work including 'The Leech Gatherer', 'Immortality Ode', 'Ode to Duty', 'Daffodils', 'To the Cuckoo', 'The Rainbow', and completed his autobiographical poem 'The Prelude'.

The cottage dates from the early seventeenth century, when it was built as a pub, The Dove and Olive Bough, serving traffic on the old Ambleside to Keswick road (the present A591 was not built until 1831), and is a humble building with stone walls, lattice windows and a slate roof. Wordsworth never knew it as Dove Cottage.

Here William, Dorothy and Mary Wordsworth carried out a spartan lifestyle, William devoted to gardening and chopping wood, Dorothy doing the housework – the epitome of 'plain living and high thinking'. It was evidently a little too basic for Sir Walter Scott, who longed for a civilised breakfast while staying here: one morning he stopped his bedroom door with a chair, sneaked out of the window and walked to the Swan Hotel, where he got something a bit more palatable than anything the Wordsworths could serve.

The cottage's low rooms were dark and chilly; the children's room was so damp that the Wordsworths papered the walls with newspapers to mitigate the problem; the papers survived until a few years ago, but the trustees of the cottage have now repapered it in the same style.

Only a little of the original furniture is in the cottage, but much of Wordsworth's furniture has been donated to the trustees of the cottage by members of Wordsworth's family, and the cottage has much the same character as it had in Wordsworth's day. One of the poet's favourite objects, a cuckoo-clock which used to hang at Rydal Mount, is now installed here; Wordsworth died on its twelfth stroke of midnight in the winter of 1850.

The cottage garden was a beloved place for the Wordsworths, who transplanted local flora picked from the lakeside and the neighbouring fells, farmland and woodland (Dorothy was particularly interested in mosses). William himself spent increasingly more time writing out here. They were appalled when Thomas De Quincey, who moved in here with his wife from Nab Farm at Rydal (now Nab Cottage) after they left, demolished the summerhouse (now reinstated) and chopped down trees in the orchard. De Quincey, whose best-known work is *Confessions of an English Opium-Eater*, kept up his habit here: his opium scales are on display at the cottage. De Quincey left in 1830, but continued to lease the cottage until 1836, after which various tenants took the cottage. Attempts to buy the cottage for the nation were made in 1862, 1870 and (successfully) 1890. Viewing is by guided tour, but you are permitted to walk freely around the cottage afterwards (time and space permitting). In summer, try to visit early in the day as it can get extremely busy.

Annexed to Dove Cottage is the excellent **Wordsworth Museum**, which is imaginatively set out, giving displays about the discovery of the 'picturesque', a reconstructed farmhouse room typical of the Grasmere district at the time the Wordsworths would have known it, and a lucid exhibition about the life and works of the poets associated with Grasmere, with numerous original manuscripts and pictures. Among the more light-hearted items is a glass case full of Wordsworth's effects, including his buckles, his 'ww' monogrammed socks, his silk umbrella and his purse.

Grasmere **church**, dedicated to St Oswald, has a dull pebble-dash exterior belying an interior which has an appealingly frank rusticity about it. It dates from the fourteenth century and is thought to be the third church on this site, one traditionally held to be a spot where St Oswald preached in the seventh century. The building was enlarged in about 1500 by making arches in the north wall and adding a new north aisle, called the Langdale Aisle because attenders from that valley sat in it. Its lovely roof, with bulky cross-beams, is seventeenth century. Before it was paved in 1841, the floor was covered with rushes; a rush-bearing ceremony, in which bearers of new rushes, brought in to provide fresh flooring, were rewarded with ale and gingerbread, is still carried out annually on the Saturday nearest to St Oswald's Day (5 August), when a band leads a procession of village children bearing rush crosses, and a special service for the rushbearing is held.

Primarily, though, it is for the Wordsworth connections that the church is best remembered. Above the nave is a memorial to the poet; his prayer book is preserved in a glass case near the organ. In the churchyard behind the church are the graves of William, his wife Mary and his sister Dorothy,

Catherine and Thomas Wordsworth (the poet's children, who died in infancy in Grasmere) and Dora Quillinan (née Wordsworth, the poet's daughter). Also buried here are Hartley Coleridge (Samuel Taylor Coleridge's son), and Sarah Nelson (of gingerbread shop fame).

The Old Parsonage, opposite the church, was where Wordsworth and his family lived from 1811 to 1813. It stood on undrained land with an 'ugly white wall' (Dorothy Wordsworth's description). While they lived here, the Wordsworths lost two of their children, Catherine and Thomas; the damp and poor sanitation were probably a major cause of the deaths.

By the church lych-gate is Sarah Nelson's famous gingerbread shop, operational for 130 years and selling authentic Grasmere gingerbread (more like a shortbread than ordinary gingerbread). This building housed the village school from 1668 to 1854: Wordsworth, who saw universal education as the key to eliminating poverty and ignorance, taught here for several months, as did Dorothy Wordsworth, Mary Wordsworth and Sara Hutchinson (Mary's sister).

In August (to be precise, the third Thursday after the first Monday in August), the **Grasmere Sports**, the biggest traditional sports event in the Lake District, are held. These include Cumberland wrestling, races up the fells, hound-trailing and cycling. It is extremely popular, so parking, never easy at this time of year in the village, can be impossible, and you may do better to park in Ambleside and take a bus.

Standing under Helm Crag at the north end of the village is **Allan Bank** (not open), a large white house which was home to the Wordsworths from 1808 to 1811. They left after disputes with the landlord and because the chimney smoked too much. The house can be seen from the lake.

Easedale is a short valley north-west of Grasmere, explorable only on foot. This is one of the most popular walks from Grasmere, with three attractions: first the valley itself, quite an impressive one with the pyramid of Helm Crag (whose summit rocks are unofficially nicknamed The Lion and the Lamb and The Old Woman Playing the Organ) on its north side, then Sour Milk Gill, which rushes down cataracts at the head of the valley, and finally (best of all) Easedale Tarn, in a supremely fine setting under the shadow of steep craggy slopes. Easedale can be reached by walking up Easedale Road opposite Sam Read's bookshop in Grasmere village; it is pointless to drive up as there is no parking at all along this road. The total distance to the tarn and back is about 3½ miles.

Tarn Hows and Hawkshead

Situated three-quarters of a mile north of the B5285 from Hawkshead to Coniston, **Tarn Hows** is a very pretty part-man-made tarn, formed in the early years of the century by joining together two tarns to form one and landscaping its shores and islets with mixed woodland. From the slopes along its east side is a view over the tarn with Wetherlam in the distance, a veritable picture-postcard classic. If you want the place to yourself, and in season it gets *very* crowded (to the extent that the approach to it has necessitated an elaborate one-way system), go first thing in the morning or towards dusk. The walk around the tarn is a mile and a bit, and is totally on the level. One satisfying way of reaching Tarn Hows is by walking up through the forest from near Yew Tree Tarn on the A593 (see walk on p. 253), which takes in a fine waterfall on the way.

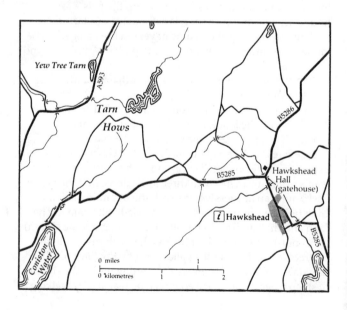

Returning to the B5285 and continuing a few miles east, **Hawkshead** is soon reached. Quaint alleys, odd-shaped yards entered by archways and flanked by white-rendered cottages, the ubiquitous craft and woollen shops and scarcely a cobblestone or hanging basket of flowers out of place, this village out of season is thoroughly engaging, and it seems probable that most visitors would rate it as the Lakes' most attractive place of its size. The car-park – roughly the size of the village itself – is the obligatory starting-point, since Hawkshead is traffic-free, a necessary measure to cope with the throngs of visitors. Cottagey tea-shops (try the Grandy Nook for fine baking) and old pubs (the Queen's Head is excellent for lunch or dinner if you can squeeze in) abound; if anything, Hawkshead is too self-conscious, but it is still a delight.

The manor of Hawkshead was one of Furness Abbey's most valuable estates. A grange was established here in the thirteenth century, in what had up to then been a modest Norse-Irish settlement, and a hall was built half a mile from the village centre. After the dissolution of the abbey, the need arose for a market centre for the important local woollen industry; suitably sited for this role, Hawkshead gained a charter for a weekly Monday market and a biannual fair in 1608 and became a busy market town. The wool trade declined in the nineteenth century, and Hawkshead never grew after that. It no longer has a market, though its market hall (also known as the town hall), built in 1790 to replace the 'market shambles' (or meat market), still stands in the old market place.

A tour around the village scarcely needs directions. From the car-park, the way into the village is past the **information centre**. Directly opposite is the old **Hawkshead Grammar School** (open Easter to Oct, Mon to Sat, 10 to 12.30 and 1.30 to 5; Sun, 1 to 5), officially named The Free Grammar School of Edwin Sandys, Archbishop of York, where Wordsworth studied from 1779–83 before going up to Cambridge. The old classroom survives pretty much as it was; the school operated from 1585 until 1909, after which it was used among other things as a Sunday school – yet it has retained a very strong sense of the past. Wordsworth, as pupils of the time were actually encouraged to do, carved his name on his desk, and it's still there, though some way below the level of the rest of the desk, the top of which has been progressively renewed over the years. Upstairs, by a windowsill, is the carved name of Wordsworth's brother John. There is also a display about the school which includes some old school mark registers and reports. The present building dates from 1675, and its sundial of that date is a memorial to Edwin Sandys, its founder; the strange mullion windows were inserted in 1891.

The **church** is built on a grassy hillock of boulder clay; a deliberate siting by the monks of Furness Abbey who built the original chapel here to ensure it would become the focal-point for the community. It was rebuilt in the fifteenth or sixteenth century, though it is thought that parts of the old chapel were incorporated into the present structure. Wordsworth saw the 'snow white church upon its hill, sat like a throned Lady sending out a gracious look all over its domain'; though the building is no longer whitewashed externally, its view of Helvellyn, the Kirkstone Pass, Latterbarrow and Wansfell is as good as ever. The inside is distinguished by two features: its white walls covered with colourful murals and inscriptions in 1711, and its massive arcades (which look vaguely Norman but are probably fifteenth century). By the north door is an ancient certificate of 'burial in woollen', harkening back to the days of Hawkshead's former days as a wool centre.

On the central square is the **Beatrix Potter Gallery** (open mid-Mar to early Nov, Weds to Sun, 11 to 5), where original illustrations are on display in the former house and office of William Heelis, whom Beatrix Potter eventually married; the solicitor's office has been carefully reconstructed. About 150 of her pictures are shown at any one time, but the exhibition is changed annually over a three- or four-year cycle. Entrance is by timed ticket, as the building's capacity is fairly limited, but usually the wait is a matter of minutes rather than hours.

In tiny lanes leading from the market square are a number of highly photogenic corners, including Anne Tyson's cottage (Wordsworth lodged with the Tysons, though it is uncertain whether he stayed here or over the fields at Colthouse, where the Tysons had another house) and Spout House, blessed with a never-failing supply of pure water which tumbles into its yard.

Half a mile north of the village, immediately north of the junction of the B5285 and the B5286, is the site of **Hawkshead Hall**, the mansion of the abbots of Furness. The hall has been

demolished, but the gatehouse (just visible from the road)
survives; above the gatehouse is the room where the
manorial court of the abbey used to be held. (The National
Trust centre in Hawkshead has the key, for those who are
really interested, though there is nothing to see inside.)

Grizedale to Force Falls

South of Hawkshead is **Grizedale**, the largest area of
Forestry Commission plantation in the Lake District. It looks
quite different from anywhere else in the region, with
clearings on the valley floor and forest covering the side of
the valley and over the skyline – a reversal of the normal
pattern. After the Forestry Commission acquired the estate
in 1936, it increased the size of the forest (then comprising
ancient oak and conifers) from 400 hectares to 1700 hectares.

The **Grizedale Visitor and Wildlife Centre**, in Grizedale
village, run by the Commission, is the starting-point for
waymarked forest walks; coloured posts mark five routes of
varying length, from one to nine and a half miles, the longest
being the Silurian Way which ascends Carron Crag (1030
feet), the highest point in the valley and a good viewpoint.

Red and roe deer frequent Grizedale (there are public
hides for watching wildlife in the forest), but what
distinguishes a forest walk here for most visitors is the
presence of forest 'sculptures' – made by artists who have
used local materials (chiefly wood and rock) and the forest
setting to create a kind of naturalistic modern art gallery,
adding a touch of enchantment to the forest. The sculptures
are widely scattered along the forest's maze of tracks and
paths, and many of them are easily missed since they blend
so much into the landscape. Accordingly, it's worth
investing in a map, obtainable from the visitor centre,
showing where to find them. The centre also sells forest
maps, more detailed than the OS one for the area, which are
essential if you intend to walk without sticking to the
waymarked routes, as it is easy to get alarmingly lost.

Opposite the visitor centre, the Theatre in the Forest,
which seats just over 200, is the venue for regular concerts,
plays, films and lectures. Adjacent is a playground of mildly
startling appearance, with a gigantic wooden bird concealing
a slide and a roundabout involving a perpetual hare and
hound race. The other building on the site is a craft

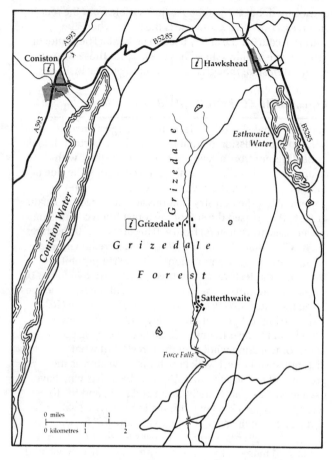

workshop and display room which has changing exhibitions. On the other side of the road a picnic site and car-park mark the site of Grizedale Hall, which was used in the Second World War as a POW camp for high-ranking German officers, one of whom successfully escaped. The hall was later demolished.

Continue southwards to **Satterthwaite**, a quiet if unexceptional village sited in the valley floor clearing. After Satterthwaite a sign announces the end of Grizedale Forest. Immediately on the west side of the road the somewhat tautologically named **Force Falls** used to power a small complex of mills and forges. In the sixteenth and seventeenth centuries there were three 'bloomeries' here, where iron smelting took place, and in the eighteenth century finery forges, producing high-quality iron, were installed. Iron is thought to have been produced here for nearly 500 years; operations ceased in 1822. A bobbin-mill worked here until 1923, when it burnt down. This corner, now just a farmhouse and the waterfall, is still called Force Mills. There were three more forges further downstream.

Grange-over-Sands and Cartmel

The National Park boundary south of the A590 between the estuaries of the Leven and the Kent wavers oddly, missing out Cartmel and Humphrey Head Point yet taking in a low-lying and largely inaccessible chunk of land abutting Morecambe Bay to the east of Grange-over-Sands. Thus it is not necessary to stick religiously to the boundary as a guide to what is and what isn't worth seeing in this area. Morecambe Bay, whose northern side is best seen in its entirety by taking the train from Ulverston to Arnside via a spectacular series of low viaducts, is a huge area of sands and swiftly changing tidal waters, rich in birdlife.

Lindale, a large, diffuse village of no special character, is made moderately pleasant by its hilly site. On its eastern side, on the B5277, is a cast-iron obelisk to 'Iron Mad' John Wilkinson (1728–1808), who owned iron furnaces at Backbarrow, near Haverthwaite. His principal iron works were near Coalbrookdale in Shropshire, and it was he who cast the parts for the world's first iron bridge, erected in 1779 at Ironbridge, a mile from Coalbrookdale; the bridge survives as a symbol of the birth of the Industrial Revolution. The obelisk was transferred here from Castlehead house near Lindale, where Wilkinson lived for a time.

Grange-over-Sands is a sedate retirement resort clinging to one of the series of low wooded hills that encompass Morecambe Bay. The town, which grew up after the opening of the Furness Railway in 1857, looks best from the esplanade, from where there is an illusion that the town's grey gabled Victorian villas are cluttered together and peer over the top of each other; in reality, though, the town is a little too spread out to have a strongly unified sense of identity – a lot of it just feels like outskirts. Its one main shopping street makes a dog-leg at the comical clock tower, the focal-point; along here is a restaurant called At Home, a bistro done up in cheerful homely décor and serving good-value evening meals (also open for coffee and snack lunches). Grange has a few of the trappings of a small resort – a swimming-pool, bowls, tennis courts, an ornamental garden and a number of Victorian hotels and guest-houses. Grange's natural site is its main attraction, however – not just the mile-long esplanade but the walk up **Hampsfield Fell** (or Hampsfell as it is also called), the hill, whose top is covered with crags and limestone pavements, rising immediately behind the town. From its hospice on the summit is an exceptional view over the bay and the southern fells (on a really clear day you might see Snaefell, on the Isle of Man, and Snowdon). The hospice itself is an engaging oddity; its inside walls are hung with moralistic nineteenth-century verses giving advice along the lines of how to enjoy the view without vandalising the hospice. See walk on p. 253.

OS maps show a strange phenomenon south-west of Grange-over-Sands at **Kents Bank** – a public pathway crossing Morecambe Bay, a 7½-mile route to Bolton-le-Sands (south of Carnforth). This route was popular with early tourists to the Lake District, and was used by stagecoaches until the middle of the last century. Because of the danger from quicksands and swift incoming tides, the walk can be attempted only with a guide; for details ask at tourist information centres.

Humphrey Head Point, a headland of cliffs topped with turf and woodland, juts out into Morecambe Bay, sloping down to sea-level at its southernmost point. There is public access to all of it, but the easy way to walk on to it is to start by the outdoor pursuits centre's driveway (made prominent from the road by an Access Area sign), then turn right just before reaching the gate that leads into the centre. This is one walk around the bay which really feels like a *cliff* walk, and it's a delightfully exhilarating one. Parking is easiest at the end of the road, which reaches the edge of the sands (from where it is a short walk back to the outdoor pursuits centre). Resist temptations to follow the cliff down to sea-level at its southern end and to walk back along the beach, as it is possible to get cut off by the tide.

Flookburgh, a plain and unassuming village, devotes itself to the fishing industry (although the shore is a mile to the south), notably for Morecambe Bay shrimps and flukes or

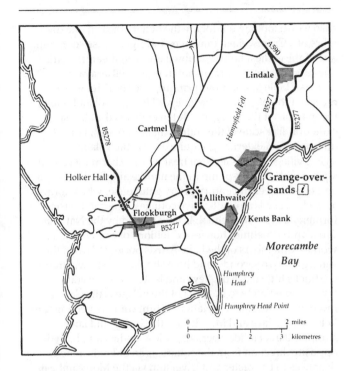

flounders – hence the name.

Cartmel, a couple of miles west of Grange-over-Sands, is
one of Cumbria's prettiest villages, quite precious in
atmosphere but nowhere near as overrun as it would be if it
were more central to the Lakes. The marvellous priory
church was founded in 1188 for canons of the Augustinian
order by William Marshall, Earl of Pembroke, though it is
traditionally held to have been founded by Irish monks who
received a divine message that they had to find a valley with
water flowing north and south. The building was saved after
the dissolution of the monasteries because the village needed
it as a parish church. The great east window (inspired by a
window in York Minster) in the Perpendicular style, with 18
main lights and 80 tracery lights, has fragmentary stained
glass; some pieces of the glass have been installed in
Bowness church. Two other glories of the church are
exquisitely carved misericords and the fourteenth-century
Harrington tomb whose outstanding stone carving includes
a frieze of tiny mourning figures (*pleureurs*) around its base.

Also worth looking out for are the bullet holes on one door, relics of a Cromwellian rampage, and a glass case containing one of the earliest known umbrellas (an eighteenth-century one, used by vicars at rainy funerals) as well as a rare 'vinegar' bible (a notorious printing error of 1716, which recorded the parable of the vineyard in the Book of Luke as the 'parable of the vinegar'). But overall it is the almost cathedral-like scale of the church that impresses, both internally and externally; it quite dwarfs the village.

The village itself is a visual treat, with a charming central square with a water-pump in the middle and flanked by pubs and the fourteenth-century priory gatehouse, which forms an arch over a lane of attractive cottages. The gatehouse, formerly a grammar school, is now owned by the National Trust and sometimes houses exhibitions of contemporary works by members of the Lake Artists Society. Also in the square are two second-hand bookshops, and strewn around Cartmel's little maze of alleys and lanes are a few craft shops, while immediately to the west of the village is the Cartmel racecourse, the smallest National Hunt course (meetings are held on Sundays and Mondays at the spring and late summer Bank Holiday periods). Close to the church, in the opposite direction from the square, is an old milestone giving distances to Lancaster and Ulverston via the Morecambe Bay sands. St Mary's Lodge nearby offers high-quality teas in its guest-house dining-room.

West of Cartmel is **Holker Hall** (open Easter to Oct, daily exc Sat, 10.30 to 6, last admission 4.30), former home of the Dukes of Devonshire (now resident at Chatsworth House in Derbyshire) and in the same family for more than 300 years. The house was partly destroyed by fire in 1871, and, though part of the seventeenth-century house survives, what the public sees is entirely Victorian. But no expense was spared in the rebuilding of 1874, executed by Paley and Austin, fashionable architects of the day; this is reckoned to be their finest domestic design. The style is extravagant mock-Elizabethan, with marble fireplaces, mullioned windows and a cantilevered oak staircase (each of its balusters, which number over a hundred, is carved differently) which leads up to a richly furnished long gallery. There are some discreet touches attuning the house for comfortable living, including radiators disguised to blend in with the oak panelling, and electric light switches hidden behind dummy books. The house is sumptuously furnished throughout (and there is a welcome lack of roping-off). Pictures include a Van Dyck self-portrait and two early views of Whitehaven. In the grounds are 23 acres of formal and woodland gardens; the formal garden was laid out in the 1720s and has topiary. Joseph Paxton, the gardener at Chatsworth and designer of the Crystal Palace, advised on the redesigning of part of the garden.

Holker Hall also has many family-type side attractions, foremost among which is the **Lakeland Motor Museum**, which many (not just enthusiasts) will find highly entertaining. As well as a sizeable collection of cars through the ages, there is a reconstructed pre-war garage, lots of old advertising signs and a group of antique slot machines (which visitors can try out). Highlights include a 1914 Dennis fire engine, an 1885 Rudge Rotary (a bicycle of highly eccentric design), and a full-size replica of Donald Campbell's *Bluebird*. Nineteen-twenties dance music throbs in the background.

The Winster Valley

Not a huge river, but a pleasant, soft and undulating landscape of green meadows and patches of woodland, with the intrusion of a vast limestone cliff on the east side, make the Winster Valley and its labyrinth of narrow lanes well worth exploring – an unworrying north–south route which makes a much better drive than the A592.

Turn south from the A5074 at **Winster**, and you soon get into the heart of the valley. At **Strawberry Bank**, just to the west of the river, is the Masons Arms, a splendid pub with traditional furnishings and an enviable view over the valley; its renown for good pub food and an amazing array of bottled and draught beers means that it can get very crowded. Just up the road, to the west, you can get tea and cakes at Lightwood Farm (see p. 207).

Virtually every other signpost hereabouts seems to point the way to **Cartmel Fell Church**, sited obscurely in a dip at the end of a cul-de-sac. It was built in about 1504 as a chapel of ease in Cartmel parish, serving a scattered community of hill-farmers and their families: Cartmel itself is some seven miles away (see p. 189), and until Cartmel Fell was licensed for burial in 1712 corpses were taken to Cartmel. The

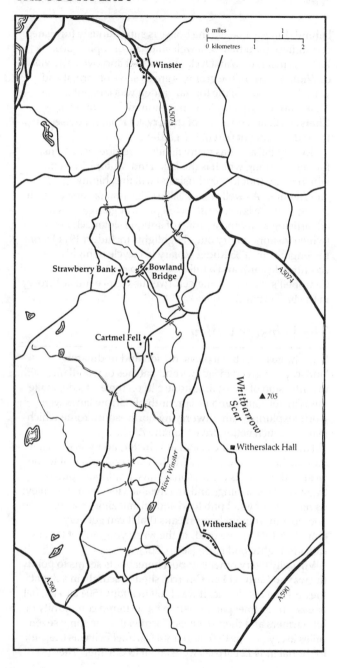

churchyard was used for many years for archery practice (look out for the grooves on the porch; these were probably made by people sharpening arrows). Inside the church are some interesting survivals, notably a three-decker pulpit and the Cowmire Pew (for the family from Cowmire Hall), actually made out of the old chancel screen: a bench inside the pew has an old children's game carved on it, probably the game of 'fox and geese' – a relic of the days when the church doubled as the village school. Behind the Cowmire Pew is a box pew dated 1696.

Like all the other settlements in the valley, **Witherslack** is effectively a scattered hamlet, though it does have its own church, a plain Gothic design of about 1669 with a screen consisting of two Ionic columns; the building was erected under the terms of the will of Royalist John Barwick, who was imprisoned for his beliefs in the Tower of London, and whose initials can be seen on the sundial.

Witherslack Hall, a nineteenth-century mansion which is now a school, lies a mile to the north of the church and is the most convenient starting-point for walks up **Whitbarrow Scar**, the natural wonder of the Winster Valley. See walk on p. 255.

The Lyth Valley

The northern end of the valley of the Rivers Pool and Gilpin (there is no river Lyth) has strong similarities to the Winster Valley – winding lanes over a patchwork of grassy fields punctuated by small groups of trees, with the distant backdrop of an abruptly rising limestone cliff to the east. Further to the south, the dale becomes less appealing as it broadens out and its floor is flat and fen-like. The principal road along the valley leaves the B5284 at Crook and heads south towards Brigsteer and Levens before reaching the A590.

Villages are large and shapeless, predominantly whitewashed houses and cottages, but there's nothing especially of note. Both **Crosthwaite** and **Underbarrow** are in lovely countryside, though have no particular intrinsic interest.

The Lyth Valley is famous for its damsons, which grow wild in places; Kendal used to hold a special annual damson fair for the sale of these.

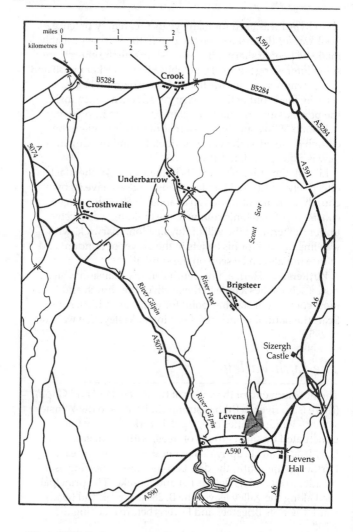

East of Underbarrow, the Kendal road rises up **Scout Scar**,
which like Whitbarrow Scar (see p. 193) is a cliff of
carboniferous limestone running north to south for several
miles. The limestone features on top of the cliff are much less
striking than Whitbarrow's, but the view of the Pennines and
Morecambe Bay is much more easily obtained. At the top of
the slope is a car-park; the path along the crest of the ridge is
opposite and slightly to the right, and it requires little effort

194

to reach the 'mushroom shelter', erected in 1912 to commemorate the coronation of George v.

Close to the junction of the A590 and A6 towards the southern end of the valley is **Levens Hall** (open Apr to mid-Oct, Sun to Thurs, 11 to 5; steam collection 2 to 5). The hall was built around a Norman peel tower, mostly extended from about 1570–90 by the Bellinghams, who transformed it into an outstanding Elizabethan mansion. Colonel Graham, a cousin of the family, bought it after the Bellingham fortune had been lost on gambling, and was responsible for much of the fine furniture the house now contains. Its limestone walls and mullioned windows give it something of the external appearance of a Cotswold manor (providing you ignore the peel tower!), while inside are fine carved overmantels, plaster ceilings and gracious period furnishings. Its yew topiary garden, one of the most celebrated in the country, was laid out in 1690. Purists may shudder when they hear that the present owners are marketing it as a family attraction, with steam traction rides for children to the playground at the far end of the grounds, plus a collection of scale model working steam engines, but it's all fairly restrained; an endearingly out-of-tune fairground organ is often in operation in the car-park. Across the road from the hall is the deer park, where black fallow deer and a rare breed of long-horned Bagot goats are to be found. Teas and light lunches are available in the house, and there is a gift shop.

Sizergh Castle (open Apr to late Oct, Sun, Mon, Weds and Thurs, 2 to 5.45) is further north, just off the A591 towards Kendal. Home of the Strickland family (staunch supporters of the Stuarts) for the last 700 years (although it is now actually owned by the National Trust), this is another house of ancient foundation which has been enlarged and modified into a delightful country house of predominantly Elizabethan character. Its 58-foot-high peel tower and remodelled Tudor great hall of 1450 have both been integrated into the later design. Of the Elizabethan work, the carved overmantels are outstanding, and there is much heavy panelling, although the finest of it (which hung in the Inlaid Chamber) was sold in the last century to the Victoria and Albert Museum. The house has a good collection of period furniture and family and Stuart portraits, including one by Romney. The gardens, laid from the eighteenth century onwards and completed in

1926, include a terrace from which steps lead down to a lake, a rock garden with ferns and dwarf conifers, and a 'wild' garden containing local limestone flora; to the side of the house are a rock garden and rose gardens. Teas and cakes are available in the house.

South of the Kent estuary

The north-east side of Morecambe Bay, south of the Kent estuary, lies outside the National Park boundary but has been designated an Area of Outstanding Natural Beauty. Like the bay's north side, it is characterised by low wooded limestone hills (offering some astonishing panoramas), lush farmland, and grey-stone towns and villages. The area around Arnside and Silverdale has some large caravan sites, but these are well screened from the coast and are reasonably unobtrusive.

From Milnthorpe to **Arnside** the B5282 runs close to the water's edge for much of the way, getting close-ups of the 50-pier Kent Viaduct (completed in 1857). Arnside itself has ancient origins as a fishing port, but is very much a nineteenth-century small-scale resort in character, with a cluster of guest-houses along its esplanade. At weekends it fills up with visitors, most of whom come for the scenery. Morecambe Bay's finest shoreline walk extends from Arnside southwards to Silverdale, and provides opportunities of viewing Britain's largest wader population (over 200,000 in the bay). Arnside Knott, the hill rising immediately behind the town, has lovely views of the bay and the southern fells, and is signposted from Arnside. Arnside Tower, just south of Arnside Knott, is a five-storey peel tower, thought to be fifteenth century, which can be seen from the top of the hill or from the road.

Silverdale, a smaller village, is not really on the bay: a road signposted to the shore from the village centre leads down to a huge area of marsh, across which a track makes its way to the sea (half a mile at low tide). There is a craft shop, Wolf House Gallery, to the south of the village, which has a textile workshop, art gallery and coffee-room.

Between Silverdale and Yealand Redmayne, **Leighton Moss** is an RSPB reserve, situated on an area of reed-beds and meres, with special hides for birdwatchers; literature about the reserve is available from the **visitor centre**. Among the

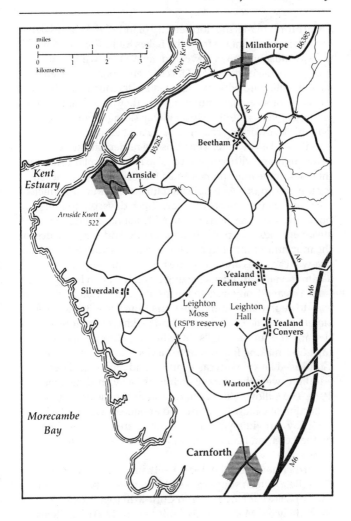

rarities are several pairs of bitterns (the only regular breeding colony in northern England) and water rail. The site is also fascinating for flora and fauna, offering a good illustration of the stages of natural succession from fen to mature woodland, and red deer and otters are found here. The reserve is open all year; day permits are available from the visitor centre, and there is free access along a public footpath which crosses the reserve.

Carnforth marks the northern tip of industrial Lancashire, but merits a pilgrimage from the Lakes for its **Steamtown** railway museum (open all year, daily, 9 (11 in winter) to dusk). The Lake District and its close environs have been steadily filling up with various steam attractions, but this is *the* place for steam locomotives. Here they are crammed into an unheated engine shed in a railway siding, dominated by Britain's last working coaling tower, next to the main London–Glasgow line. The locos are rather hard to see, being high up, with a dearth of raised viewing platforms, but there are some fine engines and a few carriages (unlabelled for the most part). A complicated timetable indicates which parts of the museum are open on which days; on 'full operating days', sections of line with standard and miniature steam engines are open, giving unlimited rides up and down the museum's mile of track – for 10 minutes you can sit in pre-war carriages and recapture the taste of long-distance steam travel, with 125s whizzing by on the main line.

At Yealand Conyers is the turn-off for **Leighton Hall** (open May to Sept, daily, 45-minute tours from 2 to 4.30), a small stately home nicely set in parkland looking over Morecambe Bay and the southern fells. In 1810 the Gillow family (of furniture-making fame) adapted a Georgian house into a Gothicised fancy, with castellations and pinnacles; later additions were the work of architects Paley and Austin in 1870. The Gillows still live here, and the house has a good collection of Gillow furniture and antique clocks. At 3.30 each day, providing it is not raining, there is a flying display by the Leighton Hall eagles, and visitors can volunteer to handle the birds.

Further north, off the A6, is **Beetham**. This lies on the River Bela, which supports a still-functioning paper-mill, on the opposite bank from **Heron Corn-Mill** (open Easter to Sept, daily exc Mon, 11 to 5), built around 1750 on a site that has had a mill on it since the thirteenth century. The mill closed in 1955 but has been restored to working order by a charitable trust. A 14-foot waterwheel turns four pairs of millstones, producing stone-ground flour and oatmeal which are on sale in the shop; there is also an exhibition about the history of the mill.

Just west of the village, on the Arnside road, a signpost points to **Fairy Steps**, a limestone cleft in an attractive wooded spot, with a natural flight of 'steps'.

Kendal

The largest town in the old county of Westmorland, and one of the most prosperous manufacturing centres of pre-Industrial Revolution England, Kendal is still very much a busy country town – home of the Kendal Mint Cake, K Shoes and Provincial Insurance as well as a regional centre for shopping. But despite some not very sensitive redevelopment which has nibbled away at the unity of the 'auld grey town', Kendal has plenty of historic survivals. It's also one of the best-endowed towns of its size in northern England for museums, and has a lively arts centre. In late August to early September the annual Kendal Gathering is held, a festival with lots of carnival-style events, including competitions, a torchlight procession, live music and exhibitions. Other events include the Westmorland County show in September and the Lakeland Rose Show in July.

Because Kendal is some way from the centre of the Lake District (in fact, a mile outside the National Park boundary), it tends to feel much more down to earth and less conditioned to tourism than the likes of Bowness-on-Windermere and Ambleside. There is so much of the old town meriting exploration – a lot of it is easily missed because of its complex layout – that it is best dealt with as an extended walkabout (see walk on p. 250).

Early Kendal was developed to the south of the present town centre: the Romans established a camp, Alauna, by the River Kent at a point where the river could be forded easily. Medieval Kendal grew up around Kirkland, which is now effectively the southern end of the main street around the parish church, where many ancient buildings have survived. The town began to be an important regional market from 1189, and the wool trade that became the key to Kendal's prosperity began to flourish in the thirteenth century (hence the town's motto, *Pannus mihi pani*, 'wool is my bread'). Green cloth, made for foresters, known as 'Kendal green', used to be manufactured here; it was the livery of Robin Hood and his men, and was mentioned in Shakespeare's *Henry IV (Part I)*: 'three misbegotten knaves in Kendal green came at my back and let drive at me'. Blue from woad was added to the dyer's yellow broom (which still grows in the Kent Valley) to obtain the green colouring. From the thirteenth to the nineteenth centuries many mills also operated by the River Kent, including saw-mills and mills producing bobbins, corn, paper and gunpowder.

The present-day focal-point of the town is the town hall, rebuilt in 1825 in baroque style, which dominates the main street, the section north of here being called **Stricklandgate**, and the section to the south being **Highgate**. A striking feature of this street is the number of yards leading from it, many of which were built in the 1700s to house people working in the weaving industry; there used to be over a hundred such yards, but many have been filled in by later development. Narrow openings often conceal wider alleys; many of the old yards were developed with back-to-back houses. The most interesting yards to have been retained are Dr Mannings Yard, Collin Croft (whose recent restoration won a Civic Trust award), Shakespeare Yard (which once had a theatre), New Inn Yard and the Old Shambles (which formerly housed a meat market; restored rough stone-walled cottages, cobbles and a handsome porticoed building sealing off the end). There are several reminders of the wool industry: examples are Sandes' Hospital (charitable almshouses built for widows of men who worked in the wool industry), the Fleece Inn (look for its coat of arms made up of wool-hooks and teasles) and Woolpack Yard.

The main street has some period shop-fronts. Two of the best of these are the pharmacy in Highgate and Farrer's tea and coffee shop, which has an iron doorway and eighteenth-century bow windows (there is also a cafe at the back of the shop). Above an estate agents door, opposite the library in Stricklandgate, is a curious shop-sign in the form of a hog with a bristle on its back, which used to advertise a brushmaker formerly on this site.

The **Brewery Arts Centre**, towards the southern end of Highgate, has a lot going on, and it is worth picking up a leaflet giving the month's programme. The centre usually shows several different films in one month, and theatrical events and concerts (predominantly rock, folk and jazz) are held here. Additionally, there is often a photographic exhibition, and there is a bar and cafe. A three-day folk festival is held at the end of August.

Off Stricklandgate to the east is a complex of streets around the **Market Place**, which leads into the sloping and cobbled street of Branthwaite Brow, where some buildings are fronted with iron. Market days are Saturday and

Wednesday, but there is also a flea-market on Monday. The New Shambles is a tiny alley with single-storey shops along one side, topped with improbably heavy-looking slate roofs. Like the Old Shambles, this was a meat market – Kendal's many slaughter-houses (there were over 10 in 1849) were far from hygienic, and probably contributed to a high mortality rate; the yards deliberately sloped so that blood and offal could drain from them.

In Stricklandgate's shopping centre a new Kendal Heritage Centre is due to open during 1989.

West of Stricklandgate and Highgate is a now pleasant area of back streets and ginnels (passageways or alleys between or through buildings) climbing the hillside. Some of Kendal's worst slums were once here, concentrated around a warren of lanes and stepped paths known as Fellside. Much of the area has been cleared away and redeveloped, but there is still quite a bit of character around Sepulchre Lane and its offshoots. To the south are some agreeable tree-lined streets built around long greens; the triangular green enclosed by Bankfield Road, Greenside and Brigsteer Road is thought to have been a former market place. From the county hospital, Captain French Lane slopes downhill, with a long row of cottages on its southern side. Ginnels from the north side of this lane lead to the site of Castle Howe, Kendal's first castle, built in around 1092 by the third baron of Kendal, Ketel de Tailbois. It is now just a grassy hillock, capped by an obelisk erected in 1788 to mark the centenary of the revolution which led to William of Orange taking over the throne from James II. This memorial was built by Webster's, a local building firm whose work now makes up much of the streetscape in the town centre, especially Stricklandgate and Stramongate.

Kirkland, the southern end of the main street, has quite a few ancient houses (most of which have been altered through the ages) as a reminder that this was the old centre. George Romney, a fashionable portrait painter of his day, lived at what is now known as Romney House at the southern end of Kirkland; a plaque records his death here in 1802. Kendal's parish church has the distinction of being the second widest in the country (at 103 feet it's only seven feet narrower than York Minster). It dates from the thirteenth century, though it has undergone a thorough nineteenth-century going-over. Three features of the church are the Parr Chapel (Catherine Parr's family lived at the 'new' castle), a memorial to George Romney, and a helmet and sword which traditionally are thought to have belonged to Robin, the Devil of Belle Isle, Windermere, who in the days of the Commonwealth rode into the church to avenge a Colonel Briggs who had besieged his house only to lose his helmet and sword here when he was struck down. The Ring o' Bells pub adjacent to the church was opened in 1741, initially functioning as a refreshment place for the church wardens.

Abbot Hall, next door to the church, comprises two-thirds of Kendal's excellent museum complex (open all year exc Christmas and Good Fri, daily, 10 to 5.30; 2 to 5 Sat and Sun). Combined entry tickets, giving admission to three museums for the price of two, are available, and there is no time-limit on when they must be used. The hall itself houses the **Art Gallery**, notable both for its paintings and for the rooms in which they hang. The house was built for Colonel George Wilson in 1759, who wanted an approximation of a country house in the heart of the town. Its eighteenth-century décor has been restored and the house filled with antique furniture, silver, glassware and porcelain. An important collection of paintings by Romney, including *The Gower Family*, forms the hub of the display, but there are several other major works, including Turner's *The Passage of the St Gothard* and watercolours by eighteenth- and nineteenth-century British artists, including Ruskin. Upstairs is a gallery devoted to contemporary art (the display changes, but there are often works on show by Ben Nicholson and German Dadaist Kurt Schwitters, late of Ambleside) and rooms for temporary exhibitions. There is a coffee shop around the side of the building.

The **Museum of Lakeland Life and Industry** sets out to present a picture of the Lake District's people, their work and lifestyles in the eighteenth, nineteenth and early twentieth centuries. It succeeds admirably: it's hard not to get swept up in the enthusiasm that the museum has obviously put into the displays, which are predominantly cleverly reconstructed scenes using objects that came from all over the Lake District – a printer's office (with some of the original proofs and printing-blocks for the Wainwright guides), a traditional farmhouse parlour (with eye-strainingly dim light giving the feel of what long winter evenings must have been like), a Victorian pharmacy, and numerous industries once typical of village Lakeland. Apart from a little shrine-like collection dedicated to the life and works of Arthur Ransome (his life's supply of pipes seems to be here), there is scarcely a glass case in sight. The museum has opted for a policy of minimal use of labels; most of the exhibits speak very well for themselves, but the museum guidebook is nevertheless recommended to enable you to get the most from a visit. Outside, reached through a door leading from the craft shop, is an annexe containing a farming gallery.

The third museum run by Abbot Hall, the Kendal Museum of Archaeology and Natural History, is on the north-east side of town (see p. 204).

East of the River Kent there is less to see in the way of historic streets, though the river and surrounding nineteenth-century residential roads are pleasant enough. The Lancaster Canal, which used to run roughly parallel to the river on this side, has now been filled in for the final stretch from Natland, two miles south of the town. After it opened in 1819, the canal provided a vital transport link with Lancaster, a key to Kendal's continuing prosperity in the early nineteenth century. An industrial complex grew up around Canal Head, near the junction of the head of the canal and the River Kent, close to the town centre.

Kendal's 'new' castle (always open) stands on a hill commanding a view of the whole town plus the Pennines, and is well worth taking in just for the panorama. It was built in around 1180 by Gilbert Fitz Reinfried, probably as a replacement for Castle Howe (see p. 201) which had been burnt down in a Scots raid in 1210, but it was probably a fortified manor house rather than a garrison. It was owned from the thirteenth to the sixteenth centuries by the Parr family (Catherine Parr was born here), but soon after that it fell into disrepair; its ruins now are scant, but some of the curtain wall survives, along with arches which formed the ground-floor store-rooms of the manor house and the remains of two round towers (one partly rebuilt in the nineteenth century).

In Wildman Street is **Castle Dairy**, the oldest inhabited house in Kendal, and also the house with the smallest window. It dates from the fourteenth century, and was refurbished in 1564 by Anthony Garnet. It's now an evening-only restaurant, but from Easter to October can also be visited on Wednesdays from 2 to 4. Close by in Station

Road is the **Kendal Museum of Archaeology and Natural History**, in which there is a room devoted to archaeology (including a scale model of Galava Roman Fort at Ambleside and various minor hoards), a world wildlife gallery with a large and slightly eerie collection of stuffed animals (including a multitude of animal heads staring down at visitors) arranged by continent, and (upstairs) a display giving the geological and natural history of the Lake District. This is by far the oldest of Kendal's museums (dating from 1796, when it was a private collection of curiosities), though one suspects it has now been somewhat eclipsed by the more prestigious Museum of Lakeland Life and Industry across the river. Nevertheless, it makes a good way of finding out about aspects of the Lake District, and most children will find the world wildlife display absorbing.

In Stramongate, the Corner Spot cafe and the (mostly vegetarian) Eat Fit are good value for lunch and tea; for dinner, Moon, in Highgate, is a small friendly restaurant with tasty wholefood cooking.

Kentmere and Longsleddale

This area is reached by taking the A591 northwards from Kendal. Kentmere and Longsleddale are both long, quiet valleys in hill-farming country; remote, and reminiscent of the Pennines. They are not much visited, as there are no sights and the scenery is not spectacular. The area's main devotees are hill-walkers wanting to get away from the bustle of the central Lakes.

Staveley, just off the A591 at the entrance to Kentmere Valley, has little distinction as a village, but its church is worth a look for its Burne-Jones east window, with gorgeously coloured glass depicting angels against a background of midnight blue.

The road up **Kentmere** is signposted from the centre of Staveley, and ends a mile beyond Kentmere village, after which point the Nan Bield Pass continues northwards on to the High Street range. Kentmere Tarn was made by draining a lake in the last century. Deposits of clay in the lake bed are now excavated for industrial purposes. A pleasant walk is to take a path from the church to Kentmere Hall (which has a fourteenth-century peel tower), just before which turn left along a track leading past the Tarn to the works, where the

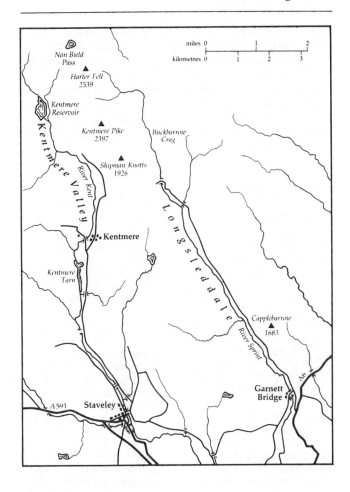

road can be picked up. Fragments of the primeval forest that once covered most of the Lake District are found in Kentmere, and because of their rarity value have been designated Sites of Special Scientific Interest.

If you are travelling from Staveley or Windermere towards Penrith or vice versa, a recommended scenic route is to take roads following the National Park boundary, using minor roads from Staveley to the hamlet of Garnett Bridge then north to Shap via the A6. Garnett Bridge is the access point for **Longsleddale**, which holds little for the motorist just wanting to drive up it; there is no settlement of any size and the best scenery, at its northern end, can be enjoyed only on foot. But it's a remote and lovely dale: a maze of mostly unsignposted lanes have to be followed to reach the valley's entrance, at Garnett Bridge, and the lane soon narrows further. Walks from here into Kentmere Valley can be made into circular routes, and it is quite possible to take in part of the High Street range as the highlight of a day's walking. Barren and virtually featureless moorland lies to the east of Longsleddale.

Where to stay

For a key to prices, see p. 10

Ambleside

Nanny Brow, Clappersgate, Ambleside, Cumbria LA22 9NF. Tel Ambleside (053 94) 32036
A secluded and immaculate Edwardian country-house hotel, in a woodland garden setting a mile west of Ambleside. The style is chintzy-traditional in the main house, modern-luxurious in the garden wing extension. £££

Kirkstone Foot Country House, Kirkstone Pass Road, Ambleside, Cumbria LA22 9EH. Tel Ambleside (053 94) 32232
Quietly set above Ambleside, a converted seventeenth-century manor house comfortably traditional in style and relaxed in atmosphere – until the rather formal set dinner at 8. Leave room for a choice of delectable puddings. ££

Rothay Manor, Rothay Bridge, Ambleside, Cumbria LA22 0EH. Tel Ambleside (053 94) 33605
Genteel luxury here, in a graceful Georgian house (a listed building) just out of Ambleside and not entirely free from traffic noise. The deep-pile comfort extends to the cuisine: rich and plentiful, with wonderful afternoon teas. £££

Wateredge Hotel, Borrans Road, Waterhead, Ambleside, Cumbria LA22 0EP. Tel Ambleside (053 94) 32332
The lake's the thing here: views down the length of Windermere from the public rooms and most (but not all) of the comfortable bedrooms. There are lakeside lawns, and boats for guests' use. The older part of Wateredge was a pair of fishermen's cottages, and the excellent dinners are served under low beams. A modern extension holds more spacious suites. ££

Cartmel

Aynsome Manor, Cartmel, Cumbria LA11 6HH. Tel Cartmel (053 95) 36653
A friendly, family-run hotel in a mostly Georgian manor, with older history in its cellars and appealing attic. Aynsome sits in open countryside, the great

priory in view. The polished, panelled, candle-lit dining-room is a memorable setting for high-quality cooking, and the assorted bedrooms have been made comfortable with no loss of character. ££

Uplands, Haggs Lane, Cartmel, Cumbria LA11 6HD. Tel Cartmel (044 854) 248
'In the Miller Howe manner' claims the brochure, and indeed it is, though less flamboyant. It's a restaurant (of considerable repute) with rooms, up the hill from Cartmel village, in green, quiet countryside. The lounge and dining-room are elegant and confidently done, with pastel pinks and greys, fine arts posters, classical music and plenty of comfortable corners. Rooms are on the small side, and there are just five of them; the flair of the set dinner is the point here. ££££

Cartmel Fell
Lightwood Farm, Cartmel Fell, Cumbria LA11 6NP.
Tel Grange-over-Sands (053 95) 31454
A 300-year-old farmhouse, attractively furnished with polished old bits and pieces; makes a friendly base for exploring southern Lakeland. Simple bedrooms, augmented by a couple of new ones. £

Crosthwaite
Crosthwaite House, Crosthwaite, Kendal, Cumbria LA8 8BP.
Tel Crosthwaite (044 88) 264
A three-storey Georgian building, just outside the village on a B-road which carries very little traffic, with rolling views beyond Crosthwaite church. Square rooms, stripped wood and fresh décor, comfortable and cheerful, is the style. The dining-room has stripped floorboards and a marble fireplace; the lounge has an open fire, big armchairs, knick-knacks and a loud cuckoo clock. Bedrooms are not huge, but uncluttered and sensitively decorated. All this, plus the copious five-course dinner, adds up to very good value. £

Grasmere
White Moss House, Rydal Water, Grasmere, Cumbria LA22 9SE.
Tel Grasmere (096 65) 295
Formed from three eighteenth-century cottages between Ambleside and Grasmere, this caring small hotel makes up for little rooms by providing many pleasing extras, from maps to White Moss lavender. Two bedrooms are in a peaceful annexe. The set dinners are excellent: interesting British cooking, with fine wines – a Muscat for dessert – and a splendid choice of cheeses. ££££

Hawkshead
Field Head House, Outgate, Hawkshead, Cumbria LA22 0PY. Tel Hawkshead (096 66) 240
A friendly country-house hotel about a mile outside Hawkshead, in pretty grounds that include the vegetables featuring strongly in the host's excellent and imaginative cooking. Two comfortable lounges allow you to enjoy or avoid the introductory pre-dinner drinks. £££

Queen's Head, Hawkshead, Cumbria LA22 0NS. Tel Hawkshead (096 66) 271
Guests staying at this whitewashed old inn in the pedestrianised centre of Hawkshead are given free passes to the village car-park. Bedrooms are neat, creaky and charming, and there's an oak-panelled restaurant behind the popular pub and snug. No children under 10. £

Rydal

Nab Cottage, Rydal, Ambleside, Cumbria LA22 9SD. Tel Grasmere (096 65) 311
Keeping much of its character from the time it was home of Hartley Coleridge and Thomas De Quincey, Nab Cottage offers farmhouse cooking in a very central location. It overlooks Rydal Water, and considerable daytime traffic; and it's cosy rather than comfortable, with no private bathrooms. £

Troutbeck Bridge

Quarry Garth, Troutbeck Bridge, Windermere, Cumbria LA23 1LF. Tel Windermere (096 62) 3761
Close to Brockhole, between Ambleside and Windermere, and just off the main road – muted traffic noise is audible from the front windows. The grounds are very pretty, with a stream, shrubberies and a terrace; and the house has Edwardian solidity, a rendered structure of the Arts and Crafts style, with oak panelling in the lounges, and old-fashioned brass fittings on the doors. The owners have kept the style plain, letting the building speak for itself; like the building, the cooking is competent and traditional. Bedroom size varies considerably, and rooms at the front of the building are lighter than those at the back. £££

Windermere

Miller Howe, Rayrigg Road, Windermere, Cumbria LA23 1EY. Tel Windermere (096 62) 2536
Celebrated as a gourmets' paradise – and also for its thoughtful service – Miller Howe is perched above the lake with wonderful views of the peaks beyond. Accommodation is sumptuous, and the food is internationally acclaimed; dinner is served with theatrical flamboyance, breakfast preceded by Buck's Fizz. No children under 12. £££££

Witherslack

The Old Vicarage, Witherslack, Grange-over-Sands, Cumbria LA11 6RS. Tel Witherslack (044 852) 381
A secluded little late-Georgian house in gentle walking country. William Morris fabrics contribute to its attractive style, and bedrooms are very comfortably equipped. Bread is home made, and breakfast is particularly good; the imaginative set dinners are high-quality English cooking. £££

Bed and breakfast

The area east of Windermere, notably the Trout Beck, Winster and Lyth Valleys, is quiet and unspoilt and makes a good base for anyone wanting to escape from the busier parts of the district; this is not true upland landscape, however.

Hawkshead and Near Sawrey and Far Sawrey also have plenty of accommodation, and the surroundings are very attractive (though a little more overrun). Grasmere has the advantages of scenic splendour and a central position, so not surprisingly it thrives as a guest-house resort; in summer the place gets very busy, but its facilities (on a par with a small town) are useful. For anyone prepared to forgo the convenience of centrality for the pleasure of staying in a delightful village, Cartmel is recommended. Accommodation in the resort towns – Ambleside, Windermere and Bowness – is plentiful and convenient, but mainly much of a muchness, and the towns themselves are not that special. Kendal is too far from the lakes to appeal to most people.

Walks

The Lake District's fame as a walking area derives from the immense scenic variety found over a relatively small area, all at a scale made for walking. The network of paths is dense, and many are well marked on the ground, and there is open access over many of the fells; accordingly it is impossible to exhaust the area's possibilities in one stay. Even when mist denies a walk on the fell tops, there is huge scope for excellent easy low-level walks – along valley floors, by lakesides or through woods to see a waterfall. In better visibility it's worth making an effort to get up to a viewpoint; by no means are these ascents all arduous. If you have little experience as a fell-walker, be sure to walk well within your abilities – start with easy strolls before gradually progressing to more challenging walks.

This chapter describes the best walks in the district. The ones with directions and a map can be attempted without the use of an Ordnance Survey (OS) map (assuming the weather is good). Others, listed under Walks in Outline for each section, are summaries – full directions are not needed either because the routes are easy to follow (they nevertheless require the appropriate OS *Outdoor Leisure Map* (see p. 265), and it's prudent to take a compass on all walks, particularly on the fells) or because the walks outlined refer to *The Holiday Which? Good Walks Guide*, which describes the walks in full. This guide is also edited by Tim Locke and published by Consumers' Association and Hodder & Stoughton.

A second walks guide – *The Holiday Which? Town and Country Walks Guide* – edited by Tim Locke and published by Consumers' Association and Hodder & Stoughton is also available. It features a further seven walks in the Lake District.

If you are venturing on to the fells, it's worth bearing in mind some basic rules of mountain safety. Each year, people are killed on the fells – often through carelessness. The Mountain Rescue Teams, staffed by volunteers, have frequent call-outs to the fells, sometimes in dire conditions. Whenever you plan on walking the fells, follow these precautions:

Dress sensibly Wear walking-boots with a good sole; falls on slippery rock or even grass can result in a twisted ankle or worse.

Carry waterproofs (including leggings) to keep out wind as well as rain. Take a spare jumper and spare socks in case you get cold or wet. Don't wear jeans (they restrict movement when wet). Hats are invaluable in cold weather (most of the body heat escapes through the head).

Watch the weather It can be a great disappointment to arrive for a week's walking in the Lakes and be confronted daily with dismal weather. Except for hardened hill-walkers and self-confessed masochists, few will derive pleasure from a slog up a mist-enveloped peak in a howling gale; instead, you would probably do better resigning yourself to lower-level walks. What is more of a problem as regards safety is the seemingly delightful day which changes for the worse. The Lake District can show astonishing changes in weather from one valley to the next – thick mist on one side of a

Difficulty

All the walks are graded for difficulty with a figure from 1 to 5. In assessing the degree of difficulty, the conditions underfoot, any steep slopes and the length of the walks have been taken into account. Grading sometimes straddles two categories.

Difficulty 1 *Very easy*
Mostly on the level; suitable for anyone who can manage a few miles – families with small children, for example. Wear stout shoes or wellingtons.

Difficulty 2 *Easy*
Within the capabilities of most occasional walkers; be prepared for stiles, gentle slopes and occasional roughish terrain. Wear stout shoes or wellingtons.

Difficulty 3 *Middling*
Suitable for moderately keen ramblers: no major ascents. Walking-boots strongly advisable.

Difficulty 4 *Energetic*
Within the capabilities of a reasonably experienced walker, but be prepared for some sizeable ascents and descents. Walking-boots and suitable clothing essential.

Difficulty 5 *Demanding*
For fit and reasonably experienced walkers only, and not to be attempted in poor weather. Expect major hill or mountain ascents. Walking-boots and suitable clothing essential.

The timings given are for an average walker, in good weather. They do not include stopping times.

ridge, bright sunshine on the other. National Park information centres display the day's forecast (including cloud levels) in their windows; for recorded weather forecasts telephone Windermere (096 62) 5151. When planning a fell walk, allow for an escape route if the weather turns against you.

Take food and suitable equipment Take more than enough food and drink for the time you think you will be away. Essential gear includes first-aid kit (particularly plasters for blistering feet), torch, compass, whistle (six blasts once a minute is the distress signal), OS map and survival bag.

Tell people where you are going Leave your day's itinerary at your hotel or youth hostel so a rescue party can be sent out if you fail to return. Don't forget to announce your safe arrival at the end of the day.

Walk carefully Zigzag up and down slopes (keeping to the path if there is one) – this is not only less tiring but causes far less erosion. Don't walk too fast uphill: a rhythmic plod without too many stops is a more effective way of covering ground than a breathless rush interspersed with breaks for rest. If the weather turns nasty, put your spare clothes on; in extreme cold, huddle together with other members of the party and improvise a shelter against a wall or crag.

If someone in your party has an accident Blow a whistle or flash a torch six times a minute. Then get someone to stay with the injured person (if he or she can't move), and go for help, noting the precise location of your companions (taking a grid reference if possible). Telephone the police, who will call out the Mountain Rescue Team.

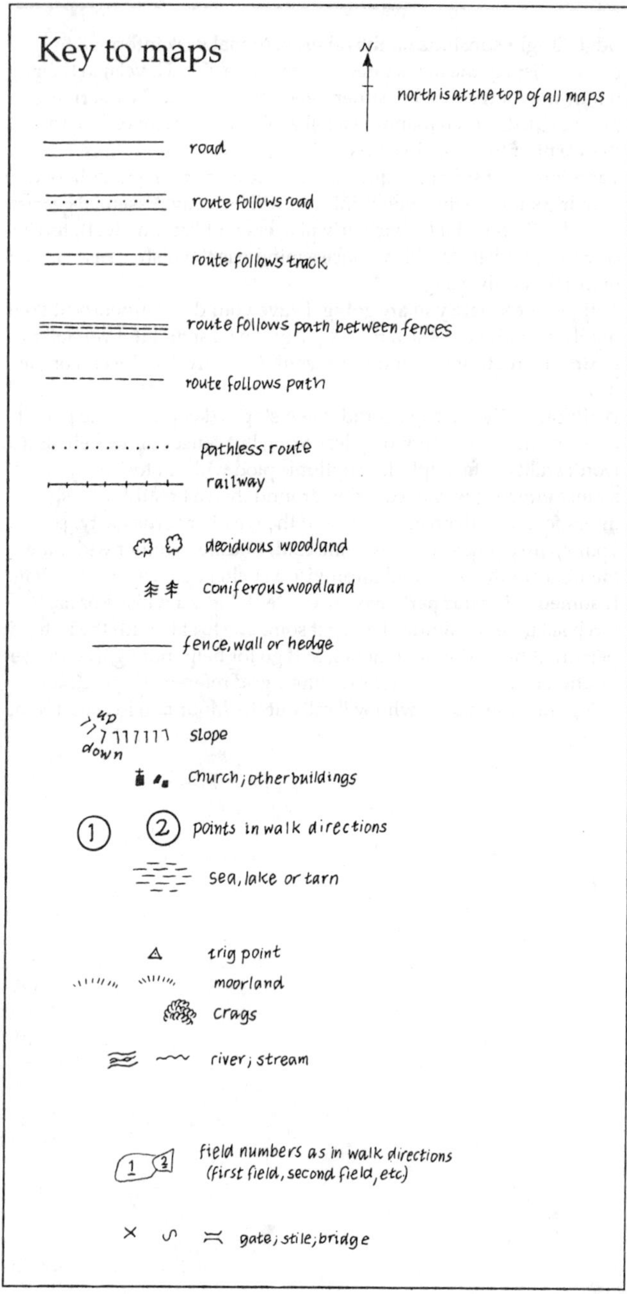

Key to maps

N

north is at the top of all maps

——————— road

············· route follows road

======= route follows track

========= route follows path between fences

– – – – – – route follows path

············· pathless route

+—+—+—+ railway

❀ ❀ deciduous woodland

⌇ ⌇ coniferous woodland

——————— fence, wall or hedge

slope *up / down*

▮ ▪ Church; other buildings

① ② points in walk directions

sea, lake or tarn

△ trig point

moorland

crags

river; stream

field numbers as in walk directions
(first field, second field, etc)

× ∿ ⌒ gate; stile; bridge

THE NORTH-WEST

Easy walks

Buttermere and Rannerdale Knotts

A figure-of-eight-shaped route which can be treated as two separate short walks. The first section is the circuit of Buttermere, one of the most satisfying lake circuits and just about the easiest, all on the level and with no real problems of route-finding; expect crowds on fine summer days. The surrounding fells give the lake its appeal, with the high wall of the Red Pike–High Crag ridge to the south, the jagged outline of Haystacks to the south-east and the milder green slopes of High Snockrigg to the north. One short section through a tunnel adds further to the interest of the route.

Rannerdale Knotts is the group of small crags at the end of Low Bank, a grassy ridge which makes an excellent fell walk in miniature, on a par with Cat Bells but less well known; views of Lorton Vale and the Cumbrian Coast.

Buttermere circuit

Length 3½ miles (5.5 km), 1½ hours **Difficulty** 1
Refreshments Bridge Hotel, Fish Inn and a snack bar, all in Buttermere
Start Buttermere village car-park. Alternatively, start at Gatesgarth (free car-park) at point ③
Directions ① From Buttermere car-park, take road past Fish Inn to B5289 by Bridge Hotel, and turn right along road. After 50 yards, turn right through farm (signposted lakeshore path). ¼ mile later, turn right in front of gate, signposted lakeside path. ② At road, continue forward along it to reach Gatesgarth. ③ At Gatesgarth, take track on right by post-box, signposted to Buttermere. Pass through farm, then immediately fork right. Track heads towards stone wall that skirts base of fell ④; turn right (signposted Buttermere). Soon reaching a point level with lake, proceed, ignoring all left forks, and keep as close as possible to lakeside. ⑤ At end of lake head for footbridge 50 yards away to right. Then follow clear path (later becomes track) to Buttermere village.

Rannerdale Knotts circuit

Length 2½ miles (4 km), 1½ hours **Difficulty** 2–3 (2 if returning same way from Rannerdale Knotts)
Directions ⑥ Start on B5289 and find signposted path by NT sign for Ghyll Woods, opposite Bridge Hotel. Path leads up through woods: keep along left side of stream. ⑦ At end of wood, leave by ladder stile. Beyond it, take path opposite and slightly to left. This ascends; after 7–8 minutes you will be level with nearest crags. Beyond them, fork left: your objective is the low humpy ridge to the left (soon comes into view), with rocky knob at far end. Clear path leads along

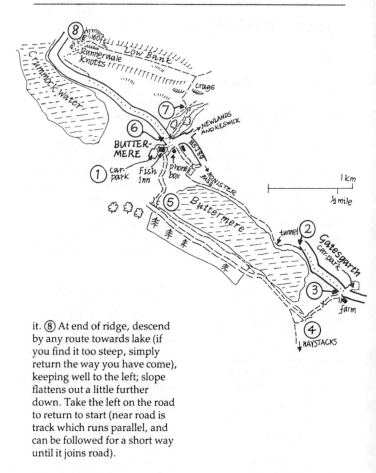

it. ⑧ At end of ridge, descend
by any route towards lake (if
you find it too steep, simply
return the way you have come),
keeping well to the left; slope
flattens out a little further
down. Take the left on the road
to return to start (near road is
track which runs parallel, and
can be followed for a short way
until it joins road).

Loweswater

Quite a rewarding walk around the lake, which borrows the fells
around Crummock Water for its backdrop. Optional detour up
Darling Fell, the fell which dominates Loweswater as you look
across from its southern side. Hardly anyone goes up there; it's a
rather tedious 25-minute ascent, but the views are extraordinary,
with the heart of the Lakeland fells to one side, and a flattish plain
leading to the coast, and with the Scottish Lowlands beyond
on the other.

Length (lake circuit only)
3 miles (5 km), 1¼ hours
Difficulty 1

Length (lake circuit plus ascent
of Darling Fell) 4 miles (6.5 km),
2¼ hours **Difficulty** 3

Start 300 yards after the north end of the lake: there's a wide verge on the west side of the road for parking, close to a Public Footpath sign and nearly opposite Mossergate Bridleway sign

Directions ① Standing with lake behind you, take signposted public footpath on left into field; route across fields is well waymarked. In first field, follow right edge until stile on right into second field; then proceed slightly diagonally across second field to footbridge; maintain direction in boggy third field, aiming for gate/stile in corner ②. From here, proceed forward (half-left) on tarmacked lane, uphill. At next farm, proceed forward (signposted Holme Wood). ③

After leaving wood, when you reach a farm, keep left on track. ④ By car-park, where track becomes tarmacked, keep left. ⑤ Turn left at T-junction with road. Follow this along north-east side of lake, back to start or ⑥ fork right after one mile, up lane signposted to Mosser (unsuitable for motor vehicles). ⑦ ¼ mile after lane emerges from trees, cross stile up on right, signposted Foulsyke. Ascend to summit (easiest way is to turn immediately left and proceed alongside fence). From top, return down to stile, then turn right on lane. ⑧ After ¼ mile, take signposted track on left between fences and descend to road. Left at bottom and return to start.

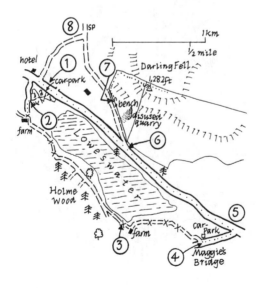

Derwent Water: Friar's Crag, Great Wood and Castle Head

This walk takes in the shores of Derwent Water at their most magical, fine woods frequented by red squirrels, and a view summing up this mellow and richly varied landscape from the top of Castle Head.

Length 4 miles (6.5 km), 2 hours **Difficulty** 1
Refreshments Cafe near Lakeside car-park
Start Lakeside car-park, Keswick. To reach this on foot from centre of Keswick (well signposted), take Lake Road (behind Moot Hall, and by Barclays Bank), turn right opposite Four in Hand pub, under subway at end of road, alongside park, join road and continue forward to car-park

Directions ① Left out of car-park, taking road along lakeshore. Road soon becomes track, passing landing-stages and entering woods. Continue

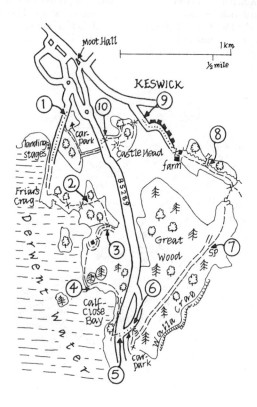

along lakeside, past Friar's Crag (NT sign). Path soon emerges into meadow then enters woods by gate. ② 75 yards after gate, fork left, soon crossing footbridge. ③ Pass through next gate into meadow. Immediately turn right on track; soon pass through another gate. 50 yards later, fork left as signposted, on path, where main track bends right to house. Follow path through next group of trees to reach Calfclose Bay ④. Half way across bay is footbridge; 100 yards later, path enters woods; 150 yards later, pass wooden bench and keep left, close to main road. ⑤ After further 80 yards, find 'squeeze stile' (a deliberate gap in the wall) giving access to road. Turn right on road, then immediately left on tarmac track (No Entry sign refers to vehicles). ⑥ At car-park, take gate on right-hand side of car-park, signposted Walla Crag and Ashness Bridge. 70 yards later, turn left (uphill) by signpost for Walla Crag. Follow track for ½ mile. ⑦ Fork right, signposted Walla Crag and Rakefoot. Path soon leaves forest by stile, then proceed on enclosed path to reach T-junction of paths. Turn left, downhill. ⑧ 30 yards after path turns right, into woods, keep left (avoiding footbridge away to right). Descend dingle, with stream on right. At bottom, pass through farm, then continue along residential road. ⑨ After ¼ mile, opposite Wood Close House, take path on left inconspicuously signposted to Castle Head Wood. Enter woods by gate, and immediately keep right. Skirt right edge of woods, detouring left via obvious route to summit. Return to same path and leave woods by gate on far side ⑩. Turn left on road, then right after 100 yards on fenced path between fields. At woods, turn right and follow woodland path to car-park.

Borrowdale: Castle Crag

Borrowdale's finest close-up vantage-point: a precipitous wooded crag which dominates the valley; also good views north of Derwent Water and Skiddaw. Looks almost impossible to climb when you first see it after emerging from the woods by the River Derwent, but there is a fairly easy winding path to the top. Quite a bit of spoil from the abandoned slate quarries in the final stages of the ascent, but this presents no problems providing you are sensibly shod.

Length 2 miles (3 km), 1 hour **Difficulty** 2–3 **Refreshments** In Grange **Start** Grange (Borrowdale) **Directions** ① Take signposted bridleway roughly opposite church. ② Take first turning on left (after ¼ mile). ③ Reach river, continue for 100 yards, then at signpost for Honister and Seatoller (in front of dry-stone wall) fork right, soon leaving forest by gate ④. Castle Crag is the fell immediately to the left: continue past it to a large cairn, where the main path crosses a stream by a stone slab ⑤. Bear half-left here, to leave main path. Path is faint at beginning. After 50 yards, bear sharp left heading towards bench and memorial stone 100 yards ahead. Beyond wall before you, path becomes clear. Ascend to top (through quarry spoil for last section). Return same route.

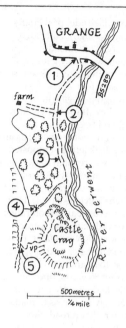

St John's in the Vale

A well-varied route with excellent distant views in the opening sections, notably northwards towards Skiddaw, then later the unspoilt, more intimate scenery of St John's in the Vale – at its best from this path. Three ancient packhorse bridges en route – near Bridge End Farm, near the A591 and at Sosgill.

Length 5 miles (8 km), 2¼ hours **Difficulty** 2
Start Car-park at Legburthwaite (½ mile north of the A591, beyond the northern end of Thirlmere). Not very well signposted, so take the B5322 south of Legburthwaite for 100 yards until you reach a large wooden outbuilding on the west side of road; turn off here into car-park
Directions ① Exit via back of car-park on to lane, and turn left along it to reach A591. Take minor road directly opposite,

signposted Public Road Around Lake. 75 yards later, fork right into Bridge End Farm. In farmyard, turn right opposite farmhouse, pass through pen and small gate, and descend through field aiming for stone bridge ②. After bridge, path soon enters field: turn left as signposted along edge of this and next field. In third field, proceed 30 yards and then take entrance into derelict farm on left. Pass through farmyard, through gate on other side, then along track to road ③. Turn right on road, then take hard track on left after 50 yards. Follow this for ½ mile; woodland eventually appears on both sides. ④ Shortly before woodland ceases on right, fork right on to grassy track (signpost on it, facing other way, for long-distance footpath to Dunmail). Follow into next

farm, and keep right at end of farmyard. 100 yards later, just before cottages up on left, turn right on track and follow to main road ⑤. Left on road for 100 yards, then take minor road sharp right. After 80 yards, take gate on left, follow grassy track for 50 yards, and as it veers right take gate on left. Follow path across hummocky

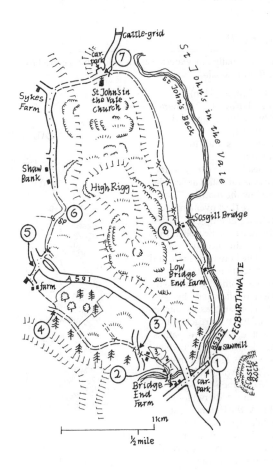

ground, heading towards nearest house, ⑥ ignoring signpost pointing to left (towards ladder stile) after 300 yards. At house, proceed along tarmacked lane; keep straight on at next junction, signposted St John's in the Vale Church, then take hard track on right (again signposted to church) where lane leads into Sykes Farm. ⑦ At church, proceed along lane, then, when level with end of churchyard, take signposted bridleway on right. Follow for 1 mile. ⑧ Where sign indicates route ahead is for Low Bridge End, you can take gate on left close by low stone barn, to take in Sosgill Bridge, an old stone bridge. The two routes rejoin just before next farm. Follow path, which soon runs along river again, to main road. Left and left again to return to car-park.

Taylor Gill Force

An exceptionally fine waterfall at the side entrance to a broad valley just off Borrowdale.

Length 2 miles (3 km), 1 hour **Difficulty** 2 (generally level but a little boggy and rough in places)
Refreshments Cafe in Seathwaite
Start Seathwaite car-park. If car-park is full, start at Seatoller and follow the road to Seathwaite (just over a mile)
Directions Entering Seathwaite from Seatoller, turn right opposite second cottage, taking gate between barns, and follow track to footbridge. Cross the footbridge and then turn left to follow path by brook. The path passes patches of woodland then reaches a ladder stile. From here, path is slightly less clearly defined, but route is easy. Head for trees at foot of Seathwaite Fell – the detached dome-shaped fell straight ahead; do not lose height. At the last moment, waterfall appears. Short (optional) scramble a few feet up to a gate for close-up view. Return the same way.

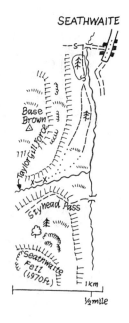

SEATHWAITE

Easy walks in outline

Derwent Water The paths around Friar's Crag and near Brandelhow Park offer majestic views of the lake and its islands.

Watendlath can be reached from Rosthwaite (see p. 53) and elsewhere in Borrowdale. *The Holiday Which? Good Walks Guide* walk 133 is a circular route taking in Watendlath, the Lodore Falls and the Bowder Stone. Borrowdale itself is beautiful throughout, and there are several excellent walks in this valley. A fine ramble which more or less keeps to the valley floor is from Seatoller to Grange via the River Derwent and back via the route to Castle Crag mentioned on p. 219.

Latrigg gives good views of Derwent Water, its surrounding fells and Borrowdale: an easy one-mile stroll from the Skiddaw car-park; longer and less pleasant (because of traffic noise from the A66) if starting from Keswick (see p. 46).

Scale Force The tallest waterfall in the Lake District is reached from Buttermere or Loweswater (see p. 56).

Whitehaven to St Bees The coastal section between these two places (both well worth visiting in their own right) has a clifftop path, which makes for good walking. St Bees Head is an RSPB nature reserve with special platforms for birdwatching. Throughout the walk there are views of the Isle of Man. The Whitehaven end passes a strange landscape of coal spoil from the now-closed coal-mines and won't appeal to everyone. Inland, the scenery has nothing to offer the walker, so the return route must be by bus or train (check times before travelling; note the train does not run on Sundays). See *The Holiday Which? Good Walks Guide* walk 124.

Walla Crag is the highest point (1234 feet) close to the east side of Derwent Water, where rolling moorland suddenly breaks off at great (near vertical) crags just above the top of the forest, from where there are lovely views of the lake, Skiddaw, Bassenthwaite Lake and the Derwent Fells. Start at Great Wood car-park, off the B5289 on the east side of Derwent Water. Return either down Cat Gill or continue on to Ashness Bridge.

Lanthwaite Hill (see p. 58) is an easily reached hillock near Crummock Water, a short distance from the road, with a good panorama of Lorton Vale.

Spout Force (see p. 60) is on a waymarked Forestry Commission two-mile walk in the Whinlatter Pass.

Thornthwaite Forest (see p. 60) offers waymarked walks of various lengths, from the 1½-mile Forest Trail to the excursion up Lord's Seat (1811 feet), giving views of Skiddaw and Bassenthwaite Lake. A map is available from the visitor centre.

Ennerdale Forest has three waymarked forestry and lakeside walks – the Smithy Beck Trail, the Nine Becks Walk and the Liza Path – with thorough waymarking and with maps displayed on boards;

alternatively, buy a map from an information centre (note that there is no information centre in Ennerdale).

In the grounds of *Mirehouse* is a waymarked walk taking in a section of the shore of Bassenthwaite Lake. Details of the house are on p. 65.

Dodd Wood (p. 65) has Forestry Commission trails; the longest ascends the 1647-foot summit.

In *Whitehaven*, leaflets about the well-conceived town trail are available from the tourist information centre.

There are walks along the west shore of *Thirlmere* with trails for Launchy Gill and Swirls Forest (the latter on the A591 side of the lake).

Guided walks start at the Moot Hall, Keswick, and Buttermere car-park; details from the National Park information centres.

Fell walks

Whiteless Pike and Whiteside

Whiteless Pike and Whiteside, with Grasmoor, are a notable trio of peaks joined by a complex of ridges, giving a wonderful walk on the grassy ridges high above Buttermere, Crummock Water and Coledale. Grasmoor dominates Crummock Water, but in this route the ridge leading to Whiteside is the grand climax, with astonishing views of the Cumbrian coast and across the Solway Firth into Scotland.

Length 7½ or 9 miles (12 or 14.5 km), 4 hours or 4¾ hours, depending on whether detour is made on to Grasmoor and back

Difficulty 4–5 (some loose stones in final, very steep descent. Route-finding quite easy in clear weather; OS map not very helpful in early stages)

Start Cinderdale car-park on the B5289 by Crummock Water

Directions ① From car-park, with lake on right, follow road 50 yards to next car-park. Take signposted track out of car-park. Track almost immediately crosses stream then runs along the level, eventually veering gently left and soon passing through gate. ② Beyond next gate, track

ends: continue forward, along bottom of wide valley; your objective is lowest point of pass ahead, formed by Whiteless Pike to left (with pointed peak) and Low Bank to right. Before you reach it is a fence/wall; cross wall 100 yards to left of where it meets fence (there is a hurdle here, but fence still requires stepping over); then proceed up to top of pass where ③ turn sharp left on to well-defined path, ascending Whiteless Pike. ④ From summit, path proceeds along Whiteless Edge; Grasmoor, the closest major summit, is on the left. ⑤ Reach crossing of paths: straight on is continuation, left is optional detour to Grasmoor. Route continues along slight

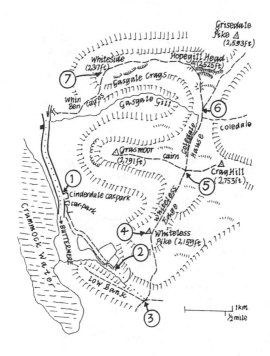

valley (Coledale Hause), with Hopegill Head visible ahead. ⑥ Suddenly, big view opens up on right down valley of Coledale: keep left here (right ascends Grisedale Pike). Path ascends minor summit of Sand Hill and continues up Hopegill Head, then continues left along ridge to Whiteside. ⑦ At end of ridge, keep to left, looking for a steep cairned path dropping down towards Whin Ben, a pronounced ridge far below. Beyond it route is obvious in clear weather. At bottom, cross footbridge, left on stony track, then left on road and follow back to starting-place.

Cat Bells, High Spy and Newlands

A walk of contrasting halves, offering gentle walking in the Newlands Valley then, after a 1500-foot haul up to High Spy, a long and glorious ridge section, slightly downhill for three miles. At High Spy the views are distant and the foreground heathy and only just undulating, but the ridge tapers almost to a knife-edge at Cat Bells

225

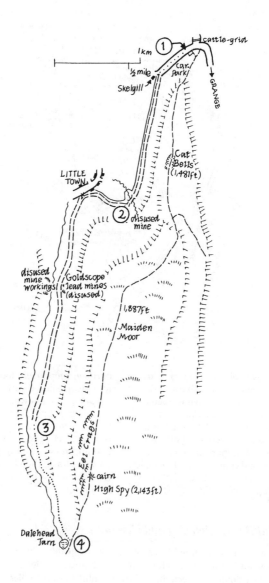

(where some care is needed with footing), from where there is a classic panorama of Derwent Water and Skiddaw. See also *The Holiday Which? Good Walks Guide* walks 134 and 136 for routes along this ridge, taking in Borrowdale and the shores of Derwent Water.

Length 7 miles (11 km), 4 hours **Difficulty** 3–4
Start Cat Bells car-park (between Grange and Portinscale)
Directions ① With car-park on left, follow road to Skelgill (house). At house, road ends: pick up stony track on left (initially ascending), alongside wall. ② As soon as track crosses footbridge, it swings right, still alongside wall, getting close to road by hamlet (Little Town), but not quite reaching it. Track then enters valley. Towards end of valley ③, track becomes intermittent narrow path and soon becomes indistinct; make your way to lowest point in skyline at head of valley, keeping stream away to right. ④ At top, turn left along well-defined path and ascend further to cairn on High Spy, the highest point on this walk. Then follow ridge path all the way. Ridge eventually narrows and culminates in a series of dramatic humps (Cat Bells). Follow to end of ridge, and descend to car-park.

Fell walks in outline

Skiddaw is most easily ascended via a broad track from Keswick, crossing the A66 by a footbridge and continuing to a car-park near Underscar Hotel (this car-park is an alternative starting-point, though it fills up early in the day in summer). No route-finding difficulties: just follow the crowds. There are good views, but these are behind you all the way up its 3054 feet. More varied but much less frequented and a little more challenging is the western approach from the Ravenstone Hotel on the A591 and along the ridge via Ullock Pike; from the summit bear north to Whitewater Dash to join a track leading westwards to the road. See also p. 45.

Grisedale Pike (2593 feet) and *Crag Hill* (2753 feet) make a horseshoe-shaped ridge walk from Braithwaite, with good views and slopes plunging far below. Crag Hill is the highest point on the route, but Causey Pike, the prominent summit near the end of the walk, is probably the best-loved feature of the range. See *The Holiday Which? Good Walks Guide* walk 137.

Red Pike (2479 feet) and *High Stile* (2644 feet) are best walked from Buttermere village: a steep but constantly interesting ascent over wild terrain, following Sour Milk Gill up to Bleaberry Tarn, and then up on to the ridge, whose south side drops steeply down to Ennerdale. A nice, unworrying return route along the shore of Buttermere provides a total contrast. See *The Holiday Which? Good Walks Guide* walk 135

Haystacks, at 1900 feet, is not the tallest fell in the area by any means, but one of the most climbed, and it is easy to see why as soon as one catches sight of Haystacks' jagged outline. On top there is a profusion of pointed crags, tarns, marshy areas and screes, plus a view of Lorton Vale and Ennerdale. It is only just over 1000 feet of ascent from the car-park at the top of the Honister Pass. A more satisfying round walk, but still a relatively easy one, can be made by starting from Gatesgarth (just south-east of Buttermere; Haystacks is directly south of Gatesgarth), taking a track by the post-box (signposted Buttermere), crossing flat meadows until the base of the fell is reached, where the Scarth Gap Pass heads up diagonally to the left. From the top the route continues east before striking downhill via Warnscale Bottom.

THE NORTH-EAST

Easy walks

Binsey

Binsey, at 1467 feet, gives a magnificent northern view of the Lakes; it is not at all difficult to ascend and is very little known.

Length 1 mile (1.5 km), ½ hour **Difficulty** 2 (no bogs or difficult terrain, although there is no defined path to the summit)
Start Take the A591 Keswick–Bothel, turn right at the signpost for Bewaldeth, north of Bassenthwaite Lake, and, a mile later, park on the roadside at a group of cottages and a farm (Fell End)

Directions Take gate on left just beyond the last cottage as approached from the A591. Binsey is ahead; make straight for a fixed gate in wall (there is a movable gate 100 yards to the left of it, but this was in a state of near disintegration at the time of inspection), then make your way up to the top.

Shap Abbey and Keld

A short stroll through stone-walled pasture, getting views of the Shap Fells – austere and incredibly empty. Use this as a link route between Shap Abbey and Keld chapel (see p. 111). Return the same way.

Length 1½ miles (2.5 km), ¾ hour **Difficulty** 1
Refreshments Tea-room in Keld

Start Shap Abbey car-park
Directions ① Make your way back up road. After 100 yards, opposite the first house, take

track on right, heading to gate; from the gate, proceed forward with fence on right. At end of field ignore a small gate (to right) but take stone steps into next field. Keep alongside wall on the left (at top of field), past a group of some half-dozen trees, then 50 yards later take stone steps on left ②. Immediately, turn right to continue alongside wall in previous direction, until reaching corner of wall. Here, continue forward, keeping to right of corner of another wall 50 yards ahead ③. Then forward, towards houses, with wall on left, soon reaching Keld.

In the other direction the route can be confusing although you are returning by the same route. The following directions may be helpful, and enable you to start from Keld if preferred.

Start at last house on left (with the slope behind you), at top of village, opposite a turning signposted to Thornship. Keep alongside wall to right of the house, signposted Shap Abbey. After a stile you will soon emerge into pasture. Continue forward, with wall on right until it reaches a corner, then keep forward to right of corner of another wall 50 yards ahead. Proceed along this wall for 100 yards, then take stone steps on left. Immediately, turn right to continue previous direction. In next field, continue forward, with fence on left. At next gate proceed forward to house, then left on lane to abbey car-park.

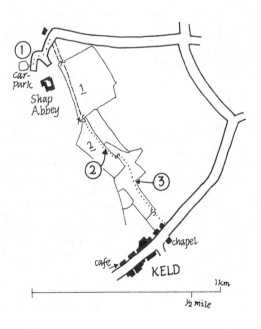

Lowther Castle and Askham

The best of the quiet and unspoilt limestone landscape of the
Lowther Valley, passing close by the eerie ruins of Lowther Castle
and through Askham, one of the Lake District's prettiest villages
(see p. 107).

Length 5½ miles (9 km),
2½ hours **Difficulty** 1–2
(you can shorten the walk by
½ mile by following the road to
Askham from where it is joined
just after ⑥)
Refreshments Pubs in Helton
and Askham; shop in Askham
Start Helton, which is just off
the Askham to Bampton road
Directions ① With Helton Inn
on left, follow the road through
the village. Opposite last house
on right (Holywell guest-
house), turn left to reach the
main road. Cross road, take
bridleway opposite, signposted
to Whale, and follow enclosed
path. ② After ⅓ mile, and 30
yards before the gate across the
path ahead, take gate on left and
cross field to a stile with a
waymarker arrow. Do not cross
this but turn right, following
edge of field (past another
waymark) to reach a
footbridge. Cross the
footbridge; beyond it, proceed
to a big footbridge over river
and cross it. ③ On other side,
take stile on right, then
immediately left alongside
wall, soon to be joined by track.
At top, exit via gate on to lane
at T-junction. Continue
forward, signposted Whale. ④
In centre of Whale, by the grass
triangle, cross some rough
stone steps on left, immediately
after last house on left. Pass
into back yard of this house
(this is a public right of way),
and proceed forward with wall

on right, to leave by gate at
end. Emerge into open pasture,
keep forward, ⑤ soon crossing
stile on right into forest, where
you join track. Turn left on
track, and follow it for 1¼ miles
until you reach front of
Lowther Castle ⑥. Leave track
and keep close to castle wall,
immediately passing through
gate, then proceed forward
along avenue of trees, heading
for houses. Emerge by houses
via ladder stile or gate. Turn left
on road, and keep left at next
two road junctions, following
signs for Askham. Then *either*
follow road all the way to
Askham, rejoining route at ⑦
(takes in Lowther church and
gets a pleasant view from the
river bridge) *or* take next estate
road on right (marked No
Entry, This Road Is Private; this
sign refers to road vehicles only
– it is a public right of way).

If taking the latter route,
follow this estate road, then
just beyond cattle-grid, fork
left, down to bridges. Cross the
left-hand bridge (a stone one),
and on the other side of river,
just before the tracks over the
two bridges merge, take
narrow woodland path on left.
The path soon rises to give a
good view of castle and church
from the top, and eventually
leaves woods via a gate. Bear
half-left across field to a gate in
the corner, beyond which turn
left on track into Askham
(views of hall from rear). Turn

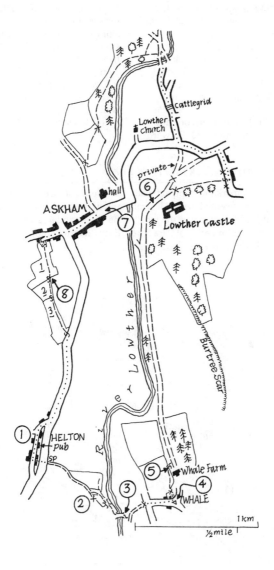

right on village street.

⑦ Walk up village street. By general stores, keep straight on by turning right and immediately left (by phone box). 100 yards later, fork left near No Through Road sign. Turn left immediately before second to last house (a grey stone building), crossing stile into back yard, then continue forward to enter field. Forward to end of this long field, finding steps over stone wall ⑧, then forward in second field, alongside wall on left. Cross stone steps over wall into third field, and again proceed alongside wall until it bends left, where keep forward 50 yards to cross stone steps over wall. Turn right on road and follow to Helton.

Gowbarrow Park and Aira Force

This is a remarkably compact walk, considering its scenic variety, with magnificent views of Ullswater and of the countryside towards Great Mell Fell; it makes the most of the woods and a series of waterfalls culminating at Aira Force. Easy underfoot, and route-finding poses no problems.

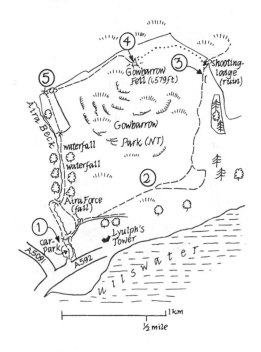

Length 4 miles (6.5 km),
2 hours **Difficulty** 2–3
Refreshments NT cafe close by
Aira Force car-park
Start Aira Force car-park on
A592, just east of junction with
A5091
Directions ① Take gate into
woods at back of car-park, soon
crossing river; path rises, then
take next fork right, which runs
along wooden fence. Just after
wooden fence is replaced by
metal one, take stile on right.
Path ascending the front of
Gowbarrow Park (the hill
straight ahead) is visible; take
this, forking left ② higher up
(both forks lead to the same
place, but views are better from
the upper path). Path skirts

hillside, curving around to left,
then ③ drops towards ladder
stile over a wall by a ruined
shooting-lodge: do not cross
stile but fork left by
shooting-lodge. Path becomes
indistinct, but the wall away to
your right is a guide. Keep
forward, aiming for trig point
on Gowbarrow Fell – the tallest
hillock on this hummocky
ground ④. Thereafter, pick up
clear path by wall away to
right. The path soon descends;
when you reach corner of wall,
cross via stone stile by
signpost, heading for signpost
90 yards away, where ⑤ turn
left on path. Follow path back
to car-park via woods and
waterfalls.

Hallin Fell and Ullswater

Without doubt, *the* walk in Martindale Common and the most
satisfactory of the really short circular walks on the east side of
Ullswater. The walk uses the lakeside path, plus the optional short
ascent of Hallin Fell at the end for a very lovely aerial view of
the lake.

Length 3 miles (5 km),
1½ hours including ascent of
Hallin Fell, which adds
½ hour **Difficulty** 1 without
Hallin Fell, 2 with
Refreshments Howtown Hotel
Start At St Peter's Church,
Martindale: car-parks on both
sides of road. Alternatively,
take the lake steamer from
Pooley Bridge or Glenridding
and start at Howtown pier:
from pier, with the lake on the
right, follow the lakeside track
until No Entry sign ahead,
where you take the gate on the
left signposted Sandwick: up
steps, through gate, and turn
left on the path beyond to join
walk directions at ④

Directions ① Standing on
road with church on left, make
for gate ahead and above road,
about 50 yards away. Beyond
it, cross field, following
waymark, to next gate.
Continue in the same direction
(waymarked) in the next field
(don't lose height) to a gate.
Beyond gate, turn right, uphill.
② Just before wall on right
reaches a corner, fork left
towards the corner of another
wall. The path runs along this
wall, soon descending into
woods and reaching the
lakeside path ③. Turn right
and follow this lakeside path
for a mile. Just after first house
away to left, ignore gate on left

(unless you have come from Howtown pier, in which case this is the return route), and, ④ 50 yards later, fork right and follow the path to the road ⑤. Turn right on this road. On reaching car-parks by St Peter's Church, you can ascend Hallin Fell (optional): take path opposite church, to left of small car-park, going straight up hill, initially with a wall on left. Where wall bends left, fork left and follow grassy path to summit; return by the same way.

Easy walks in outline

The Howk A 10-minute walk from Caldbeck to a romantically set waterfall spouting down a limestone gorge (see p. 98).

Ullswater (eastern shore) The walk described on p. 237 also takes in parts of this exceptionally fine lakeshore route, but it is possible to follow it in its entirety from Howtown to Glenridding, using the lake steamer for the outward or return leg. Note that ferry services may be cancelled without warning (accordingly, it is safest to take the ferry from Glenridding, then do the walk). See *The Holiday Which? Good Walks Guide* walk 132.

A very gently rising track leads to the rather sombre **Bowscale Tarn** (see p. 95). The views are unchanging, but it's a peaceful valley. Start from Bowscale (near Mungrisdale).

Guided walks start at Glenridding car-park and at Pooley Bridge information centre. Details from National Park information centres.

Fell walks

Fairfield

Fairfield's 2863-foot summit is large and disappointingly flat, but it's nevertheless a superb vantage-point, and there are good close-up views of Grisedale Tarn and Striding Edge. This is a less walked route than the Fairfield Horseshoe (the southern approach from Rydal), but nevertheless a very fine one, with a surprise section along the topmost ridge, with a sudden panorama opening out over the southern lakes. The ridge walk on the return half via St Sunday Crag is excellent, the outward leg over Hartsop-above-How enjoyable if not quite in the same league. The path is intermittent in some sections; in anything but thick mist, however, the route is obvious most of the way. Some roughish terrain on St Sunday Crag.

Length 8½ miles (13.5 km), 5 hours **Difficulty** 4–5
Refreshments Shop, hotel and pub in Patterdale
Start Patterdale, parking either close to the White Lion Inn (very limited) or near the village hall (signposted from the road; fee payable). If parking at the latter, you can avoid some road walking by taking a track by the village hall by a sign for Side Farm, then turning right at the farm and, ¼ mile later, by houses, taking a left turn signposted Hartsop; you join the route directions at ②. Alternatively, start at Deepdale Bridge (marked as Bridgend on some maps), 1 mile south of Patterdale, on the A592, where there is parking by a telephone box; with the telephone box on the right, walk along the road for 360 yards and join the route directions at ④. If really pressed to find parking space, start from Glenridding and walk along the road to Patterdale village hall, where you can pick up the directions above

Directions ① With White Lion Inn on left, proceed down road and take first left, by a 6'6" road restriction sign. 400 yards later, at houses, turn right, signposted Hartsop. ② Just before farm (Crookabeck), path deviates off to left, opposite a barn, over a stile (signposted Hartsop); soon, however, it rejoins main track. ③ ½ mile later, turn right, signposted Deepdale Bridge. The track soon crosses a bridge; immediately after next gate, take stile on right (marked Growing Crops, Keep To Path).

Head across two fields, aiming for gates. In second field, gate you want is near the left-most house ahead. Go through gate, then turn left on road and follow it for 360 yards. ④ Take gate on right (permissive path signposted Fairfield via Hoggill Brow; the right of way has been diverted). Immediately, bear left towards a fence and pick up clear path ascending a wooded slope. Soon, you emerge into open land, with Hart Crag (left) and Scrubby Crag (right) towering ahead at the end of a ridge. Using the wall on the left as a guide (the path is generally very clear), ascend steadily to Hart Crag (ascent takes about 2 hours) ⑤. At Hart Crag, turn right along ridge to Scrubby

Crag, then proceed to grassy summit of Fairfield ⑥. Turn right, and walk down to ridge of St Sunday Crag (which soon rises). Later, near end of ridge, path keeps well to left (follow cairns), passing around a foothill (Birks) and finally descending sharply to a wall and gate ⑦. For Glenridding take track beyond gate, and you will soon emerge on a lane, where you turn right; follow lane to main road and turn left on the main road. For Patterdale do not pass through gate but turn right, with wall initially on left. Where track divides, keep left and descend to Patterdale.

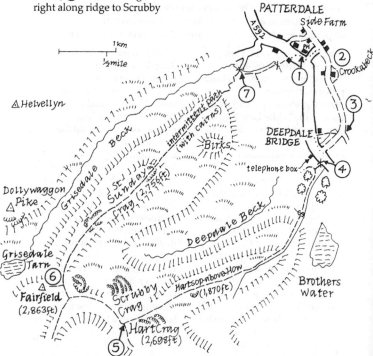

Place Fell

A 2154-foot-high fell whose steep western edges plunge down to Ullswater's south-eastern shores. All the climbing is at the beginning and is well graded, then, near the summit, the view over the lake and east to the Pennines suddenly opens out and accompanies the route for the next 1½ miles gently downhill over springy turf. The final section along the intermittently wooded lakeshore path is a delight, one of the best walks of its kind in the Lake District.

Length 6½ miles (10.5 km), 3½ hours **Difficulty** 3–4
Refreshments Shop, hotel and pub in Patterdale; soft drinks and sweets available at Side Farm
Start Patterdale village hall in the adjacent car-park (fee payable), just off the A592

Directions ① Take the track signposted Side Farm. At the farm, turn right along track and continue until you soon pass a cottage and then through a gate shortly beyond it. ② Immediately after gate, take the first of two gates on left, signposted Boredale Hause and

Angle Tarn. 50 yards later, ignore a sharp left turn but continue up front of fell: where path divides, take either fork (they rejoin at top). ③ At top of pass the path bends left and reaches a cairn by path junction, with a ruin away to right. Take path to left of a metal water cover. Soon, route up Place Fell becomes apparent: ascend to trig point ④. Beyond trig point, keep forward on a well-defined path: beyond final mini-summit (with cairn), the path drops towards a ruined sheep-fold near base of a grassy hill (High Dodd). ⑤ Turn left just after this sheep-fold, taking a grassy track which soon passes a ruin by a disused quarry and descends towards Ullswater. ⑥ At bottom, join track running alongside a wall and turn left along it. Follow track back to Side Farm, ignoring side turnings.

Fell walks in outline

Helvellyn (see also p. 91), at 3116 feet, is the third highest peak in the Lake District and the most frequently climbed. The easiest route is from Thirlmere, but much more interesting is the eastern approach from Glenridding via Striding Edge, then north from the summit for an effortless ridge walk. See *The Holiday Which? Good Walks Guide* walk 138.

High Street (see also p. 110) is a grassy whaleback, endowed (like Helvellyn) with a craggy eastern face, and with a long and lovely ridge walk along the top (2719 feet). Its chief disadvantage is that its best starting-point, Haweswater, is so inaccessible from the rest of the Lake District. A convenient, though much less dramatic approach is to the west from Hartsop (near Patterdale), via Hayeswater Gill and The Knott. Ascents are steady rather than steep, and much of the terrain is quite easy-going underfoot. See *The Holiday Which? Good Walks Guide* walk 131.

Blencathra or *Saddleback* (2847 feet) To the east of Blencathra the fells stop abruptly, so there are tremendous views into the Pennines. But as the Lakeland views are to the south and west, it's best walked east to west. The spurs and scooped-out hollows which give this fell such an individual southern face offer tough ascent routes, most of them simply unpleasant. However, the path via Hall's Fell and Narrow Edge (aptly named) is a rewarding way to the top. Much easier, but nevertheless excellent, is the path up Doddick Fell, which immediately gets views on both sides and of the summit itself, from where you should follow the edge south-westwards, descending either from Knowe Crags (the end of the edge) or returning the same way. It is also worth making a detour north from the summit to get close-up views of Scales Tarn and Sharp Edge (more razor-like in character even than Striding Edge on Helvellyn).

THE SOUTH-WEST

Easy walks

Stanley Ghyll Force

This is an attractively set waterfall (also called Dalegarth Falls) in Eskdale woodland; don't miss the view from the top of the precipice. You can reach the Force either as a there-and-back walk or, slightly shorter, as a round trip, using stepping-stones on the return journey; these stepping-stones may be submerged after wet weather but are otherwise easy to cross.

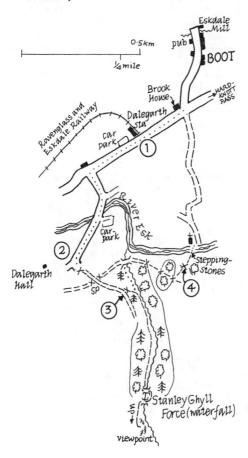

Length 2 miles (3 km),
1 hour **Difficulty** 1
Refreshments Brook House
(tea-room and restaurant)
in Boot
Start Dalegarth railway
station, Eskdale
Directions ① With station
behind you, turn right on road.
300 yards later, opposite
Eskdale Centre, take lane on
left. This crosses the River Esk,
passes a car-park and becomes
unsurfaced. ② At fork, bear
left (right goes to house), and
follow track past a signpost to
Boot (left) and Eskdale Green
(right), ignoring both
signposts. Carry on up and
take next gate on left, into
wood, where there is a Stanley
Ghyll Force sign ③. The
woodland path leads right, up
stream to falls. At final
footbridge at bottom of falls,
continue up path to the right of
stream until you reach the top
of the precipice (to see the
view, get on all fours and
cautiously peer over the edge).
Return downstream, past the
point at which you joined
stream at ③, until you cross a
wooden footbridge. The track
then leads out of woods, over
pasture, through more woods
to join the River Esk by a gate
④. Cross river by stepping-
stones (if these are submerged,
you have to retrace your steps),
and pick up track between
stone walls to right of church
100 yards later. Ignore a left
fork and proceed to road. Boot
village is straight ahead;
Dalegarth station is to the left.

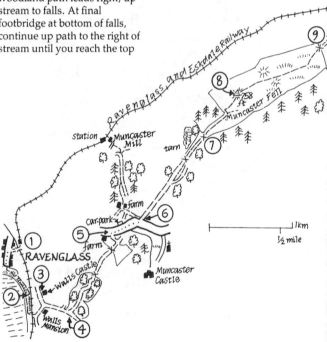

Eskdale

Eskdale harbours a rich variety of attractive walks, both lowland and upland in character. This route covers a number of permutations: a short walk from Ravenglass to Muncaster Mill, returning by the Ravenglass and Eskdale Railway, and a longer walk from Ravenglass to Eskdale Green (which also returns by train). You can shorten the latter by starting from Muncaster Mill, or lengthen it by continuing to Boot via Stanley Ghyll Force and returning from Dalegarth station (see *The Holiday Which? Good Walks Guide* walk 125). The finest part of the walk scenically is Muncaster Fell, from where there are excellent views of the central fell group and the Cumbrian coast. See also pp. 123–8.

Length Ravenglass to Muncaster mill: 2½ miles (4 km), 1 hour; Ravenglass to Eskdale Green: 5½ miles (9 km), 2¼ hours **Difficulty** 2 **Refreshments** Shops and pubs at both Ravenglass and Eskdale Green
Start Ravenglass railway station
Directions ① From station, cross bridge over BR line and continue forward into village street. Turn left along street to reach beach at end. Forward across beach. Just after last

house, pick up a path beyond a stone wall up a slight bank. ② Where railway line becomes visible on left, drop down on to beach and follow shore until a railway arch appears on left. Pass under the arch, then take a left on the other side. You soon pass a house (Walls Mansion); ignore (for the moment) any right turns, but continue 200 yards to see ruins of Roman Bath House (Walls Castle) ③. Return towards Walls Mansion, but take first left, a broad track running just inside woods. ④ After ¼ mile (soon after passing under power lines), take track on left (signposted Footpath; ignore a minor unsignposted left turn *immediately* after power lines). Walk through woods, then across fields and into more woods, where immediately keep left (right is private) and proceed to road ⑤. Turn right along this road, past entrance to Muncaster Castle. ⑥ Leave road at next right bend.

For Muncaster Mill turn left (signposted Bridleway) on track and proceed up to farm. Turn right in farmyard to enter woods. Path soon joins a forest track: keep forward. Where a view opens out, take centre of three paths and descend to crossing-track, where you turn right (signposted Mill) and then almost immediately left to reach the mill.

To join route from Muncaster Mill take path between mill buildings, keeping right at top (signposted Castle) and ascend through scrubby woodland. At top, when you reach mature forest, keep forward on track. ¼ mile later, fork right on to path, ascend to farm, then turn left. Follow track alongside a fence (ignore right turn which crosses field) until you reach corner of road.

To continue the route, take bridleway signposted Eskdale and Hardknott. Follow track, ignoring occasional side turns, for a mile (following signs for Eskdale). ⑦ Emerge by a gate on to open land (Muncaster Fell). Continue along track with forest fence on left. Soon, a multitude of tracks appears: head for the trig point which is prominent ahead – a clear path leads to it. ⑧ Beyond trig

point, keep forward (do not bear too far to right). Down to the left (though not visible) is a fence; ahead, beyond nearest hillocks, is a wall – your objective is the corner formed by these ⑨. Beyond the wall, a clear track continues ahead, initially with a wall on left. Track soon leaves the wall and heads over the right shoulder of Silver Knott, the large hillock ahead, then snakes down to reach a gate. Beyond gate, proceed until you reach a T-junction of tracks ⑩. Turn left (for Irton Road station, from where you can take a train back to Ravenglass, keep along this track all the way). For The Green station, where you can also catch a train, turn right at a signpost after 300 yards, where corner of a fence is reached on right. Path (which can be boggy) runs alongside this fence, over footbridges, over railway, through an entrance in a stone wall, and then reaches a track ⑪. Turn left on track, then at junction by some houses turn right and follow lane to reach station.

Wallowbarrow and the Duddon Valley

A nicely varied walk, with a short ascent near the beginning, then a section along a track through elevated country giving views of the major peaks close to the Duddon Valley, then finally two river sections, looking down into the wooded precipice of the Duddon at its most spectacular. The route is easy to follow, but it can be rocky underfoot in sections and can be spongy; there's one set of stepping-stones to cross (which can be avoided in wellingtons by using an adjacent ford).

Length 3½ miles (5.5 km), 1¾ hours **Difficulty** 2 **Refreshments** Newfield Inn **Start** Newfield Inn,

Seathwaite, Duddon Valley; there's roadside parking a few yards in either direction of the inn

Directions ① With pub on left, follow road for 200 yards, then take a stone stile on right by a signpost opposite second house on left. Follow path down to a stream, where path turns right alongside it, soon crossing it and a wider stream

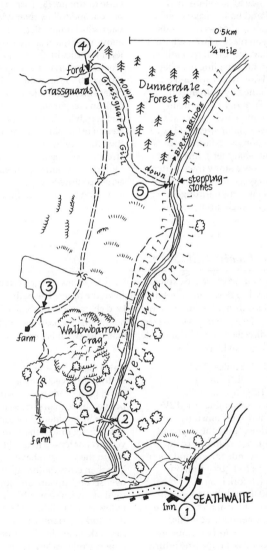

by footbridges. Path doubles back left and soon joins the River Duddon and runs close to it. ② Cross stone bridge over river, and bear half-left on other side to a well-defined woodland path. Leave woods by a gate and cross two fields until you reach a farm, where you take gate on right. Path rises gently heading for a big crag, Wallowbarrow, and is soon joined by a stream on right. Fork right on to main path immediately after path crosses a minor stream. ③ At a T-junction (with farm close behind, sharp left), turn right and follow a stony track. After second gate plus a ladder stile, track bends right through a gate. ④ Reach farm

(Grassguards), continue across stream (cross by ford or stepping-stones) then 20 yards later turn right (avoiding gate ahead into a forest) to descend close to stream. ⑤ Turn right at bottom and follow riverside path which immediately rises above river (path along river itself is difficult). ⑥ At bridge crossed earlier, cross it again, then continue straight on the other side, alongside a wall. Path snakes through a wood and rough land, reaches a stream by an old sluice and then turns right along the stream, crossing it by footbridge. Continue forward across pasture to a gate, emerging by Newfield Inn.

Tilberthwaite Gill

A short but worthwhile exploration of a little ravine gouged out by the Yewdale Beck – up one side and down the other. The path ascends only a little, but gets true upland character at the base of Furness Fells, an impressive craggy mountain, and has views in the other direction towards Langdale. Suitable footwear is needed to cross a stream by boulders.

Length 1½ miles (2.5 km), ¾ hour **Difficulty** 2
Start Tilberthwaite Gill car-park, on a minor road 2½ miles north of Coniston
Directions Take the steps out of car-park and follow path, which ascends the gill and soon reaches a fork (by a ruin on right): left fork is a continuation, but detour right to a footbridge at foot of ravine is recommended; after this, return to fork and continue up around top of ravine (the return route can be seen away to

right). Soon, another footbridge is visible away to right; path heads towards this, but you have to first cross a stream by boulders (these are not difficult unless they are very wet or icy – if in doubt return the way you have come). You then cross footbridge itself over second stream, and fork right at a cairn soon after. Then follow path (avoiding a later right fork, as signposted) to car-park, emerging by former miners' cottages and an old cottage with a spinning gallery.

Irton Pike

Irton Pike, a 751-foot hill, gives views over Wasdale, Eskdale, Sellafield and the coast. The hill is covered with Forestry Commission plantations, but the route up is quite easy. Driving from Eskdale Green to Santon Bridge, park on the road where it enters forest and where Forestry Commission gates appear on both sides of the road (the gate on the south side has a 15mph speed restriction sign on it). Take the gate to the north side, fork right after 100 yards, then 20 yards later take a steep, narrow path on the left. This reaches a T-junction with another path: bear right here, and the path soon veers left, steeply uphill to the open summit. Walking time there and back is somewhat short of half an hour.

Easy walks in outline

A wealth of industrial archaeology can be found at *Coniston copper-mines*, which are on the eastern side of The Old Man of Coniston and approached by a track running alongside Church Beck from Coniston. The landscape is not at all pretty, as it was mined intensively for nearly 350 years, but the area has been designated one of historical and scientific interest. See *The Holiday Which? Good Walks Guide* walk 126.

At 836 feet, the highest point in the hummocky ground that constitutes the Blawith Fells, just south of Coniston Water, is *Beacon*. Start at Brown Howe car-park on the A5084 at the southern end of the lake; turn left on the road then first right on a narrow, twisty lane; after half a mile leave the lane as it bends sharp right, and take a path half-left, under power lines and heading to a minor summit from which the path to the top can be seen. Beacon gives an excellent panorama of Coniston Water and its associated fells.

Little Langdale offers plenty of scope for short walks in charmingly varied scenery, with Langdale Pikes in the distance. The best objectives are Blea Tarn and Colwith Force, and extra interest is added by taking in Elterwater (lake and village) in Great Langdale. See, for example, *The Holiday Which? Good Walks Guide* walk 128.

The Abbotswood Nature Trail runs two miles in the countryside around *Furness Abbey*. A leaflet is available from Barrow tourist information centre.

There's a town trail around *Vickerstown*, Barrow's model garden suburb. A leaflet is available from Barrow tourist information centre. The best way of walking close to Coniston Water's eastern shore without using the road is to take the trail through the estate of *Brantwood* (Ruskin's house; see p. 147).

There's a nature trail in the grounds of *Muncaster Castle* (see p. 126).

Nether Wasdale Nature Trail The full route is 3½ miles, along the

shore of Wastwater, and by riverside and in woods. Leaflet from
Cumbria Trust for Nature Conservation, Church Street, Ambleside.
Guided walks start at Campbell Memorial in Coniston and from
car-parks (National Park and railway) in Ravenglass. Details from
National Park information centres.

Fell walks

Pillar, Steeple and Yewbarrow

Commonly known as the Mosedale Horseshoe (not a very helpful
name, given there are so many places in the Lake District called
Mosedale), these three great ridges, with Pillar (2927 feet) the
highest point, have dramatic crags on the northern side and views
into Ennerdale, plus panoramas of Scafell and Great Gable. The
easiest way up is to take the well-graded Black Sail Pass (one of
Lakeland's least demanding mountain routes) to Pillar and to return
by the same way – but this misses the charming minor summit of
Steeple as well as the breathtaking view of Wasdale from the far end
of Yewbarrow. The short but steep climb up the last-named peak,
which is unfortunately followed by a tedious (though not
unmanageable) descent over scree, can be missed by descending
gently from Dore Head. The Wind Gap turn-off is too steep to be
pleasurable.

Length 9 miles (14.5 km),
5½ hours **Difficulty** 5
Length (omitting
Yewbarrow) 9 miles (14.5 km),
5 hours **Difficulty** 4–5
Length (up Pillar and back,
using Black Sail Pass both
ways) 6 miles (9.5 km), 3¾
hours **Difficulty** 4
Refreshments Wasdale Head
Inn; the adjacent outdoor shop
sells sweets and soft drinks
Start Wasdale Head. Note that
the car-park can fill up early in
the day (there are a number of
other car-parks along
Wast Water)
Directions ① Take signposted
path for Black Sail Pass, which
leads round back of Wasdale
Head Inn to a stream, then turn
right along the stream (do not
cross the stone bridge). The
Black Sail Pass enters the valley

of Mosedale and, after ¾ mile
along the level, begins to
ascend gently to the head of the
pass, which is ahead and to the
right, crossing a stream on the
way. ② At top, by a cairn, turn
left along ridge. The horseshoe
shape of the walk is now
apparent (unless you're in thick
mist!): ridge ascends to the trig
point on Pillar ③. Turn left
here and continue to Scoat Fell,
where a stone wall joins path.
④ Here route bends left (away
from wall) for return route, but
before taking ridge on left,
make a detour to Steeple, a
prominent bell-shaped summit
10 minutes away to right;
return and proceed forward to
Red Pike, the first summit on
the final section of ridge. The
best views are on left side of
ridge. ⑤ At Dore Head, you

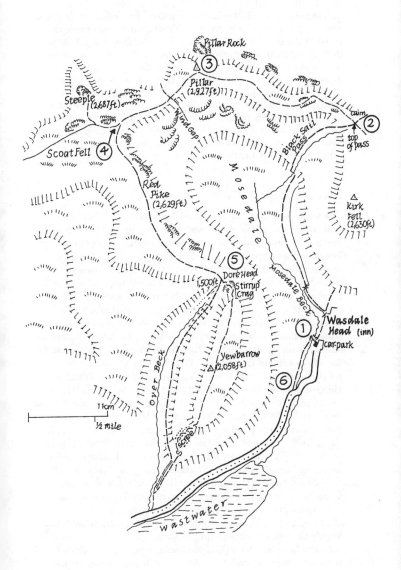

can omit the ascent of Yewbarrow, whose rocky face towers up in front of you, and tu:n right into valley – take the descending path, keeping to left-hand side of valley; it eventually reaches a wall and drops further to road. Otherwise, scale Yewbarrow carefully; it is steep, and you will need to use your hands, although the ascent is not as difficult as it looks and there is a friendly grassy ridge to follow. At far end, route down is steep and made a little tricky by scree. Descend patiently, eventually crossing a ladder stile, then proceed down an easy path alongside a wall to lakeside road, and turn left along it. ⑥ Just before road bends right and crosses a bridge you can keep straight on along a path to Wasdale Head.

Fell walks in outline

The south-west Lake District is a relatively small area that offers a vast choice of outstanding fell walks. There is unrestricted access to much of the area, and most peaks have numerous routes to the top. The easiest way up *Scafell Pike* (3206 feet) (see also p. 132) is via Brown Tongue, the mountain's west flank, but all the views are behind you on the way up. The Corridor Route approaches Scafell Pike from the head of the Sty Head Pass (from the north) and is an exciting, though reasonably safe way up via a shelf in harsh and exacting terrain dissected by ravines; it can be reached by starting at either Seathwaite (Borrowdale) or Wasdale Head. The vicinity of the summit is highly dramatic and has challenging rock climbs, notably the 400-foot cliff of Esk Buttress. Piers Gill gouges out a rocky precipice and can be perilous. A sample round route is Wasdale Head – east to Sty Head – south on Corridor Route – Scafell Pike – west to Lingmell Gill – north to Wasdale Head. Its twin peak, *Scafell* (3162 feet), can be climbed from Wasdale or Eskdale.

Another hugely popular walk, but also quite a demanding one, is up *Great Gable* (2949 feet) (see also p. 130). Start from Wasdale Head, Gatesgarth (by Buttermere), Seathwaite (Borrowdale) or from the top of the Honister Pass. The Wasdale route goes via Sty Head Pass, then directly up or via Aaron Slack. The direct south-west ascent via Great Napes involves walking over scree in the later sections and is not recommended. A very enjoyable walk ascent, involving less climbing, is from Seathwaite or Honister Pass via Green Gable and Windy Gap: steady rather than gruelling.

To reach *Langdale Pikes* (2415 feet), most people go up Stickle Ghyll from the Dungeon Ghyll New Hotel, and (to a lesser degree) the well-defined path that leads north-west to Loft Crag, visible from the valley as a route making a diagonal course around the front of the fell; the latter makes a good ascent route as it is easily graded, and after the delights of the summit – the mini-peaks of Harrison Stickle and Pike of Stickle (with its adjacent Stone Age axe 'factory') and the cliff of Pavey Ark presenting an awesome scene, with Stickle Tarn brooding below – you can join the crowds and descend via Stickle Ghyll.

Bow Fell (2960 feet) and *Crinkle Crags* (2816 feet) (see also p. 119), two summits which are effectively part of the same ridge, arguably Lakeland's finest, can be climbed in the same day. The easiest way on to Crinkle Crags is from the Wrynose Pass, from where it is only 1650 feet up to the top along a well-graded path. From Great Langdale, a spur called The Band provides an unproblematic and enjoyable route from the valley floor up to the ridge, starting at Stool End Farm. Good round routes from Dungeon Ghyll in Great Langdale are, for Bow Fell, west up Mickleden Beck via Cumbria Way – Angle Tarn – south to Bow Fell and Three Tarns – east on The Band to Stool End Farm and back to Dungeon Ghyll; for Crinkle Crags, Stool End Farm – Oxendale – south-west to Great Knott – Crinkle Crags – north to Three Tarns – east on The Band and back to Stool End Farm.

There are two peaks named *Harter Fell*; one is near Haweswater, but this one (2140 feet) rises gracefully above the southern side of Eskdale. Its eastern base, the Duddon Valley side, is heavily afforested, but the Forestry Commission has waymarked the route to the edge of the forest, from where the way to the summit is obvious. More absorbing is the ascent from Eskdale, via Spothow Gill and the west side of the fell; it is best to start from Dalegarth station, take the path along the north bank of the Esk east to cross the river at Doctor Bridge, striking south a mile later down the Spothow Valley.

The Old Man of Coniston (2635 feet) (see also p. 146) is one of the easier fells to climb, owing to clear tracks all the way up. The best route is generally agreed to be via the Walna Scar 'Road' to the west of the village; where the road metalling ceases after ¾ mile there is parking space. From here head up to Goat's Water, around which keep to the right and ascend to the summit; a longer version keeps along the Walna Scar Road until the ridge, then heads north via Brown Pike and Dow Crag, giving a good ridge section. Return the same way or via the track on the mine-despoiled eastern slopes, via Church Beck.

Black Combe (1970 feet) (see also p. 134), at the very south-western tip of the Lake District, is a sprawling fell with its toe nearly in the sea. It tends to get ignored in favour of the more accessible central fells, but its summit is an excellent viewpoint, reached by a gentle grassy track – an undemanding, though long (2½-mile) ascent. Start at Whicham on the A595, ¼ mile north of the junction with the A5093. Park opposite a footpath signpost to Silecroft; the gate marking the start of the walk is signposted to Black Combe but is not very visible from the road. The route starts by crossing two fields diagonally, then joining a lane behind a farm; fork right just after this.

THE SOUTH-EAST

Easy walks

Kendal

Kendal has a complicated layout, and it is possible to miss some of
its major features during an unstructured visit. The town is
described in full on pp. 199–204, but the main points of interest are
briefly listed here.

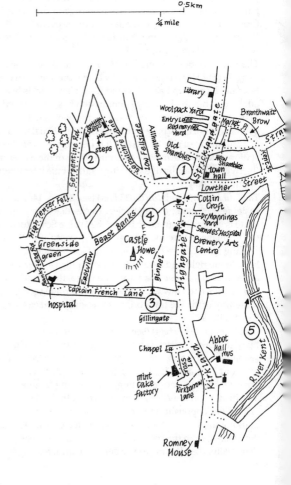

Length 1½ miles (2.5 km), plus detours, 1½ hours excluding time needed for museums
Difficulty 1
Refreshments Plenty

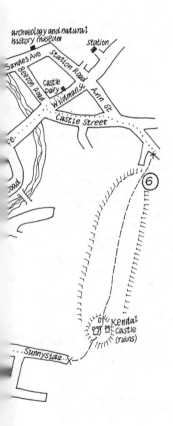

archaeology and natural history museum

station

Sandes Ave

Station Road

Beezon Road

Castle Dairy

Wildman St.

Ann St.

Castle Street

6

of Kendal Castle (ruins)

Sunnyside

Directions ① From town hall [**a**], turn left into Lowther Street [**b**]. By river, bear left into Kent Street and walk up Branthwaite Brow and the Market Place [**c**]. Turn right along Stricklandgate to see the bristling hog sign above the estate agents [**d**], then return along Stricklandgate, past the Old Shambles [**e**] to the town hall. Turn right into Allhallows Lane, then first right, where the shops end, then first left into Sepulchre Lane [**f**]. At a fork by some modern houses, bear left, ignore steps soon after on left, but just after a row of cottages called Church Terrace, take steps on left. ② Reach Serpentine Road, turn left on to it and follow signs to county hospital (keeping right with road markings at next fork, over Greenside then along Bankfield Road) [**g**]. Beyond hospital, follow road marked with No Entry sign, descending Captain French Lane [**h**] (ignore left fork half-way down). ③ Near bottom, opposite gate numbered '2' and just before advertising sign for Hayes and Parkinson undertakers, take path on left (Garth Head). Soon, make a detour left up some steps to see Castle Howe [**i**], then return to path, proceed to Allhallows Lane, and turn right; 30 yards later, just after house number 13a, turn right into Collin Croft (it looks like a private garden at first sight) [**j**]. ④ Reach Highgate, and turn right along it [**k**] (it soon becomes Kirkland). Opposite entrance to Abbot Hall [**l**], turn right into Chapel Lane (under arch), then first left into Cross Lane, past

251

Kendal Mint Cake factory [m], then take path on right immediately before reaching a housing estate. Follow path [n] back into Kirkland [o], where you should continue to right. Pass church [p], then continue up towards bridge (optional detour to Romney House [q]: keep straight on for a short distance); immediately before bridge turn left on to riverside path [r]. ⑤ Cross next bridge, turn right on road then immediately left into Parr Street and walk up to top of road, then continue on path to castle [s]. Pass through central circle of castle, head across to left of largest fragment of castle ruins, picking up path along top of a long grassy ridge (town centre is away to left). ⑥ At the end, drop down to the gate, then turn left along Castle Road and left at T-junction into Castle Street (ignore one-way signs indicating right turn for traffic into Ann Street). At river bridge, make a detour to right up Wildman Street to see Castle Dairy [t/u], then return to bridge and cross it. Head back along Stramongate to town hall, passing New Shambles [v] on right.

Key to features

[a] Town hall rebuilt 1825, now the town's central point. [b] Sign on snuff factory. [c] Cobbled market place, iron-fronted buildings; flea-market on Mondays. [d] Advertising sign for brush factory once on the site. [e] Preserved street, formerly a meat market, with cobbles and a porticoed building at the end. [f] Part of Fellside, Kendal's former slum area and still a warren of alleys. [g] Grass triangle was probably once a market place. [h] Attractive row of cottages on one side of Captain French Lane. [i] Kendal's original castle (a wooden stockade); here reached by one of the town's many ginnels. Obelisk commemorates the Glorious Revolution of 1688. [j] Picturesque yard, whose recent preservation won a Civic Trust Award; formerly housed a brass foundry, a tobacco factory and a printing works. [k] Several yards to look out for leading off Highgate: Shakespeare Yard (unpreserved; once had a theatre), New Inn Yard and Sandes' Hospital (almshouses) on the right, and Dr Mannings Yard on the opposite side. The Brewery Arts Centre is also on the right. [l] Museum of Lakeland Life and Industry; Abbot Hall Art Gallery. [m] Wilson's Kendal Mint Cake factory, plus shop and the ever-present sweet whiff of mint cake. [n] One of the most ancient ginnels in town. [o] The original town centre. [p] Parish church, heavily Victorianised but notable as being the second widest parish church in England. [q] Home of George Romney, portrait artist. [r] Pleasant riverside walk by River Kent. [s] Kendal's 'new' castle, once home of Catherine Parr, and now in ruins; good view of the town and its surroundings. [t] Kendal's oldest house. [u] Can detour to Kendal Museum of Archaeology and Natural History (see map). [v] Another quaint yard, formerly butchers' shops and retained for commercial use.

Tarn Hows

This somewhat over-visited beauty-spot is reached on this walk from the west by an ascent through woods and past a waterfall – by far the most satisfying way of getting there, and relatively unknown. The ascent is not particularly steep, but the ground is a bit uneven.

Length 2½ miles (4 km), 1 hour **Difficulty** 2
Start On the A593 between Skelwith Bridge and Coniston, at any of three small car-parks by a wooden signpost to Tarn Hows, on the left-hand side of the road as you come from Skelwith Bridge, and ¼ mile south of Yew Tree Tarn
Directions There are three signposts (one for each car-park). Take the one for Tarn Hows, keeping along the left-hand side of the stream and ascending through woods. You will soon reach the confluence of streams – do not cross, but keep left, with stream on right; you soon pass a waterfall and ascend to the top. Emerging at Tarn Hows (a small lake), make a mental note of where you have emerged as you will return that way, and turn left on track around tarn; ignore left forks.

Hampsfield Fell

The extent of this hill's wonderful view is attributable to its position at the northern side of Morecambe Bay rather than its height (just 727 feet). Its limestone pavement and whimsical hospice provide further diversions. The ascent is gentle going, through pleasant mixed woodland, and there is a bracing start to the walk from Grange-over-Sands (see p. 187) along the esplanade.

Length 3½ miles (5.5 km), 1½ hours **Difficulty** 1–2
Refreshments Plenty in Grange-over-Sands
Start Clock tower, Grange-over-Sands
Directions ① Take alley opposite clock tower, between Halifax and Nationwide building societies. Cross railway, then turn left on esplanade. ② Just after station, go under subway, then turn left on main road. After 100 yards, turn right into Windermere Road (marked by signpost to Windermere). 300 yards later, immediately after houses end, turn left on a woodland path signposted Routen Well and Hampsfield. Follow signposts to Hampsfield Fell (also called Hampsfell) throughout the wood – over two driveways (bearing half-left at second one), then ¼ mile later ③ forking right, close to derelict concrete pits on right. ¼ mile later, fork left, immediately reaching a stone stile at edge of woods. Continue forward, across open land; path peters out, but keep on uphill; eventually a wall appears on left, and shortly before it reaches a corner cross by steps

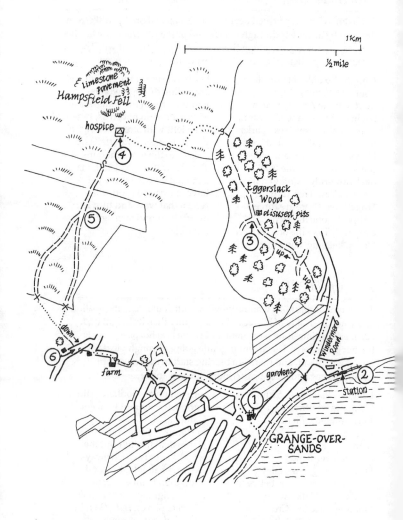

and continue up, to reach
hospice (tower), hidden from
view until the last moment ④.
Turn left (from the top of the
hospice it is possible to see the

broad grassy track you are
heading for), soon crossing a
wall by steps, then forward on
already-mentioned broad
grassy track. ⑤ At fork, bear

254

left, follow the track to a wall,
after which path disappears.
Continue forward for 100 yards
(to where scrub begins), then
turn left on to a track heading
to left of a small, square,
covered reservoir building. ⑥
Emerge on a lane, take
signposted stile opposite, and
head for gate just to left of
house. Turn right on track and
proceed down to farm;
immediately before farm, take
stile on left and proceed
forward, walking up right edge
of field alongside a wall. At
end, leave field and pick up
enclosed path which soon
disgorges on to the corner of a
residential road ⑦. Turn left on
to unmade lane, keeping right
40 yards later. At next junction,
turn right, to reach road
junction. Turn left here, and
200 yards later keep straight on
at junction (on road barred to
through traffic); turn right at
bottom and follow to town
centre.

Whitbarrow Scar

Whitbarrow Scar is a splendid limestone cliff which looks daunting
from the bottom, but can be ascended in a few minutes by woodland
paths. It is excellent for views – the Pennines, Morecambe Bay,
Fairfield, Langdale Pikes, Scout Scar – plus the limestone pavement
and nature reserve. See also p. 15.

Length 2 miles (3 km), 1 hour,
there and back to Lord's Seat,
the summit; the walk can be
extended northwards along the
ridge if desired
Difficulty 2–3
Start Witherslack Hall in the
Winster Valley; the Hall is
1 mile north of Witherslack,
on the easternmost road
in the valley
Directions Take track to right
of school (Witherslack Hall)
driveway, signposted
Whitbarrow Scar. Shortly

reaching a gate, turn half-left
on to a stony track. 200 yards
later, fork right, and, on
reaching gate into woods, turn
left, signposted Whitbarrow
Scar and Lord's Seat. 220 yards
later, turn right by a signpost
and ascend to top of edge.
Follow path until you soon
emerge from dwarf woodland
into the open. The summit
cairn on Lord's Seat is visible
away to right, and shortly take
a cairned path leading to it.

Elter Water and Rydal Water

A walk memorable for breathtaking beauty and scenic variety, with a
sequence of classic views, including Grasmere from Loughrigg
Terrace, and Loughrigg Tarn and Elter Water against the formidable
outline of Langdale Pikes. Other features include Rydal Water, some
pleasant hill-walking over Loughrigg Fell and the waterfall, Skelwith
Force. Route-finding is moderately easy, but special care is needed at
⑦. See also pp. 119, 143 and 177.

Length 7 miles (11 km),
3½ hours **Difficulty** 3
Refreshments Skelwith Bridge
Hotel and Kirkstone Galleries
coffee shop, Skelwith Bridge;
shop and Britannia Inn,
Elterwater

Start Skelwith Bridge; there's
roadside parking on the B5343
at the rear of Skelwith Bridge
Hotel.

Alternatively, start at Rydal:
turn off the A591 on to minor
road by bridge at east end of

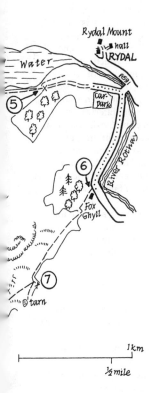

Rydal Mount

hall
RYDAL

Water

Car-park

River Rothay

Fox Ghyll

tarn

1 km

½ mile

Directions ① From Skelwith Bridge, follow the A593 in the Coniston direction (signposted), but just after Skelwith Bridge Hotel turn right by a sign for Kirkstone Galleries. 50 yards later fork right, passing slate workshops, where a slate signpost indicates route of path (straight ahead). You soon pick up the riverside path, passing Skelwith Force (waterfall), then proceed through pasture, past Elter Water (lake), and along river again to reach Elterwater village after 1½ miles from the start. ② Take road to right of village shop. At a T-junction, cross road and pick up path running uphill alongside a wall. After 75 yards, cross a stream on left by a slab (leaving wall) and continue up: your objective is grassy path which reaches a low point in skyline just to right of fells ahead – lowest point on skyline is a little further to right than this and is marked by a small conifer plantation. Half-way up, cross road and continue ascent, soon passing electricity sub-station. ③ From skyline, path descends to a gate, then soon you'll see walls parallel away to left and right. Pass through another gate and immediately take kissing-gate on right into woods. Turn right on reaching road and proceed along it for 75 yards, then turn left into woods down a path. On leaving woods, path runs nearly level (ignore right ascending fork up fell) along Loughrigg Terrace, with superb views of Grasmere. ④ Path later descends to a stone wall: keep forward alongside this

hamlet, marked by a two-ton weight restriction sign, then immediately turn right. Car-park is up on the left. To start walk, return to the T-junction, turn right along the minor road by the river and join directions at ⑥ (ignoring sharp left turn, and ignoring right fork 25 yards later), with Rydal Water soon appearing on left. You soon join edge of lake. ⑤ Just before woods ahead, fork right and follow path (which soon becomes a lane) to a T-junction. Turn right, alongside River Rothay. ⑥ After ½ mile, where river bends markedly left and road is about to enter between stone pillars, take stile on right. Path leads through woods and soon passes through a gate on left by a signpost and over a small footbridge. Path then rises and soon reaches open land; a stream is on left, and later a wall is apparent up on left. ⑦ Where wall bends left, your objective is to keep forward parallel with slope on right: however, as ground is boggy it is easier to continue alongside wall round to left for 50 yards to gate. Before gate, turn sharp right on to a well-defined path (avoid ascending slope, which is now on your left). Soon, path descends towards base of a fell (Ivy Crag) 400 yards ahead and skirts it. Soon, path is joined by a stone wall, which it follows around south side of Ivy Crag. ⑧ When you reach a crossing of tracks, ahead (signposted Langdale and Elterwater) is continuation of walk, but first take a sharp right turn, by cottage, to see Loughrigg Tarn (a 200-yard detour). Return to main route and descend to reach end of tarmac lane. Turn left (right goes to Tarn Foot Farm), reaching a T-junction by a post-box 50 yards later. Turn right, then first left, and descend to Skelwith Bridge.

Easy walks in outline

Scout Scar, a limestone cliff above the Lyth Valley, gives impressive views, obtained by the easiest of 10-minute strolls from the road. See p. 194.

Orrest Head and *Gummer's How* are two fine viewpoints on the east side of Windermere. See pp. 165 and 168.

Latterbarrow, another hill giving fine views over Windermere and the fells to the west, can be climbed in about 15–20 minutes. See p. 164.

Windermere (western shore) See p. 161 and *The Holiday Which? Good Walks Guide* walk 127.

Humphrey Head Point, the coastal headland near Grange-over-Sands, has a ¾-mile-long walk (see p. 188).

There are numerous Forestry Commission trails, marked with coloured hoops around wooden posts, in *Grizedale Forest*: mixed woodland, forest sculptures and a viewpoint. Maps are available from the visitor centre. See p. 185.

A variation on the walk on p. 255 is to follow the water's edge of both *Grasmere* and *Rydal Water*, completing a circuit by taking a path from Dove Cottage to Rydal Mount. See *The Holiday Which? Good Walks Guide* walk 129.

Easedale Tarn (see p. 181) A magnificently sited tarn above Easedale.
Take the Easedale road, opposite Sam Read's Bookshop in Grasmere
village, keep straight on at the next road junction; the tarn is soon
signposted to the left. In true Lake District manner, the tarn doesn't
come into view until the last moment. Return the same way.
Arnside Knott, near Arnside, on Morecambe Bay: wooded, except
for one grassy slope, but the trees around the top have been kept
down to give the view north into the Lakeland fells; there is no
southern view (unlike Hampsfield Fell), but the walk around the
shore at the base of the hill is very attractive. See *The Holiday Which?
Good Walks Guide* walk 123. There is also a nature walk; leaflets are
available from local bookshops and newsagents.
The west edge of Kendal has a one-mile nature trail in *Serpentine
Woods* with views across the town. A leaflet is available from Kendal
tourist information centre.
A 2½-mile nature walk on *Loughrigg Fell* starts at Bridge House,
Ambleside (from where leaflets can be obtained), and gives views
over Rydal Water and Ambleside.
Brockhole (see p. 165) has a nature trail through woods and along
the shore of Windermere (early March to early November).
White Moss Common A nature walk, ¾ mile long, in woods just
south of Rydal Water. Leaflets are available from National Trust
information centres in Ambleside and Grasmere and from Cumbria
Trust for Nature Conservation, Church Street, Ambleside.
Guided walks start at the tourist information centres in Ambleside
and Waterhead, the Skelwith Bridge Hotel on the A593, Grasmere
village centre, Hawkshead car-park and Bowness Bay information
centre. Details from National Park information centres.

Fell walks in outline

Wansfell is actually higher, but *Wansfell Pike* (1581 feet) gets the
best of the view of Windermere. A good 'practice' fell, which feels
like the real thing but is quite a friendly ascent providing you go up
from the Troutbeck side. It's convenient for Ambleside, too, and the
walk can take in Stock Ghyll Force (see p. 173), Jenkin Crag and
Town End (see p. 175). The full route is described in *The Holiday
Which? Good Walks Guide* walk 130.
Helm Crag (1299 feet), north-west of Grasmere, is also known as The
Lion and the Lamb because of the shape of the crags on its summit.
The shortest ascent is from the southern (Grasmere) side via
Lancrigg. It's not a high fell, but the walk is interesting because of
the rock-strewn terrain at the top, and has a lovely view over the
Rothay Valley.

Information

Tourist information centres

*Open summer only

*__Ambleside,__ The Old Courthouse, Church Street. Tel Ambleside (053 94) 32582

__Barrow-in-Furness,__ Town Hall, Duke Street. Tel Barrow-in-Furness (0229) 870156

__Bowness-on-Windermere,__ The Glebe, Bowness Bay. Tel Windermere (096 62) 2895

__Brockhole National Park Visitor Centre.__ Tel Windermere (096 62) 6601

*__Cockermouth,__ Riverside car-park, Market Street. Tel Cockermouth (0900) 822634

*__Coniston,__ 16 Yewdale Road. Tel Ambleside (053 94) 41533

__Egremont,__ 12 Main Street. Tel Egremont (0946) 820693

*__Grange-over-Sands,__ Victoria Hall, Main Street. Tel Grange-over-Sands (053 95) 34026

*__Grasmere,__ Red Bank Road. Tel Grasmere (096 65) 245

__Grizedale Forestry Commission Visitor Centre.__ Tel Satterthwaite (0229) 860373

*__Hawkshead__ main car-park. Tel Hawkshead (096 66) 525

__Kendal,__ Town Hall, Highgate. Tel Kendal (0539) 725758

__Keswick,__ Moot Hall, Market Square. Tel Keswick (076 87) 72645

__Maryport,__ Maritime Museum, 1 Senhouse Street. Tel Maryport (0900) 813738

*__Millom,__ Millom Folk Museum, St George's Road. Tel Millom (0229) 772555

__Penrith,__ Robinson's School, Middlegate. Tel Penrith (0768) 67466

*__Pooley Bridge,__ The Square. Tel Pooley Bridge (076 84) 86530

*__Ravenglass,__ Ravenglass and Eskdale Railway Station. Tel Ravenglass (0229) 717278

*__Seatoller,__ Seatoller Barn, Borrowdale. Tel Borrowdale (059 684) 294

*__Ullswater__ main car-park, Glenridding. Tel Glenridding (076 84) 82414

__Ulverston,__ Coronation Hall. Tel Ulverston (0229) 57120

*__Waterhead__ car-park, near Ambleside. Tel Ambleside (053 94) 32729

__Whinlatter Forestry Commission Visitor Centre.__ Tel Braithwaite (059 682) 469

__Whitehaven,__ Civic Hall, Lowther Street. Tel Whitehaven (0946) 695678

__Windermere,__ Victoria Street. Tel Windermere (096 62) 6499

Recorded information

Weather report, daily. Tel Windermere (096 62) 5151

*Teletourist events line. Tel Windermere (096 62) 6363

Accommodation

There is a comprehensive range of hotel accommodation in the Lake District – from top-class luxury establishments to family-run guest-houses – and an enormous amount of it, particularly in the popular areas around Windermere and Derwent Water. Many of the most attractive places get booked up, sometimes months and occasionally years ahead. But it is practicable for much of the year to arrive in the area without booking and find somewhere to stay. There is plenty of bed-and-breakfast accommodation concentrated in Keswick, Bowness, Windermere and Ambleside, but also scattered in small villages. Almost all the tourist information centres will, for a fee, telephone registered local accommodation and make bookings for you.

Self-catering accommodation includes houses, cottages and flats, and is also most concentrated around the more popular lakes, plus static caravans, singly or in small groups, and some secluded sites for touring caravans and tents. Youth hostels, often strategically located for walkers and in the finest scenery, provide simple inexpensive accommodation: it's usually in dormitories, but some have family rooms. (Despite the name, the hostels are open to people of any age.) Membership of the Youth Hostels Association can be obtained on the spot or from Trevelyan House, 8 St Stephen's Hill, St Albans, Hertfordshire AL1 2DY (tel St Albans (0727) 55215).

The Cumbria Tourist Board, Ashleigh Holly Road, Windermere, Cumbria LA23 2AQ (tel Windermere (09662) 4444), publishes an annual *Holiday Guide* listing hotels, guest-houses and self-catering accommodation of all types; the Lake District National Park Authority also offers *Where to Stay* booklets and its own list of sites for touring caravans and tents. The Cumbria and Lakeland Self-Caterers' Association provides an illustrated booklet of members' properties and a Vacancy Advisory Service (tel Ulverston (0229) 57668). The National Trust has some farm and cottage accommodation: leaflet and bookings from the Bookings Secretary at Fell Foot Park, Newby Bridge, Cumbria LA12 8NN (tel Newby Bridge (053 95) 31273).

Entertainment

Useful publications include the annual *Places to Visit and Things to Do in Cumbria*, the monthly *South Lakeland: What's On and Leisure Guide* and the local newspapers, the *Westmorland Gazette* and *Lakeland Echo*. From the National Park office, *What's On at Brockhole* lists the visitor centre's talks, walks, films and children's events. The Cumbria Trust for Wildlife Conservation produces *Wildlife What's On*, and a leaflet from Holker Hall (near Grange-over-Sands) gives details of its

INFORMATION

summer programme which includes rallies, auctions and ballooning. For the main Lakeland events, see the calendar on p. 273.

Theatre and music

Bowness *Countryside Theatre* (tel Windermere (096 62) 2895).
Grizedale *Theatre-in-the-Forest*: drama, classical and folk music, jazz, pop and talks. Box office open Tues to Sat, 11 to 4 (tel Satterthwaite (0229) 860291); you can also book through Hawkshead post office, Coniston post office and Holdsworth's bookshop, Ambleside.
Kendal *Brewery Arts Centre* (tel Kendal (0539) 725133): drama, concerts, music workshops, folk, jazz and films in an active, well-run community centre, a good source of information about all of cultural interest in the Lakes; *Mary Wakefield Music Festival* (tel Kendal (0539) 84696): classical music (concerts and competitions) for a week in mid-May.
Keswick *Century Theatre*: designed as a mobile touring theatre, this curious construction of linked cabins in the Lakeside car-park is more comfortable than it looks. A season's productions might include Restoration comedy, thrillers, farces, plus visiting ballet and amateur opera. Book through the Moot Hall, Keswick Town Centre (daytime) or Century Theatre Booking Office, Lakeside car-park (evenings). Tel (for both) Keswick (076 87) 74411.
Ulverston *Renaissance Theatre Trust* (tel Ulverston (0229) 52299): this arts centre organises concerts, plays and shows (including touring companies) in many south Cumbrian venues.
near **Whitehaven** *Rosehill Theatre* (tel Whitehaven (0946) 692422): drama, classical concerts, workshops, talks, a good range of productions all year.
Workington *Carnegie Arts Centre* (tel Workington (0900) 602122).

The Lake District Summer Music Festival is held in August at several venues including Ambleside, Grizedale, Kendal, Keswick and Troutbeck Bridge: classical music and talks. Box office is at Museum Building, 97 Grosvenor Street, Manchester M1 7HF (tel 061-247 4149 or (0629) 823733; in August tel Ambleside (053 94) 39340.

Cinemas

Ambleside *Zefirelli's* (tel Ambleside (0966) 33845).
Barrow-in-Furness *Astra* (tel Barrow-in-Furness (0229) 825354).
Bowness *Royalty* (tel Windermere (096 62) 3364).
Kendal *Brewery Arts Centre* (tel Kendal (0539) 725133).
Keswick *Alhambra* (tel Keswick (076 87) 72195).
Penrith *Alhambra* (tel Penrith (0768) 62400).
Ulverston *Roxy* (tel Ulverston (0229) 52340).
Whitehaven *Gaiety* (tel Whitehaven (0946) 693012).
Workington *Rendezvous* (tel Workington (0900) 622505).

Shopping

There are **markets** at Ambleside (Weds), Barrow (Weds, Fri and Sat), Broughton (Tues), Cockermouth (Mon), Kendal (Weds and Sat plus flea-market on Mon), Keswick (Sat), Maryport (Fri), Penrith (Tues and Sat), Ulverston (Thurs and Sat), Whitehaven (Thurs and Sat) and Workington (Weds and Sat).

Early-closing day is Wednesday or Thursday – never the same as market day, and not necessarily a total shutdown.

Souvenir-hunting

Shops and galleries selling wooden goods, toys, arts, crafts and gifts in general are found throughout the Lake District. The following are some local specialists and good centres.

Ambleside *Adrian Sankey Glass*, Rothay Road: glass-blowing workshop and sales counter; *Hayes Garden World*: plant sales and coffee lounge in a big glassed site on the edge of town.

Cockermouth *Antique Market*, Main Street.

Coniston *Lakeland Guild Craft Gallery*, Brantwood.

Grange-in-Borrowdale *Lakeland Rural Industries* (on the B5289).

Grasmere *Sarah Nelson's Gingerbread Shop*: purveyor of the original stuff since the 1850s; *English Lakeland Perfumery*.

Kendal *Wilson's Kendal Mint Factory*, off Kirkland (sales counter).

Skelwith Bridge *Kirkstone Galleries*: slate products.

Thornthwaite *Thornthwaite Galleries*, including craft demonstrations.

Windermere *Windermere and Bowness Dollmaking Company*, College Road: antique doll specialists.

Bookshop-browsing

There are enough Lake District bookshops to keep any bookworm happy through a wet holiday. Ambleside, Bowness, Cockermouth, Grasmere, Kendal, Keswick, Millom and Ulverston all have one or more new bookshops. The following are second-hand bookshops.

Ambleside *The Little Bookshop*, 1 Cheapside: general.

Barrow-in-Furness *Mostly Books Shop*, 247 Rawlinson Street: general, shipping, technical, crafts, geology, postcards, sheet music.

Braithwaite *Book Cottage*: natural history, literature, history, topography, biography, military, paperbacks.

Caldbeck *The Book End*, Priest's Mill: small general stock, maps, prints, architecture, cookery.

Cartmel *Peter Bain-Smith*, Market Square: large general stock, including children's books, English literature, Lake District, antiquarian.

Cockermouth *The Old Storyteller's Bookshop*, 10 Old King's Arms Lane: specialises in topography, British history and natural history; *The Printing House*, 102 Main Street: general, antiquarian, Lake District, climbing.

INFORMATION

Kendal *Books and Prints*, 68
Kirkland: general; *Ewen Kerr*, 1
New Road: general, modern
first editions, Lake District,
natural history.
Keswick *The Gift Horse*, 5 St
John's Street: general,
including Lake District and
cricket.
Penrith *St Andrews Bookshop*, St
Andrews View: antiquarian,
field sports, natural history.
Whitehaven *Michael Moon's
Bookshop*, 41–43 Roper Street:
huge general and antiquarian
stock.

Outdoor equipment

Not surprisingly, there are
plenty of shops in the Lake
District selling walking,
climbing, camping, sporting
and aquatic equipment. The
biggest concentrations are in
Ambleside, Kendal and
Keswick; this is a selection
only.
Ambleside *Frank Davies (The
Climber's Shop)*, Compston

Road; *F. W. Tyson*, Market
Place; *Stewart Cunningham
Outdoor Centre*, 12 Rydal Road;
Rock and Run, 4 Cheapside;
Waterhead Marine, Waterhead.
Bowness *Stuart's Sports*, Lake
Road; *Shepherd's Boatyard*,
Bowness Bay; *Windermere
Aquatic*, Glebe Road.
**Broughton-in-
Furness** *Mountain Centre
Sports*, Market Street.
Kendal *Peter Bland Sports*,
42 Kirkland; *Lakeland Mountain
Centre*, 3 Kirkland; *Moor and
Mountain*, Waterside.
Keswick *George Fisher*, Lake
Road; *Mountain World*, 28 Lake
Road; *Heart of the Country*,
St John's Street; *Rathbone*, Main
Street; *Keswick Mountain Sports*,
Main Street; *Field and Stream*,
Main Street.
Wasdale Head *Barn Door*.
Whitehaven *The Complete
Angler*, King Street.
Windermere *Fellsman*,
2 Victoria Street.

Getting around

Maps

Several touring maps of the Lake District are published, but it's not
easy to find a well-detailed map which contains the whole of the
District. The *A–Z Visitors' Map of the Lake District* is the nearest to
achieving both goals, a clear and very informative map at the scale of
one inch to a mile. Tourist sights are highlighted, town plans are
given and nearly all the fells are named; other information includes
recreational facilities, bus routes, camp- and caravan-sites and
car-parks. Unfortunately, the map omits the northernmost tip of the
National Park (around Caldbeck) and the area to the south of the
National Park abutting Morecambe Bay. The Cumbria Tourist Board
publishes *Cumbria/English Lake District*, a touring map at the scale of
1 inch to 2½ miles; this is much less detailed than the *A–Z* map but
covers the whole of Cumbria, including the Eden Valley, the
Cumbrian Pennines and the north side of Morecambe Bay. The
Ordnance Survey One-inch Tourist Map of the Lake District is an

attractive piece of cartography (although opinions differ on the usefulness of the heavy colour shading to depict relief). Compared with the *A–Z* it has less tourist information and a more restricted area of coverage (omitting the west coast and the southern extremities of the National Park). The *Ordnance Survey Landranger Series of Great Britain* maps at the scale of 1:50,000 (about 1¼ inches to the mile) are worth buying only if you are restricting yourself to one area of the Lakes (or can't resist collecting OS maps) as you need five sheets to cover the whole of the district.

For anyone considering walking, the *Ordnance Survey Outdoor Leisure Maps* are almost essential. Four of them are published for the Lake District, covering the main part of the National Park at a scale of 1:25,000, or about 2½ inches to a mile. Field boundaries are indicated (crucial if you are following a poorly defined route across fields or enclosed uplands), although a source of potential confusion in upland areas is that the public rights of way (shown in green) often don't match up to what is on the ground; the actual route may instead be shown by a broken black line. For areas not covered by the *Outdoor Leisure* series, OS *Pathfinder* maps (published at the same scale) are available.

Using a car

In many ways the Lake District is ideal touring country. Out of season the roads are often deserted, and driving can be highly pleasurable. Scenic drives, such as the Wrynose and Hardknott Passes, the Duddon Valley, Corney Fell and Borrowdale, are among the finest in the country. Inevitably there are crowds at peak times – late July to the end of September, Bank Holidays and Sundays throughout the year – when it will be necessary to restrict the length of tours accordingly. But even at peak times it is possible to dodge the traffic jams completely by avoiding the main towns (Bowness, Ambleside and Keswick can be nightmares) and some of the more popular routes (Hardknott Pass, Watendlath, Ullswater and Windermere). Some roads, particularly around Caldbeck, Loweswater, Ennerdale, Blawith and Cartmel Fell, never get a lot of traffic.

According to surveys conducted by the National Park, one of the things visitors find most annoying about the Lake District is the parking problem. At peak times it can be impossible to park in places as popular as Hawkshead and Grasmere; unless you are prepared to queue, the only solutions are to get there first thing in the morning or early in the evening, park half a mile or so away and walk the rest, or use public transport. Be prepared for the ticket machines in Pay and Display car-parks: most do not give change, and people *are* prosecuted for non-display. Season tickets are available for the National Park car-parks.

INFORMATION

Public transport

If you plan to tour the lakes without a car, the most convenient centres for public transport are the main towns: Windermere and Bowness, Ambleside and Keswick. Public transport has its attractions even if you've come here by car, as the bus network is a useful means of avoiding high-season parking problems.

The main bus companies are Ribble (tel Kendal (0539) 733221), which also runs Minilink, and CMS Cumberland (tel Whitehaven (0946) 63222), which also runs the Borrowdale Bus. Rover tickets are available from both. Local services include Mountain Goat (tel Windermere (096 62) 5161), which also offers sightseeing tours, and Fell Bus (tel Keswick (076 87) 72403), which provides a 'hail-and-ride' service in the Borrowdale and Buttermere areas.

Tour operators

Browns (tel Ambleside (053 94) 32205 or Grasmere (096 65) 627): tours can be booked additionally through tourist information centres at Ambleside, Bowness, Grasmere and Windermere. Coach and minibus tours in the Lake District, and a few destinations outside.

Fellrunner: book at tourist information centres in Alston, Appleby, Brough, Carlisle, Kirkby Stephen, Penrith or Pooley Bridge. Tours in the north-east Lakes, Eden Valley and Pennines.

Grange Coachways (tel Grange-over-Sands (053 95) 34794): Lakeland coach tours.

Grass Routes (tel Windermere (096 62) 6760): minibus tours.

Lakeland Link (tel Blackpool (0253) 695931): trip from Windermere station/Bowness Bay pier to Holker Hall via lake steamer, Lakeside and Haverthwaite Railway and coach.

Mountain Goat (tel Windermere (096 62) 5161 or Keswick (076 87) 73962): minibus tours, often with a theme, mostly in the Lake District, plus a few trips to the Yorkshire Dales.

Ribble (tel Kendal (0539) 733221): local and outside destinations, including open-top bus tours.

Windermere tourist information centre (tel Windermere (096 62) 6499): tour of Furness, including Ulverston, Furness Abbey and Conishead Priory.

Guided chauffeur-driven car tours are offered by *Jeeves Tours* (tel Workington (0900) 603016), *Lakeline Car Tours* (tel Windermere (096 62) 4648).

British Rail

The Lake District is encircled by railway lines, but the system does not penetrate far into the area. The main way in to the Lakes by train is by the branch line to Windermere from Oxenholme (on the main London–Glasgow line), not itself a particularly interesting journey. But there are two lines of outstanding scenic interest skirting the Lakes. The *Cumbria coast line* takes 2¾ hours for the 85-mile trip from Barrow-in-Furness to Carlisle and runs beside the coast for much of the way, passing

Sellafield, St Bees and Whitehaven en route. There are no Sunday services. The *Lancaster to Barrow line*, notably the 13½-mile stretch between Arnside and Ulverston, takes in fine scenery around Morecambe Bay, crossing the northern side by a series of spectacular low viaducts.

There is also the famous *Settle to Carlisle line*, rather out of the Lake District but well worth sampling for its views over the central Pennines.

For British Rail information tel Carlisle (0228) 44711, Kendal (0539) 720397, Lancaster (0524) 32333 or Penrith (0768) 62466.

Nostalgia railways

The Lakeside and Haverthwaite Railway: steam engines haul ex-British Rail carriages along a 3½-mile reopened section of the Ulverston to Lakeside branch, now operational only from Haverthwaite to Lakeside, where steamers can be taken along the length of Windermere. Combined rail-sail tickets are available. The route runs for 18 minutes through the wooded Backbarrow Gorge. For information tel Newby Bridge (053 95) 31594.

The Ravenglass and Eskdale Railway ('Ratty'): miniature steam locomotives and diesels pull tiny carriages (many open-sided) through Eskdale. The seven-mile (40-minute) route is excellent for stopping off at stations to do some sightseeing or walking. For information tel Ravenglass (0229) 717171.

Air flights

Air Furness has nine-seater planes available for private charter for half-hour flights over the Lake District from Walney Island Airport.

Lake transport

Note that services can be subject to cancellation, particularly in bad weather

Coniston Water The National Trust's restored steam yacht *Gondola*, first launched in 1859, operates from Coniston pier to Park-a-Moor near the south-west end of the lake via Brantwood. Easter to end October, with five sailings daily in summer. The round trip takes an hour. No reduction for National Trust members. For information tel Coniston (053 94) 41288.

Derwent Water *Keswick Launch* (tel Keswick (076 87) 72263) runs motor-launches around the lake, stopping at seven piers; alternates between clockwise and anti-clockwise. Easter to mid-November, eight times daily (with additional services every 15 minutes from mid-July to end August). The round trip takes 50 minutes. Seven-day Explorer Tickets, giving unlimited travel, are available.

Ullswater *Ullswater Navigation* (tel Kendal (0539) 721626 or Glenridding (076 84) 82229) runs nineteenth-century steamers from Pooley Bridge to Glenridding via Lake Pier at Howtown. Easter to end October, with three services a day in each direction. The trip takes 55 minutes each way.

Windermere Two companies operate steamer services (Easter to end October). The *Windermere Iron Steamboat Company* (tel Windermere (096 62) 3056 or Ambleside (053 94) 32225) operates three boats – *Tern* (built 1891), *Teal* (1936) and *Swan* (1938) – running the length of the 10½-mile lake from Waterhead pier to Lakeside with a stop at Bowness. Shorter trips are also available, including 45-minute tours of the central lake from Bowness. Holiday Tickets give unlimited travel for three or seven days. The Lakeside to Waterhead trip takes 1½ hours, and there are about five or six sailings daily. The *Bowness Bay Boating Company* (tel Windermere (096 62) 3360) operates trips around the islands and to Brockhole National Park visitor centre, and also runs evening cruises.

There is a chain ferry (not operational at night or in winter) across the centre of the lake, connecting the B5284 and the B5285, a link in the Hawkshead–Kendal route. Traffic queues can be long in summer (signs tell you how long you can expect to wait), although even then this may be quicker than driving around the lake; pedestrians and bicycles can nearly always get on without queueing. Services run every few minutes.

Skippered sailing cruises are offered on the *Mistral* and the *Four Winds* (tel Windermere (096 62) 2324), with buffet lunches and evening meals available on board, and by *Lakeline* (tel Windermere (096 62) 4648).

Bicycle hire

Ambleside *Ghyllside Cycles*, The Slack (tel Ambleside (053 94) 33592); *Lakeland Mountain Bikes*, Lancet House, Kelsick Road (tel Ambleside (053 94) 34464).

Kendal *Askew Cycles*, Burneside Road (tel Kendal (0539) 728057); *Brucie's Bike Shop*, 9 Kirkland (tel Kendal (0539) 727230).

Keswick *Keswick Cycle Hire*, Braithwaite (tel Braithwaite (059 682) 273).

Penrith *Harpers Cycles* (tel Penrith (0768) 64475).

Pooley Bridge *Knotts Hill*, Watermillock (tel Pooley Bridge (076 84) 86328); *Treetops* (tel Pooley Bridge (076 84) 86267).

Windermere *Lakeland Leisure*, Spring Gardens, Station Precinct (tel Windermere (096 62) 4786).

Mopeds are available from *Lakes Moped Hire*, College Road, Windermere (tel Windermere (096 62) 4853.

Outdoor activities

The Lake District has practically every pursuit on offer, watery or dry. Riding and pony-trekking are particularly popular, and a long list of places is available from information centres. You can go sailing, canoeing, rock-climbing and orienteering; there's grass-skiing near Windermere, a parachuting centre at Flookburgh and a gliding club at Barrow-in-Furness. If you tire of scenery and want some exercise, there are sports centres and indoor swimming-pools at Cockermouth, Kendal, Keswick and Whitehaven.

On the fells and on the lakes, every level of experience can be catered for; this is an excellent area for trying something new or for putting an energetic day into your relaxed touring holiday. The following places offer day courses or short sessions of most things in their range; booking is usually necessary.

Adventure Awareness/West-morland Watersports (tel Windermere (096 62) 5756): most activities, from abseiling to water-skiing.
Bigland Hall Country Sports Ltd (tel Newby Bridge (053 95) 31361): riding, fishing, shooting, stalking, archery, windsurfing.
Calvert Trust (tel Keswick (076 87) 72254): activities for the disabled, including climbing, fell-walking, canoeing, angling, orienteering, birdwatching.
Claife and Grizedale Riding Centre (tel Windermere (096 62) 2105): riding and riding instruction.
Limefitt Park (tel Ambleside (053 94) 32564): grass-skiing, pony-trekking.
Motherby House Activities (tel Greystoke (085 33) 368): abseiling, rock-climbing,

orienteering, canoeing, scrambling, fell-walking, caving, sailing, windsurfing.
Pleasure in Leisure (tel Windermere (096 62) 2324): windsurfing, sailing, canoeing, riding, fell-walking, climbing, orienteering, archery, clay-pigeon shooting.
R&L Adventures (tel Windermere (096 62) 5104 or Staveley (0539) 821499): canoeing, climbing, hill-walking, orienteering.
Royal Hotel, Ullswater (tel Glenridding (076 84) 82356): canoeing.
Summitreks (tel Ambleside (053 94) 41212): canoeing, hill-walking, climbing, abseiling.
Wynlass Beck Stables (tel Windermere (096 62) 3811): escorted rides.

Angling

The Lake District offers excellent fishing, not only in its lakes but in tarns, rivers and reservoirs. First you need a North-West Water Authority rod licence, available from most tackle shops. In most places you will also need a fishing permit, usually a National Park one, although some waters are free: enquire locally. A useful source of information is the little *Angler's Guide to the Lake District*, published by the *Westmorland Gazette* and available at bookshops and information centres. It covers all fishing waters, with details of their ownership, their fish and the recommended methods of catching them, close seasons, and the availability of permits, day tickets and boats.

Boats on lakes

No private craft are allowed on Blea Tarn, Brothers Water, Elterwater, Ennerdale Water, Haweswater, Little Langdale Tarn, Loughrigg Tarn, Loweswater, Rydal Water, Tarn Hows, Wast Water or Yew Tree Tarn.

A full list of launching sites for small boats is available at information centres.

Bassenthwaite Lake No power craft allowed. Members of the Royal Yacht Association affiliated clubs may be permitted to use the Bassenthwaite Sailing Club's facilities at the northern end of the lake: contact the secretary. Canoes and rowing-boats can be hired from Peel Wyke near the north-western corner of the lake; permits are required and may not be available in the fishing season, and in any case the southern end beyond Blackstock Point is not open.

Buttermere No power craft allowed. Sailing-boats, canoes and rowing-boats are permitted. Permits and rowing-boat hire available from Gatesgarth Farm, Buttermere; permits are also available from the Kirkstile Inn, Loweswater.

Coniston Water Power craft allowed; 10mph speed-limit. They can be launched from the Coniston Boating Centre, approached from Lake Road, Coniston, where sailing-boats, rowing-boats and low-powered motor-boats are available. Non-powered craft can additionally be launched from two other sites on the lake. Permits are not required.

Crummock Water No power craft allowed. Canoes and small craft may be launched from the roadside. Permits and rowing-boat hire available from Rannerdale Farm, Buttermere.

Derwent Water Power craft allowed; 10mph speed-limit. Nichol End Marine, Portinscale, and Keswick Launch, Keswick, both offer powered, sailing- and rowing-boats for hire. Permits are not required.

Esthwaite Water No power or sailing craft allowed. Rowing-boats may be launched from the south-western shore. Permits are available and rowing-boats may be hired from Sunnyside, Near Sawrey.

Grasmere No power craft allowed. Small non-powered boats allowed: payment required from Easter to October (Mrs J. M. Allonby, Padmire, Pavement End, Grasmere; rowing-boats can be hired from here). Permits are not required.

Loweswater No private craft allowed, but rowing-boats can be hired from Scale Hill Hotel.

Thirlmere No power craft allowed. Permits for small non-powered boats obtainable from the Supply Manager,

North-West Water Authority, Mintsfeet Road South, Kendal (tel Kendal (0539) 740066).
Ullswater Power craft allowed; 10mph speed-limit. Sailing-boats can be hired from Glenridding Sailing School. Powered and rowing-boats can be hired from Tindals at Glenridding and Pooley Bridge and from Ullswater Caravan and Camping Site Marina, Watermillock, canoes from Lake Leisure, Pooley Bridge.
Windermere Power craft allowed; no speed-limit apart from certain 10mph and 6mph zones. Craft must be registered and display their number prominently; details from information centres. Permits to launch from National Trust sites are available from wardens on site. Fell Foot Farm, near Newby Bridge at the southern end of the lake, has rowing- and sailing-boats for hire. Powered and sailing-boats can be hired all year from Windermere Aquatic Ltd and Shepherd's Boatyard, both at Glebe Road, Bowness, canoes from Lakeland Canoes, Hollings Lane, Burneside, Kendal.

Because of the speed-limits imposed on all the lakes except Windermere, this is the only feasible place for water-skiing. Tuition is provided at Low Wood Ski Centre, Low Wood, Windermere (tel Ambleside (053 94) 34004), and at Westmorland Watersports (see below).

Sailing and windsurfing schools

Derwentwater Windsurfing School, Portinscale, Keswick (tel Keswick (076 87) 72912).
Glenridding Sailing School, Celleron Cottage, Tirril, Penrith (tel Pooley Bridge (076 84) 86601) or (076 84) 82541).
Lakeland Sailing and Sailboard Centre, Ferry Nab, Bowness (tel Windermere (096 62) 4366).
Top Mark Windsurfing, 110 Greengate Street, Barrow-in-Furness (tel Barrow-in-Furness (0229) 24740); operates at Fell Foot Country Park, Windermere.
Ullswater Sailing School, Landends, Watermillock, Penrith (tel Pooley Bridge (076 84) 86438).
Westmorland Watersports, Cannon Hay, Storrs Park, Bowness (tel Windermere (096 62) 5756).

Golf courses

The following clubs welcome visiting parties. Booking is essential. Penrith and Workington Golf Clubs require visitors to be members of a club and to hold a current handicap.

All courses are 18-hole except where stated otherwise.

Barrow Golf Club, Rakesmoor Lane, Hawcoat, Barrow-in-Furness (tel Barrow-in-Furness (0229) 825444).

Cockermouth Golf Club, Embleton (tel Bassenthwaite Lake (059 681) 223).
Dunnerholme Golf Club (10-hole), Askham-in-Furness (tel Dalton-in-Furness (0229) 62675).

Furness Golf Club, Central Drive, Walney Island, Barrow-in-Furness (tel Barrow-in-Furness (0229) 41232).

Grange Fell Golf Club (9-hole), Fell Road, Grange-over-Sands (tel Grange-over-Sands (053 95) 32536).

Grange-over-Sands Golf Club, Meathop Road (tel Grange-over-Sands (053 95) 33180).

Keswick Golf Club, Threlkeld Hall, Threlkeld (tel Threlkeld (059 683) 324 or Keswick (076 87) 72147).

Kendal Golf Club, The Heights, Kendal (tel Kendal (0539) 724079).

Maryport Golf Club (11-hole), Back End, Maryport (tel Maryport (0900) 812605).

Penrith Golf Club, Salkeld Road, Penrith (tel Penrith (0768) 62217).

Seascale Golf Club, The Banks, Seascale (tel Seascale (094 67) 28202).

Silecroft Golf Club (9-hole), Silecroft, Millom (tel Millom (0229) 774250).

Ulverston Golf Club, Bardsea Park, Ulverston (tel Ulverston (0229) 52824).

Windermere Golf Club, Cleabarrow (tel Windermere (096 62) 3123).

Workington Golf Club, Branthwaite Road, Workington (tel Workington (0900) 603460).

Calendar of events

THE NORTH-WEST

July

Keswick Convention: an inter-denominational Bible Convention that fills the town for two weeks in mid-July.

Cockermouth Show: last Sat in July or first in Aug. One of Lakeland's traditional agricultural shows, featuring Cumberland and Westmorland wrestling – more like Japanese *sumo* than the all-in sort – and hound trailing – in which hounds race off around a 10-mile trail prepared with rags soaked in oil and aniseed, reappearing to be frantically encouraged by their owners behind the finishing line.

August

Threlkeld Sheepdog Trials: third Weds after first Mon.

Keswick Show: Bank Hol Mon. Important agricultural show; hound trailing, Cumberland and Westmorland wrestling, crafts.

Ennerdale Show: last Mon. Horticultural show, craft-making and cookery competitions, hound trailing, dog shows, gymkhana, fell racing, evening dance. Proceeds go to a Christmas party for local children.

September

Egremont Crab Fair: third Sat. One of the most colourful events on the Lakeland calendar, dating from 1267, this starts with the Parade of the Apple Cart (apples thrown to the crowds), followed by the World Gurning Championship to find who can pull the worst face, attempts at shinning up a 30-foot greasy pole and a pipe-smoking contest; also track and field events, shows and hound trailing.

Loweswater Show: third Thurs. Agricultural show.

THE NORTH-EAST

July

Penrith Show: third Sat in July. Agricultural show: crafts, shepherds' crooks, sheepdog trials.

August

Lowther Horse Driving Trials and Country Fair: weekend early in month. Major horse driving event, with sideshows.

Skelton Show: third Sat. Horticultural and agricultural show: crafts, produce, fancy dress competitions, brass band, showjumping.

Patterdale Sheepdog Trials: Sat before Bank Hol Mon. Competitions, shows and puppy trailing as well as the sheepdog trials. All day, with a dance in the evening.

Caldbeck and Hesket Newmarket Sheepdog Trials: late Aug.

THE SOUTH-WEST

August
Gosforth Show: third Weds.
Agricultural and driving show,
gymkhana, hound and terrier
racing.

September
Ulverston Lantern Procession:
mid-month. Community
procession.
Urswick Rushbearing: Sat nearest
St Michael's Day (29th). The
annual rushbearing ceremonies
used to combine festivity with
the practical business of
covering churches' bare earth
floors with freshly cut rushes.
Nowadays they are children's
festivals: flowers and token
rushes carried in procession
behind a band, and a church
service.
Eskdale Show: last Sat. Sheep,
fell races, children's sports.

October
Wasdale Show: second Sat. One
of the leading Herdwick sheep
shows, with shepherds' crooks,
tug o' war, fell races, hound
trailing, Cumberland and
Westmorland wrestling.

THE SOUTH-EAST

May
Cartmel Races: late spring Bank
Hol, on Sat and Mon.
Steeplechasing at the smallest
National Hunt course;
fairground, stalls.
Mary Wakefield Music Festival,
Kendal: see p. 262.

July
Ambleside Rushbearing: first Sat.
Lakeland Rose Show, Kendal:
second weekend. Large-scale
flower show, with parachute
displays, military bands, crafts,
children's fairground, local
produce.
Lake Windermere Festival: one
week early in month. Events
include street parades, boat
parades on the lake and
fireworks.

August
Ambleside Sports: Thurs before
first Mon. Track events, fell
racing, Cumberland and
Westmorland wrestling,
cycling.
*The Lake District Summer Music
Festival*: see p. 262.
Grasmere Rushbearing: Sat
nearest St Oswald's Day (5th).
Grasmere Sports: third Thurs
after first Mon. One of the
biggest crowd-pullers of the
year, attracting over 10,000
spectators. Fell races,
Cumberland and Westmorland
wrestling, hound trailing,
athletics.
*Lake District Sheepdog Trials,
Ings*: Thurs after first Mon.
Vale of Rydal Sheepdog Trials:
second Thurs after first Mon.
Shepherds' crooks, hound
shows, hound trailing.
Kendal Gathering: late Aug to
early Sept over 17 days. Sports
competitions, band contests,
flower shows, exhibitions,
torchlight procession,
Gooseholme Old Tyme Fair.

Kendal Folk Festival: three days, usually late Aug. Concerts, ceilidhs, workshops, mainly in Brewery Arts Centre (see p. 262).

Hawkshead Show: mid-Aug. Agricultural (notably Herdwick sheep) and horticultural show, with handicrafts and hound trailing.

Cartmel Races: late summer Bank Hol, on Sat and Mon.

Lake Artists' Society Annual Exhibition, Grasmere: Aug and first week Sept (daily exc Sun). Mostly professional local artists.

September

Cartmel Show: early in month. Mixed livestock.

Westmorland County Show, Kendal: second Thurs. Major event featuring agricultural show, Cumberland and Westmorland wrestling, dog shows, showjumping, horse-drawn carriage driving.

Kentmere Sheepdog Trials: last Thurs.

October

Windermere Power Boat Record Attempts: mid-month.

Kendal Jazz Festival: late in month.

Windermere Marathon: Sun late in month.

Index

INDEX

279

INDEX